THE MYSTICAL PHILOSOPHY OF AVICENNA

THE MYSTICAL PHILOSOPHY OF AVICENNA

PARVIZ MOREWEDGE

Global Publications, Binghamton University
Binghamton, New York
2001

ISBN 1-58684-166-1 (paper back)
1-58684-165-3 (hard back)

Published by Global Publications
Binghamton University, State University of New York at Binghamton
Binghamton, New York, USA 13902-6000
Phone: (607) 777-4495. Fax: 777-6132
E-mail: pmorewed@binghamton.edu
http://ssips.binghamton.edu

DEDICATION

Shalahudin Kafrawi

With appreciation for
the grace of his friendship
and discussions on being,
nature, and eternity

TABLE OF CONTENTS

AN INTRODUCTION TO IBN SĪNĀ'S ONTOLOGY

SUMMARY

The enclosed collection of essays focuses on the ontology of the most important medieval Muslim philosopher, ibn Sīnā (980-1037), proffering the theses that: (a) his ontology is incompatible with monotheistic theologies; (b) his cosmogony is not derivable from either Aristotelian or Neoplatonic systems; and finally (c) the mystical dimension of his system is in accord with monistic "nature mysticism," as classified by R. C. Zaehner. In contrast to the views of a majority of contemporary scholars that ibn Sīnā's philosophy essentially follows monotheistic or Greek philosophical systems, this collection emphasizes his original contributions to ontology and meta-mysticism.

THE CONCEPTION AND THE SIGNIFICANCE OF HIS PHILOSOPHY

Ibn Sīnā (Arabic), also known as Avicenna (Latin) and Abū 'Alī Sīnā (Persian) was the most original and systematic Muslim philosopher. In this light he is mentioned by two celebrated historians of medieval western philosophy: A. Maurer states, "...his [ibn Sīnā's] philosophy is a highly personal achievement, ranking among the greatest in the history of philosophy;" and F. Copelston holds, "The greatest Muslim philosopher of the eastern group without doubt is Avicenna or ibn Sīnā (980-1037), the real creator of a scholastic system in the Islamic world."[1] Y. Mahdavi lists 244 texts attributed to him and G. A. Anawati lists 270.[2] These works envelop a multiplicity of topics such as metaphysics, poetics, animal physiology, minerals, rhetoric, mechanics of solids, Arabic syntax, meteorology, mystical treatises, and a medical treatise, and are translated into more than nineteen languages. The crown of his philosophical corpus is a set of encyclopedic collections of treatises, especially *al-Shifā', al-Najāt, al-*

Ishārāt wa al-Tanbīhāt and the *Dānish Nāmeh*; each collection contains elaborate philosophical treatises on metaphysics, physics, psychology, and logic. A standard edition of the logical texts of *al-Shifā'* alone comprises more than one sixteen hundred double size (1600) pages.[3]

How do historians of philosophy receive this massive literature? Overlooking his originality, he is often painted as the most sophisticated integrator of the Greek philosophies, especially of Aristotle and Plotinus, into a model suitable for medieval monotheism. The theme of 'integration,' is significant here. A majority of scholars, many trained in the classics, or having monotheistic biases, and lacking direct access to the Arabic and Persian texts, reflect on those elements of ibn Sīnā's thoughts that are useful to decipher relics of Hellenic and standard Islamic themes. By analogy, suppose that a panther is brought to an island where the only felines that native inhabitants have seen are lions and cats. Lion trainers and cat keepers study the new animal. Some say the new animal is a ferocious cat; others take the creature to be a tame lion. Others go so far as to say that this poor animal wants to be a cat but fails to do so. But the panther's salient characteristics are never investigated; only its similarities to other felines are noted. In a similar manner, ibn Sīnā's corpus is studied for its Aristotelian and Neoplatonic features. In addition to those preoccupied by the Greek background, a number of contemporary writers have a "monotheistic God," in mind even when they study the works of Plato and Aristotle. Often, as we shall see, Ibn Sīnā's system is torn apart and reconstructed to fit a monotheistic scheme and then is thrown out for its incompatibility with such a scheme. We shall see how L. Goodman, A. Ivry and S. Inati presuppose that ibn Sīnā's 'Necessary Existent' is the God of monotheism (which is not the case); then they claim that ibn Sīnā's ontology "fails" because the specifics of his 'God' differ from the standard 'God' of monotheistic systems! These writers seem to assume that ibn Sīnā wanted to develop a monotheistic model, but that he was unable to successfully do so; moreover, they assume that he was unaware of the differences between his system and monotheistic models. Ibn Sīnā is not the only victim of these perspectives; as is pointed out later, the monotheistic notion of God is insinuated into the pagan systems of Plato and Aristotle. Others try to read him in light of the "Greek-into-Arabic" model. As we shall point out, H. A. Wolfson claims that ibn Sīnā's original views must be due to some mysterious mistranslation, as all of ibn Sīnā's works must have originated in Aristotle. A majority of investigators, such as H. A. Wolfson, R. Walzer, and D. Gutas, restrict their analyses of ibn Sīnā's views to only classical contexts.

What are needed but absent—with a few exceptions—are studies that are outside of the blindfolds of Hellenic and monotheistic perspectives. Only by moving beyond these dimensions can one appreciate what is novel in ibn Sīnā's system. A useful approach is to search for isomorphic themes between his philosophy and recent Western thought. Such a search may provide us with new perspectives on his system. Moreover, Islamic philosophy in general and ibn Sīnā's thoughts in particular may be used to re-read some key ideas in Western philosophy. Specifically, I have reinterpreted the so-called "ontological argument" proffered by Augustine and Descartes, and illustrated that it could be re-read not as a static logical argument, but in the light of a hermeneutic of a search for the being (*wujūd*), the beholder of the experience (*anā*), the ground of being (*zati-he*), and finally a search for a unity of being (*al-wājib al-wujūd*). Another topic, his concept of the internal sense of *'wahm,'* can clarify the notion of 'prehension' in the philosophy of A. N. Whitehead; also, one can relate his "flying man" argument to the "Dasein" of M. Heidegger.[4] As stated before, traditionally ibn Sīnā's philosophy is generally considered to be the optimal synthesis of both Hellenic and Islamic thought. At least this is the prevailing opinion among a majority of thinkers in the Muslim, Jewish and Christian medieval traditions. In this tenor, when major figures such as the Muslim al-Ghazālī and the Jewish Maimonides chose to criticize the Greco-Islamic tradition, they criticized ibn Sīnā's system, which to them was a true culmination of philosophical tradition. Corroborating this thesis, M. E. Marmura states that, "The main criticisms of al-Ghazālī [in the *Tahāfut*]...have Avicenna's philosophy as their target."[5] An example of the debt of Jewish philosophers to ibn Sīnā is cited by H. A. Wolfson's statement that "With regards to the Aristotelian theory, it may also be observed that both Hallevi and Maimonides are followers of early Arabic Aristotelians like Al Fārābī and Avicenna…."[6] Subsequent Muslim thinkers such as S. Suhrawardī (d. 1119) and Mullā Ṣadrā (d. 1532) often begin by an account of the ibn Sīnian formulation of a philosophical theme in question; afterward, they present their own views and how their position follows or varies from the position of Master Sheikh—as they addressed ibn Sīnā. In this tenor, H. Ziai mentions that, "When he [S. Suhrawardī] cites 'the followers of the Peripatetic,' he is usually referring to Avicenna."[7] In another text, Ziai notes that[8]

> Finally the various works of Avicenna, apart from their direct and evident impact on the philosophy of illumination as a Whole (including logic, epistemology, and metaphysics), must be regarded as sources for al-Suhrawardī's views on the relation between prophet-hood and governance by the wise.

J. W. Morris corroborates Ziai's insight when he states,[9]

> Within the high culture of Islamic civilization, the thought and writings of itinerant Persian doctor and court administrator we know as Avicenna (370/980-428/1037) came to play similarly central role; for almost a millennium, each of the traditions of Islamic thought claiming a wider, universal human validity has appealed either directly to his work or to logical and metaphysical discipline whose forms were directly grounded in them.

Not only did Ibn Sīnā influence every subsequent Muslim philosopher, but later thinkers adopted many of his ideas as well. Ibn Sīnā's most devoted follower was a brilliant philosopher-mathematician named Nāṣir al-Dīn Ṭūsī, who systematically defended ibn Sīnā against his critics such as Fakhr al-Dīn Rāzī, and developed many of his ideas.[10] Ṭūsī formulated the master's phenomenological criticism of the doctrine of atomic substances and his theodicy, which resembles Leibniz's deterministic model.[11]

Ibn Sīnā's influence on Jewish and Christian philosophies has been well documented. For example, basing many of his Christian metaphysical theological issues, such as the essence-existence distinction, on ibn Sīnā's philosophy, Aquinas mentions the Persian philosopher over five hundred times. In this light, it is impossible to exaggerate his influence on either later Muslim philosophers or on Latin fathers of the Christian tradition.

FOUR REASONS FOR THE COMPLEXITY OF RESEARCH IN IBN SĪNĀ'S SYSTEM

Investigators of ibn Sīnā's philosophy confront four *prima facie* problems:

First, due to the extent of ibn Sīnā's writings and the comprehensiveness of this system, no text of the present size can decipher an all-inclusive account of specifics of any major facet of his system; such a limitation applies especially to his ontology, which involves issues such as being, existence, space, time, person, cosmogony, ultimate being, mind-body issues, and the like. Fortunately, a number of recent studies focus on specific topics. In this vein, N. El-Bizri, in his text titled *A Quest for Being: Avicenna and Heidegger*, compares ibn Sīnā and Heidegger's views on a phenomenological analysis of being; Shams Inati, *Ibn Sīnā on Evil: A Study of ibn Sīnā's Theodicy* identifies ibn Sīnā's 'Necessary Existent' as God of Islam, and proceeds to criticize his theodicy of evil.[12] I choose to identify one of the fundamental primitives of his system: 'being' (*wujūd, hastī*), especially the mystical dimensions of his notion of the 'Necessary Existent' (*al-Wājib al-Wujūd*), the ultimate being of his system. Why is being a central notion? It is so, because being, as clarified in the subsequent discussion, is the most primordial notion in the soul. Since Aquinas, ibn Sīnā has been identified correctly as the philosopher of being. In this tenor, A. M. Goichon notes, "Throughout the Middle Ages, Avicenna was recognized in the West as the Philosopher of Being."[13] E. Gilson corroborates these themes as he quotes ibn Sīnā, "The notion of being is the most general among...abstractions. It is an absolutely prime notion, and since it cannot be deduced from . . . [other notions], metaphysics has to take it for granted ... [T]o posit being as the first principle does not mean that there is a principle of being, otherwise, being would have to be its own principle, which is absurd."[14] The most significant case of being is the 'Necessary Existent' (*al-Wājib al-Wujūd*) because it is the ultimate cause of all existents. It is also the central theme in a major controversy as to whether ibn Sīnā's system is compatible with monotheism; counter to the views of a majority of investigators, I read his system as logically incompatible with monotheism, but instead interpret his system as a case of nature mysticism.

A second problem is that ordinary language is not suitable for comprehension of his perspective; the initial phase of introducing his system must proceed from Greek philosophical ideas and technical vocabulary. Ibn Sīnā himself is often conscious of the connection between Greek ideas, his own system, and his own original contributions. Recognizing the significance of language in philosophy, he wrote the first comprehensive metaphysical treatises written in Persian by ibn Sīnā.[15] Also A. M. Goichon has produced two monumental treatises correlating ibn Sīnā's vocabulary with the technical terms in Greek philosophy: *Lexique De Langue Philosophique d'Ibn Sina* and *Vocabulaires Compares d'Aristotle et d'Ibn Sina.*[16] For example, here is an account of how his Persian philosophical vocabulary, introduced in the metaphysics of *Dānish Nāmeh*, correlates with Aristotle's Greek, his own Arabic terminology, Aquinas' Latin, and contemporary translations of Aristotle's corpus.[17]

GREEK	LATIN	ENGLISH	ARABIC	PERSIAN
Ousia	substantia	substance	jauhar	gauhar
Poson	quantum	quantity	kammiyya	chandī
Poion	quale	quality	kaifiyya	chigūnagī
pros ti	ad aliquid	relation	iḍāfa	nisbat
pou	ubi	place	'ayn	kujā ī
pote	quando	time	matā	kaī ī
keisthai	poni	posture	waḍ '	nahād
echein	habere	possession	mulk	dāsht
poien	facere	action	an yaf 'al	kinish
paschein	pati	passion	an yanfa 'il	bakunīdan

The chart above is based on the history of the transmission of philosophical vocabulary from Greek into Arabic/Persian into Latin, and its English correspondence. It is well known that in Ibn Rushd's commentaries on the works of Aristotle, terminology was based on the Syriac and Arabic translations of Greek texts and content was based on ibn Sīnā's analysis of Greek systems.[18] Latin translations of Arabic philosophical texts resulted in a relatively standard correlation among the philosophical vocabulary of different languages. Being well aware of the significance of language, Muslim philosophers wrote a number of books of definitions, and discussed various senses of key philosophical terminology.[19] M. Mahdi's excellent edition of Fārābī's *Book of Letters*, *Kitāb al-Ḥurūf*, depicts Fārābī's clear awareness of the semantics of copula in the light of differences between Persian, Sodgian, Greek and Arabic syntax.[20] Because much of the philosophical content of ibn Sīnā's philosophy, especially his ontology, is essentially related to his Greek predecessors, I need to clarify my discussions in a specific context. Accordingly, the limits imposed in the enclosed essay are confined to selections from ancient Greek texts on ontology, especially Aristotle's *Metaphysics* and Plotinus' *The Enneads*. In a similar vein, 'mysticism' has been used in a variety of senses and its use in this collection must be specified; accordingly, our discussion of mysticism takes place in the context of categories introduced in recent controversies over philosophies of mysticism grounded in some works of R. C. Zaehner (texts such as *Mysticism, Sacred and Profane*, W. T. Stace, *Philosophy and Mysticism*, and finally, F. Staal, *Experiencing Mysticism*).[21] Focusing on 'meta-mysticism,' these essays will not be concerned with topics such as psychology of mystic states, the ethical value of mystical experience, history of mysticism, practices of mystical texts, or presence of mystical passages in monotheistic texts, such as *Ezixle* in the *Torah*, *The Book of Revelation* in the *New Testament*; and the *Sura of Light* (*Mishkat al-Anwar*) in the *Qur'ān*. I agree with Zaehner that a religious, separate mode of theistic mysticism is ontically different from the monistic type, as the former presupposes a transcendent creator, whereas the latter advocates depiction of a unified monistic cosmos. As explained in the enclosed essay, in my interpretation, theistic mysticism embeds an intrinsic alienation between a creature and his/her source (*arche, aṣl*), whereas a monistic type of mysticism proffers an agenda for de-alienation through mystical union. For this reason, I think interpreters such as S. H. Nasr, S. Inati, A. Ivry, and L. E. Goodman miss the ethos of coherence in ibn Sīnā's system; they mistake his monistic philosophical construct for a flawed monotheistic system.

A third complexity in ibn Sīnian scholarship is due to the extensive secondary literature on his work, dating from his death to the present. For instance, J. L. Janssens' *An Annotated Bibliography on ibn Sina (1970-1989)* comprises 345 pages of texts which list more than a thousand articles on ibn Sīnā written during twenty years.[22] If this were taken as a measure, then there may be tens of thousands of works written on ibn Sīnian philosophy since the eleventh century. This account is not surprising, as his system was regarded as the epitome of philosophy in Islamic culture and a base of scholasticism in Jewish and Christian thought. Thus, a concentrated focus on his work must center on a specific tradition. Most contemporary investigators of Islamic philosophy and a minority of scholars in medieval Christian philosophy and Jewish thought, such as H. A. Wolfson, make ample references to his ideas on limited topics, such as his notion of being (for example, E. Gilson) or his epistemology of internal sense (for example, H. A. Wolfson). A number of scholars have spent life-long careers investigating ibn Sīnā's work. For example, for more than forty years I have taught and lectured on his ideas in the United States, Canada, Europe, the Middle East, and Asia; as an investigator and editor, I have examined a substantial number of secondary sources on this philosopher. Still, my own interpretation of his views is intended more as a prima facie proposal for a more accurate reading of his text than as a "finding" of his "true philosophy." Indeed, for many reasons it is difficult to categorically place him in any specific school other than his own. To begin with, any evaluation of his work must take account of not only the secondary sources but the multifarious syntheses of influences on his system from Zoroastrian, Islamic, and Greek traditions. H. Corbin and Panoussi have written on the Zoroastrian dimensions of his work.[23] The Hellenic influence on his work is obvious. He himself mentions that he read Aristotle's metaphysics "over forty times;" further influence of Greek thought is evident from his severe criticism of Porphyry, as well as his adoption of a Neoplatonic type of emanation in his cosmogony.[24] I restrict my references to classics of Greek ontologies and to recent and contemporary scholars, including those with whom I disagree on three specific issues: those who read—and I think misread—the aim of his philosophy to present a system compatible to monotheism, those who approach him only as a commentator of Aristotle or a Neoplatonist, and a single writer who is unique by holding that ibn Sīnā's system has no relation to mysticism.

There is a fourth and final reason for the complexity of ibn Sīnā's system. Like Leibniz, ibn Sīnā's works are written in different styles: technical ontology, mystical allegory, and even a poem on medicine. Like a shiny stone—partly clear doctrines, partly archetypal icons—often his corpus functions like a mirror, allowing an interpreter to reflect his/her own views onto ibn Sīnā's philosophy. Perhaps the variety of interpretations is partially due to the richness of his system. For example, having studied with logical empiricists such as R. Carnap, I detect a genesis of 'reconstructionalistic' approach to ibn Sīnā's philosophy of universals; reinforcement of my perception comes from works by N. Ṭūsī, one of ibn Sīnā's followers, wherein he explicates different senses of infinite into syntactical, ontic, and pragmatic.[25] In addition to my own views, the reader finds in this introduction discussions of different perspectives on our philosopher. Nader El-Bizri finds Heideggerian themes in the works of our philosopher. Muhsin Mahdi considers him to be a disciple of Fārābī. Shams Inati, Lenn E. Goodman, S. Hossein Nasr, and Alfred Ivry read his Necessary Existent as the monotheistic God. A few, like D. Gutas and H. A. Wolfson, view him as an Aristotelian; M. Fakhry considers him a Neoplatonist; and Houben perceives him to be a non-monotheist. Below follows a clarification of some of my own methodology used to analyze his system.

METHODOLOGICAL CLARIFICATION

There is clearly legitimate justification for a classicist's interest in using ibn Sīnā to 'uncover' his Greek sources, the so-called "Greek into Arabic" approach of scholars like R. Walzer, and H. A. Wolfson.[26] Obviously, Aristotle influenced all subsequent philosophers in a manner similar to that in which Plato influenced Aristotle and the pre-Socractics influenced Plato. There is a tendency in the spirit of Hellemania to fall into a reductionalist trap of forcing the view of every non-Greek system as a corollary to some Greek ideas. Once in a while, there is an exception, such as H. A. Wolfson's monumental work on Philo of Alexandria, whose work contains the genesis of Neoplatonism.[27] This generosity is not extended to the Muslim thinkers, as exemplified by H. A. Wolfson's claims that there is nothing new in ibn Sīnā that is not in Aristotle's writing; in the same manner, D. Gutas dismisses any mysticism in ibn Sīnā because he is supposed to be a rational Aristotelian.[28] In contrast, F. Rosenthal in his excellent work, *Knowledge Triumphant: The Concept of Knowledge in Medieval Islam,* considers with an open mind the specific contributions of ibn Sīnā and other Muslim philosophers concerning the nature of knowledge and as its relation to wisdom, or as life and food for the soul.[29] While ibn Sīnā's work can be used to decipher Aristotelian themes, there are several original non-Aristotelian ideas in his philosophy. For example, M. M. Goichon reads him as an original thinker.[30] I take him to be instrumental in transforming Islamic from a predominantly peripatetic tradition to a phenomenology of processes. Nader El-Bizri has adopted some of these new perspectives in his recent book on *The Quest for Being: Avicenna and Heidegger.* Following El-Bizri's views, I hold that, in addition to the Greek traditions, ibn Sīnā's philosophy should be studied not only in the light of Greek philosophy, but also in the context of thinkers such as A. N. Whitehead and M. Heidegger. This type of perspective frees Islamic philosophy from being perceived as a fossilized relic fit only to be examined by classicists. There is another merit in this methodology. As has been illustrated in these collections, Islamic philosophy can be used to re-read philosophy, such as the ontological argument by Augustine and Descartes.[31] In this vein, ibn Sīnā presents not a static atemporal argument, but a hermeneutic return to the ground of being, through four phases: an encounter with being, being-in-the-world, the ultimate essence of existents and an agenda of care for the unity of being.

Second, I would classify his mysticism as a "natural monism," using a phrase from the works of R. C. Zaehner.[32] Zaehner contrasts the monists-nature mystics with the theistic mystics. According to his proposal, the latter aim to isolate their souls from the body in order to relate to the transcendent divine, while the former proffer integration of the self with nature. A very clear case of the nature type of "mystical therapy" is found in C. G. Jung's later doctrine of "individuation process," where the self develops through the phases of ego, shadow, persona, anima-animus, and finally through the God-Nature phase, which is the ultimate de-alienation of a person from his/her source (*arche*, *aṣl*).[33] The isomorphism between Jungian analytical psychology and sufic doctrines of self-realization is obvious. In this light, I submit this collection to challenge the views of the majority of scholarship on ibn Sīnā; my reading questions especially the position of those who tend to consider the works of all medieval philosophers as offshoots of Jewish, Christian or Islamic traditions. In the enclosed essays, experts in Islamic philosophy note opposition to various specific views of many experts; this long list includes ideas in the works of H. A. Wolfson, M. H. Mahdi, M. Fakhry, D. Burrell, D. Gutas, L. E. Goodman, S. H. Nasr, S. Inati, and A. Ivry. The above-mentioned scholars view ibn Sīnā's system either to be compatible with Islamic theology or as a simple derivative of the philosophies of Fārābī, Aristotle or Plotinus. This collection presents evidence and arguments to show that these hypotheses are not warranted. I am not alone in this task. My reading of ibn Sīnā's system concurs with the interpretation of several Muslim philosophers, such as al-Ghazālī, N. Khosrow and N. Ṭūsī. These thinkers were major philosophers who lived during the era in which ibn Sīnā's system was the major philosophical view. I am in agreement with a few modern investigators, such as M. E. Marmura, J. J. Houben, H. Ziai and N. El-Bizri.

Next, as observed by H. Corbin and S. H. Nasr and others, after the twelfth century, the methodology of Islamic philosophy changed radically.[34] Specifically, there was a conscious tendency to move away from the methodology of the peripatetic who envisioned philosophy as a realistic investigation of the world external of substances. In contrast, the new spirit of philosophy was a phenomenology of an encounter, in which epistemology and ontology were synthesized. The seeds of ibn Sīnā's philosophy were nurtured by the great systems of al-Ghazālī, Mullā Ṣadrā and others.[35]

SOME DIFFERENCES BETWEEN THE SYSTEMS OF IBN SĪNĀ, ARISTOTLE, AND PLOTINUS

Islamic intellectual tradition, insofar as it relates to philosophical themes, may be discussed in the light of three dimensions: theological, philosophical and mystical. I am aware that this tripartite division is an abstract proposal; ibn Sīnā, Ṭūsī, Suhrawardī, Mullā Ṣadrā, and a number of others wrote in all of these three different traditions. For clarification, this collection delineates the mystical dimension of ibn Sīnā's work in the light of the relation between the ultimate being of each system (God, the Necessary Existent, and the mystical one) and creatures.[36] Although ibn Sīnā did not practice mystical rituals and did not claim to have experienced any kind of mystical ecstasy, this work focuses on his meta-mysticism, as he did write a number of mystical treatises, as well as a handbook on "meta-mysticism."[37] Annemarie Schimmel expresses the views of the majority of scholars of mysticism when she asserts, "...ibn Sīnā...was as much a mystical thinker as some of those classified as ṣūfis."[38] In the same tone, H. Corbin notes, "Here the characteristic of Avicenna's mysticism becomes clear; far from pursuing the abolition of the individuality, it transforms and eternizes it. ..."[39] In fact, his meta-mystical account in the fourth book of *Ishārāt wa al-Tanbīhāt* became a sourcebook for a number of subsequent philosophers of mysticism. In the light of these data, it is quite surprising that D. Gutas is the sole scholar to express strong objections to the thesis that mysticism, which has been presupposed by Persian writers for more than one thousand years, as well as by contemporary scholars, is present in ibn Sīnā's work. It is, of course, logically possible that only Gutas is correct and that all the other scholars in the last thousand years are wrong. I shall present evidence to show that it is Gutas who is mistaken; pedagogically, there are two lines of reasoning, or rather misreasoning, presupposed by Gutas: first, he assumes that symbolism is an inferior mode of expression; second he proffers that because ibn Sīnā's system is a "rationalistic" Aristotelian system, it cannot be regarded as mystical.[40] Let us consider this quotation:[41]

> The symbolic method is appropriate for the common people; when knowledge has to be communicated to philosophers, however, the symbolic method is inadequate because it cannot convey, being inferior, that demonstrative argumentation which alone brings out certainty. The only way, therefore, in which both demonstrative argumentation can be conveyed and knowledge concealed from the common people is by presenting it in an obscure way as Aristotle did; by providing, that is, pointers which will show the way to the unexpressed conclusion or premise or middle term. The indicative method therefore has a second function which it shares with the symbolic, namely, concealment of knowledge from the unworthy.

Gutas' simple identification of knowledge with conscious, specific, picture theory type of extensional case of knowledge overlooks ordinary cases of knowledge in both science and everyday life, as well as the development of epistemological theories. It reminds me of the simple-minded statement made by H. Riechenbach in his work, *The Rise of Scientific Philosophy*, which noted that Hamlet's dilemma, "To be or not to be," is solved when one realizes that the phrase is not a question but a tautology.[42] It resembles a hypothetical case in which a mystical master gives a mirror to a novice, who does not uses it for self-reflection, but examines its material constituents. Another example is that of a silver merchant who melts an artwork of Cellini to sell as silver. The general fallacy is to take the whole to be equal to some of its material constituents and overlook the pragmatic dimensions of a sign. Gutas' position is also open to specific criticisms. To begin with, syllogistic knowledge provides at best validity and not certainty (soundness). The truth of a non-tautological premise cannot be logically demonstrated; it has to be proven by other means, such as sense perception or contextual agreement. At best, syllogism provides us with a conditional knowledge, but not a categorical one; it implies merely that if we accept the premises, then we accept the conclusion. The certainty sought by Gutas is feasible in the logical structure of a content-empty argument, not in its content, which contains empirical premises. On this point, Gutas' interpretation is due to his misreading of the meaning of the semantics of syllogism and deduction. Next, ordinary cases of cognitive epistemic states include cognitive reasoning, such as fuzzy logic, speculations on weather conditions or the stock market, and physicians' opinions about the predicted outcome of surgery. As Hume stated, certainty belongs only to the empty realm of purely syntactical domain of relation of ideas (mathematics and logic) and not to matters of fact. Moreover, there is a whole body of literature about epistemology, such as A. N. Whitehead's notion of 'prehension,' which takes warranted judgment to intentional realm; there is in fact a body of intentional logic that investigates this type of statement. Not all knowledge needs to be concerned with deduction or specific facts; L. Wittgenstein points to the inadequacy of this picture theory of language; H. Bergson and the pragmatists have analyzed the instrumental theory of knowledge; G. Ryle has distinguished between two senses of knowledge, illustrated by the difference between knowing Euclidean Geometry and knowing how to ride a bicycle. But one cannot claim that all symbolic language is for the uneducated and unsophisticated who do not understand simple Aristotelian syllogism; consider Beethoven's Ninth Symphony and Michelangelo's Sistine Chapel, both expressions of symbolic language, as well as Plato's *Dialogues* and Plotinus' *Enneads*, two primordial sources of all rationalism. There are cases of learning from paradigm, such as occurs in apprenticeship, Jesus dealing with the stoning of Mary Magdalene, and the body of scholarship on Hadith in Islamic literature. Also, icons point not just to specific designata in the world, but as C. G. Jung stated, they can be viewed as archetypal representations.[43] They clarify the interrelationship among families of related data or pragmatics of signs. As an example from literature, when Dracula is presented with a cross, he is reminded of an expansive realm of Christian ethos even more powerful than his own nonstandard lifestyle, in which he overcomes death by drinking blood as food. The symbol of the cross transmits cognitive data to Dracula. Symbolic entities like the cross are icons (the original Greek meaning 'image'), since Christ actually was crucified on the cross. The same is true of light metaphors, as the Sun in fact is the source of energy. Thus, the data transmitted are cognitive and symbolic simultaneously. This is not a simple-minded mode of communication, as Gutas' interpretation would claim. One problem with the contemporary scholarship of Islamic philosophy is that most investigators like Gutas are not professional philosophers, but classicists or linguists. Gutas' type of thinking illustrates the danger of rushing to judgment without reading the elementary school texts in epistemology.

This issue takes the discussion to the second point made by Gutas: that ibn Sīnā's system cannot contain mysticism because his system is Aristotelian, based on the precept that the Aristotelian system is rationalistic, and mysticism precludes rationalism. Here are three objections to this view:

(a) Ibn Sīnā's system differs from Aristotle's philosophy in regard to many key issues, such as the following: ibn Sīnā proffers emanation of the world by a Neoplatonic process and return; his ultimate being is not a substance; for him, metaphysics begins with the phenomenology of an encounter with being and modalities. In contrast, for Aristotle, the ultimate being, i.e., the unmoved mover is a substance and is co-eternal with the world; also for Aristotle, metaphysics is initiated with the division of 'being' into the categories of 'substance' and 'accidents.' Unlike ibn Sīnā's account of the stages of the mystics, there is no reference to mysticism in the entire Aristotelian corpus, with the exception of Aristotle's prescription to imitate the prime mover.[44] (b) The genesis of mysticism is grounded in the works of masters of rationalism, Plato and Plotinus; in fact, the allegory of the cave in the *Republic*, the ascent of love in the *Symposium* and ascent to the one in the *Enneads* are all primordial models of the way of salvation, expressed as '*ṭarīqa*' in Ṣūfis. Some Muslim mystics explicitly refer to Plato as "the Divine Plato," and to Plotinus as "the Greek Sheikh."[45] Gutas ignores both the ancient and the contemporary literature concerning the affinity between rationalism and mysticism.

The entire cultural context of ibn Sīnā's life is embedded with mystical writings, such as the works of Rūmī and Shabastarī. Obviously, this historical fact by itself cannot prove that ibn Sīnā's system is related to mysticism. But he wrote on mysticism, and never commented critically against mysticism, unlike ibn Tamiyya. It would help Gutas' case if he showed how and why ibn Sīnā differed from the majority of philosophers in his tradition; also, he needs to prove in what ways everyone else incorrectly interprets ibn Sīnā's writings.

REJECTION OF FAKHRY'S REDUCTION OF IBN SĪNĀ'S SYSTEM TO NEOPLATONISM

Having rejected Gutas' thesis, let us proceed to M. Fakhry's classification of ibn Sīnā's philosophy in the context of "Further Development of Islamic Neoplatonism," which was mostly due to ibn Sīnā's adoption of emanation over creation.[46] M. Fakhry has contributed much to scholarship concerning the relation between Greek and Islamic philosophy, as the last essay in this collection illustrates, and he should be praised for singling out Neoplatonism as the most important Greek influence on Islamic philosophy. However, I submit five key differences between the systems of Plotinus and ibn Sīnā to show that ibn Sīnā's system is not derived from Neoplatonism.

1. While Plotinus rejects Aristotle's categories [Enneads VI 1 (1-24)], ibn Sīnā adopts them as the major metaphysical tool in his encyclopedic works such as the *Dānish Nāmeh*, the *Najāt*, and the *Shifā.'* There are, however, lingering similarities, as follow. While the ultimate being of Aristotle's Metaphysics, namely, the prime mover, is a substance, neither the ultimate being of Plotinus' system nor of ibn Sīnā's ontology is a substance. I also interpret ibn Sīnā's cosmogony and return in the process language of Neoplatonism rather than in Aristotle's cosmology of substances.
2. There are several places where Aristotle states that his ultimate being is conscious of itself. Plotinus criticizes Aristotle on these points. There are passages in the Enneads (VI 9 (9), chap. 6, III 9 [13], chaps. 7, 9) implying that the One is not conscious of itself. In contrast to Aristotle, there are passages in which ibn Sīnā's ultimate being is not conscious of itself.[47]
3. Plotinus' philosophy of mathematics follows Platonic realism (*En-*

neads, VI [9] 5), while ibn Sīnā rejects this view (*Shifā,'* Chap. III).

4. Ibn Sīnā is against the standard Neoplatonic equation of identification of the knowledge with the known, as advocated by Porphyry.[48]
5. Finally, for ibn Sīnā, axiomatically, the major metaphysical concept is being; his ultimate being, unlike Plotinus' 'One,' is logically derived from a concatenation of 'being' and 'contingency.' Having the status of "supra-existence/being (*ousia*)," or "beyond-existence/being (*ousia*)," Plotinus' 'One' is to be approached by negative or allegorical theology. In contrast, ibn Sīnā clearly derives 'The Necessary Being' from the primary notions of 'being' and 'necessity.' This specific issue clarifies confusion introduced by L. E. Goodman, who states that because ibn Sīnā's 'Necessary Being' is a priori, there is no ontological argument in his system. All analytically true statements are a priori, whether they are primary or derivative from a set of tautological premises. In ibn Sīnā's system, the statement that "The notion of 'Necessary Being' implies 'The Necessary Existent'" is proven logically, independent of experience. Ontological argument belongs to the domain of syntax and not semantics.

In sum, Fakhry is indeed correct about the significance of Neoplatonism in Islamic thought. But his labeling of ibn Sīnā as a Neoplatonist is not justifiable, unless he means that in many of his ideas, ibn Sīnā followed Plotinus in the same sense that Aristotle called himself a Platonist.

DIFFERENCES BETWEEN IBN SĪNĀ'S SYSTEM AND MONOTHESIM

Consider the following arguments against the position that ibn Sīnā's system is compatible with monotheism:

(a) While all monotheistic creeds advocate the doctrine of creation, ibn Sīnā rejects the Qur'ānic cosmogony and, following Plotinus, accepts the doctrine of emanation. There are several problems with the doctrine of creation. One issue is the philosophical position that "nothing comes out of nothing." "Nothing" cannot be a subject of a proposition. Moreover, there are a host of other issues, such as the nature of time, the will of the creator and the ontic relation between the creator and the created. We note here that by accepting creation, he also rejects the Aristotelian model of co-eternity. L. E. Goodman's attempt to attribute to ibn Sīnā a "creative emanation" is never clarified, and at face value is a category mistake.[49]

(b) Whereas in all monotheistic systems the salvation of the soul depends on God's grace, again, following Plotinus, our philosopher makes salvation via mystical love dependent totally on the soul's striving for perfection, without any input from his ultimate being. No monotheistic system can take away from God His power to provide punishment and rewards to His creatures. Ibn Sīnā's views on this topic are counter to the core of monotheism.

(c) I wish to point out to the reader that my views on the incompatibility of Ibn Sīnā's system with monotheism are in line with the position of many classical Muslim theologians. A few philosopher mystics, such as Manṣūr al-Ḥallāj and Shehāb al-Dīn Suhrawardī, were murdered for their peculiar mystical positions, which offended the orthodoxy. Nāṣir Khosrow and Nāṣir al-Dīn Ṭūsī were exceptions from the rest of Muslim thought because they advocated an affinity among theology, philosophy and mysticism. Consequently, to hold that ibn Sīnā's doctrines are not compatible with Islam should not be regarded as an extraordinary position that runs against common history.

As prominent features of the 'Ultimate Being', both the notions of 'God' and the 'Necessary Existent' are complex and prima facie are not equivalent. If an investigator wishes to identify them, she/he needs to prove their equivalence in the system of the philosopher in question. It is definitely not the case that traditionally Muslim philosophers have equated them. For example, Khosrow explicitly states that neither time nor existence (*hastī*) can be applicable to God.[50] Moreover, he identifies the 'Necessary Being' (*al-Wājib al-Wujūd*) not with the 'One' of Plotinus but with the 'First Intellect.' N. Ṭūsī, the major commentator on ibn Sīnā's works, states that free will cannot be attributed to God, since free will is applicable to agents that have multiple attributes, whereas God is a simple unity.

SALIENT FEATURES OF IBN SĪNĀ'S PHENOMENOLOGICAL APPROACH

As stated above, the salient feature of Islamic philosophy is the genesis of a phenomenological approach embedded in the ibn Sīnian system that was developed by subsequent thinkers. Here are three paradigm examples in his system: (a) the primary task of philosophy is a shift from the peripatetic categorical division of 'being' into 'substance' and 'accident' to a new focus on the primary existential encounter with being; (b) instead of limiting his epistemology to the extensional experience of external senses, he preferred the intentional phenomenology of internal senses, especially '*wahm*' (prehensive imagination); and (c) his philosophy of person as expressed in the so-called 'flying man' is analogous to a Heideggerian *Dasine* rather than to Descartes' *Cogito*; the latter is open to the private language fallacy.

The first point 'a' has been covered in this introduction and elaborated in our account of the 'essence-existence' distinction. The second point, with regards to the reading of '*wahm*' as an intentional notion of "prehensive imagination," is discussed in a previous essay; this in contrast to H. W. Wolfson's reading of 'estimation,' that adopts the Latin scholastic interpretation of ibn Sīnā's epistemology of '*estimatio*.' As an intentional concept, this notion as well as other internal senses, shows that ibn Sīnā's epistemology extended beyond Aristotle's extensional epistemology. Consider an illustration of 'prehension': a sheep encounters a wolf and '*wahms*' fear by running away. Unlike apprehension (*idrak*), where the agent is conscious of an experience, '*wahm*' is prehended without a conscious awareness; the response to its encounter is a not a sense datum, nor an analytic statement; instead, the response is a pragmatically reasonable reaction, such as "running away." This notion may be an early version of the instrumental theory of learning developed later by H. Bergson and J. Dewey.[51]

The final point, 'c' concerns ibn Sīnā's metaphysics of being in the realm of experience. The philosopher constructs the case of a person who loses his senses, who is gradually abstracted out of his experience. Even though the suspended man in question does not experience a concrete datum, he is aware of being-in-the-world. I agree with El-Bizri that ibn Sīnā here does not postulate a Cogito-substance, but depicts the primordial experience of the soul-self in the manner of the Dasine of Heidegger.[52] Wittgenstein points out that Cartesian *Cogito* commits the private language fallacy, whereas ibn Sīnā's notion is free from this mistake.[53] I. Kant was aware of this dimension of the problem of the self as he postulated the noumenal self beyond experience; the phenomenal self, however, was not a substance, but was encountered in the light of the transcendental unity of apperception.[54] I have discussed elsewhere that ibn Sīnā's concept of the self can be depicted in the context of process metaphysics rather than in terms of a substance-event language.[55] Far from being exceptional, there are many cases of depiction of experience in the language of phenomenological process; an example is the notion of '*ḥāl*,' often translated as 'states,' in context of '*ṭarīqa*,' the sufic notion of self-realization.[56] The distinction made between a 'station,' and a 'state' (*maqām*) is in light not of static substantial features, but intentional attitude. For example, prior to being a parent, a person is in one station, but after being a parent her/his receptivity of the world changes. For further clarification of ibn Sīnā's notion of the self, see El-Bizri's recent publication.[57]

CARDINAL POINTS OF IBN SĪNIAN METAPHYSICS

Contemporary philosophies of logical syntax of a language distinguish between two types of primitives—one, designative types of sign, the other, rules for transformation, designation, and interpretation, and these distinctions can be applied to ibn Sīnā's system. Ibn Sīnā's two primordial notions of the soul are 'being' (*hastī, wujūd*) and the modalities [of necessity (*wājib*), contingency (*mumkin*) and impossibility (*mumtani'*)]. The notion of being is the core of his system, while the modalities specify the subset of beings that are existents. The notion of 'being' concatenated with 'necessity' point to 'the necessary being;' using the second version of the ontological argument, 'necessary being' results in 'the Necessary Existent.' The notion of 'being' concatenated with 'contingency' has two possible results: (a) if there is a cause for the case in question, then the contingency is an actual existent—for example, in the case of 'being a human,' persons are existents because they have parents; (b) in the case of absence of the cause, the results are non-actual contingencies such as unicorns. 'Impossibility' and 'being' lead to no existent, as illustrated by 'round squares,' and 'the largest number.' The key notions of ibn Sīnā's system are very clear:

'Being-qua-being' (*hastī, wujūd*) corresponds to Aristotle's notion of 'being-qua-being' in *Metaphysica* 1002a 20 (τὸ ὂν ᾗ ὄν) and E. Moody's reading of Ockham's use of '*ens*' in *Summa Totius Logicae*.[58] It signifies the most determinable concept. 'Non-being' is meaningless. We should note that all mental concepts (actual or not actual) signify a being. For this reason 'being' is different from 'existent'.

'Existent' (*mawjūd*) signifies actual entities, Aristotle's notion of first substance (*prote ousia*). There are no impossible existents. For ibn Sīnā there is only one Necessary existent, which is the ultimate cause of generation of other existents. 'Existence' itself is not an existent, but signifies those entities which are neither uncaused 'contingent beings' nor 'impossible entities.'

'Essence,' (*māhiyya*) is used by ibn Sīnā in the sense of "*ti esti*" and in the secondary sense of "*ousia*" employed by Aristotle.[59] An existent partakes of an essence; for example, the feature of a basketball can be discussed in terms of the formal properties of a sphere. An unrealized entity such as a unicorn may have an essence but no existence.

CONSIDERATION OF M. E. MARMURA'S TRANSLATION OF IBN SĪNĀ'S ONTIC TERMS

While I esteem very highly the brilliant contribution of M. E. Marmura's research in ibn Sīnian metaphysics, I disagree with his translation of '*wujūd*' as 'existence' for the following reasons.[60] For ibn Sīnā, an impossible '*mui'tani' al-wujūd*' cannot not exist. Marmura's reading implies the following absurdity, that "there is an existence which does not have existence." Marmura attempts to present a formula by which we make a distinction between actual existents and other types. But this complication could have been avoided simply by following the standard translation of '*wujūd*' as 'being.' Moreover, all of the English translations of Aristotle and medieval Christian philosophers refer to 'being' in exactly the same manner in which standard translations of ibn Sīnā's text do, using 'being' for '*wujūd*.' Adoption of the translation offered by Marmura would make cross-reference between Aristotle's and ibn Sīnā's writings impossible.

DISSENSIONS FROM NASR'S INTERPRETATION OF IBN SĪNĀ'S NOTION OF BEING

Next, the discussion turns to the works of S. H. Nasr, with excerpts from his work. The first quotation reads,[61]

> Being in itself is the cause of all particular existents without being reduced to a genre common to all of them. Being is above all distinctions and polarization and yet the cause of the world of multiplicity, casting its light upon the different and distinct quiddities (*mahiyat*) of all things. Being is the reality of each thing, as it is the source of all goodness and beauty as well as the cause of all perceptions, the quiddities constituting no more than the limitation of being.

The second quotation states,[62]

> In his [i.e. ibn Sīnā's] ontology…emphasis is on the transcendence of Being, or God, above all particular beings or creatures, in cosmogony, on the contrary, accent is placed upon relation of generated being to Being and their effusion (*faid*) from the source of all things.

The expression in the first passage makes the following category mistake: being-qua-being is an abstraction of an aspect of existents as well as notions of impossible entities or non-caused contingencies. If the cause of an entity were being, then round squares, unicorns, and the like would be actual existents, as they are cases of being. Nasr's capitalization of the 'b' in 'being' constitutes a problem; in ibn Sīnā's metaphysics there is no 'Being' apart from other entities, as there is no non-being; whatever is meaningful is also a being. For example, consider the following sentence: "Sir Thomas Hobbes wanted to square a circle;" here the notion of a squared circle is an impossible being entertained by a brilliant philosopher who apparently was weak in geometry. Such a notion has no designata. It seems that in some sense Nasr wishes to give priority to the God of monotheism in every conceivable way. In doing so, he is referring to his own system rather than to ibn Sīnā's. For ibn Sīnā's axiomatic system, the primary notions are "being" and the "modalities;" there is no "God-the-creator" in his system. 'The Necessary Being' results from a concatenation of 'being' and 'necessity;' the 'Necessary Being' does not cause being or beings and it is not a Being itself, just a being.

Nasr's statement that 'God' is a transcendence of 'Being' is in conflict with ibn Sīnā's rule of formation for being; moreover, I disagree with Nasr's interpretation, which presupposes the 'Necessary Existent' as 'God' of Islam. So, counter to Nasr's position, I argue that the 'Necessary Existent,' or whatever Nasr misinterprets as 'God,' not only is not a transcendence of 'being,' but it is derived from it. The remainder of the passages in Nasr's work dealing with "casting its light" and "goodness" are either expressions in a set of metaphors or are incorrect attributes. Since, normatively, negative entities like germs are also cases of being, goodness is not an essential byproduct of being. Nasr's writing is more like a ballet than a physiological account of ibn Sīnā's meticulous system.

DISSENSIONS FROM GOODMAN, IVRY, AND INATI'S INTERPRETATIONS OF IBN SĪNĀ

I take exception to L. E. Goodman's account of ibn Sīnā's philosophy, as well as to the style of his account of Greek philosophers. Let me begin with the problem of Goodman's metaphorical rhetoric, by which Goodman judges Plotinus' wits and Aristotle's cleverness. I am not sure what impression he intends to make—perhaps to shock the reader? Here are two examples: "The

Aristotelian answer about the nature of existence, may seem disappointedly flat, even tautologous."[63] What could he possibly mean by this attempt to degrade the first teacher of all philosophers? Here is a possible answer. Aristotle has been misinterpreted as a purely discursive philosopher who does not have a Platonic vision of process or the ethics of self-realization. But a number of distinguished scholars like F. G. E. Woodridge and J. H. Randall, who have a very "non-flat" view of existence, have praised Aristotle's depiction of nature in terms of being the source of its own motion.[64] Why should a monotheist like Goodman find a pagan system to be disappointing because it does not assume that everything emerges from nothing through creation? Here is another statement: "Despite his strident polemic against Stoic materialism, Plotinus was not slow to grasp the usefulness of ..."[65] The idea that Plotinus was not slow in his intellectual ability is like saying that Fujiyama is not a minute pile of sand, or that the sun is not too cold to shine on the earth. In light of his attack on the systems of two of the greatest philosophers of all time, imagine what Goodman might do to ibn Sīnā's system. Surprisingly, he only criticizes our philosopher for not being a good monotheist. He notes that the 'Necessary Being' is an a priori concept, and then claims that ibn Sīnā follows the creation theory.

After having incorrectly forged the idea of a monotheistic God onto ibn Sīnā's work, Goodman criticizes ibn Sīnā for not allowing a place for God in nature. As we shall document, Inati and A. Ivry also misinterpret ibn Sīnā's Necessary Existent as God and then criticize him for not assigning standard monotheistic features of God to his Necessary Existent.

Let us begin with some questionable assertions made by Inati. To begin, she identifies Plotinus' 'One' with God; then she also proceeds to write as if Plato and Aristotle actually had written about a religious notion of God that has an affinity with the monotheistic notion of God.[66] It would have been more clear to use the expression 'the ultimate being,' than God for either Plato's 'demiurge' (which is clearly a metaphorical concept and has no actuality) or the 'Form of the Good' of Plato. The same applies to the 'Unmoved Mover' of Aristotle, the 'One' of Plotinus and the 'Necessary Existent' of ibn Sīnā. I do not see any religious ethos of monotheism in Platonic texts, and agree with F. M. Cornford on the following analysis,[67]

> There is, in the first place no justification for the suggestion conveyed by 'God' with a capital letter that Plato was a monotheist...Plato's Demiurge...is not an object of worship; he is not a religious figure.... He must not be equated with the God of Bible, Who created the world out of nothing and is also The object of worship...the omnipotent Creator and the Modern notion of natural law were equally foreign to the mind of Greeks.

It seemingly never occurs to Inati that all of these philosophers were perfectly capable of using the common term for God (*Theos*, *Allāh*), but intentionally did not. Throughout the entire book, she equates the 'Necessary Existent' of ibn Sīnā with God, although ibn Sīnā does not use *Allāh*, but *al-Wājib al-Wujūd*. However, she correctly admits that the entity that she reads as 'God' (and what I read as 'Necessary Existent,' following the Arabic and the Persian term *al-Wājib al-Wujūd* rather than *Allāh*, which was not used by ibn Sīnā) creates (she uses this term, I use 'emanates') out of necessity.[68] Ibn Sīnā never uses the expression *'khalq,'* which signifies 'creation.' Having by force transformed ibn Sīnā's theodicy of the ultimate being into a monotheistic God, Inati then criticizes the philosopher for denying theistic features to the 'Necessary Existent.' In a less careful treatment of ibn Sīnā's texts, A. Ivry also presupposes without any discussion that ibn Sīnā's 'Necessary Existent' is God. Then he proceeds to say that "Avicenna in a way had his cake and ate it, ..." The world is seen to be originally, continually, and ultimately dependent on God, although it also functions in a necessary, continuous and a predictable way.[69] Here is a very interesting statement, which gives the reader a clue as to how Ivry interprets the ancient and medieval philosophers. Ivry states, "Avicenna, like Aristotle, then, is in an embarrassing position—for Avicenna—of not being the Creator of the universe in the fullest sense of the term."[70] Goodman also notes that "...Avicenna's synthesis did not hold up...[partially because of] the world's temporal creation."[71] It seems that these three interpreters of ibn Sīnā assume that he was not aware of the differences between his

Necessary Existent and the God of Islam. I assume that he was aware of the non-monotheistic dimensions of his thought and he consciously chose emanationism in order to avoid the philosophical problem of the creation theory, especially the dilemma of how something can come out of nothing. Ibn Sīnā lacked not in reasoning, but rather, perhaps, he lacked faith in a transcendent being, as do a majority of philosophers.

THE AIMS OF IBN SĪNĀ'S PHILOSOPHY

Finally, the discussion turns to the aims of ibn Sīnā's philosophy. There are a number of different positions on this issue. A distinguished scholar of Islamic philosophy, M. Mahdi mentions, "...one must begin with Avicenna, as a disciple of Fārābī, which in many ways he was, but also as a thinker who attempted to redefine the course of Islamic philosophy and channel it in new directions."[72] Mahdi interprets ibn Sīnā's system as "...what emerges [as] a philosophical interpretation of religion."[73] Finally he notes "...Avicenna took the crucial step from Fārābī's general science of religion to a science of this particular religion which is Islam."[74] I wish to address two specific issues in his claim. First, can the ordinary use of 'disciple' be applied to this case? The ordinary sense of disciple is used in a case in which a philosopher refers extensively to a previous thinker, defends his/her position against critics, and finally develops themes from the latter in his philosophy. Accordingly, it is reasonable to assert that Porphyry was a disciple of Plotinus, and N. Ṭūsī was a disciple of ibn Sīnā. It is clear that in no way could ibn Sīnā be considered a disciple of Fārābī in the above-mentioned sense. Ibn Sīnā does not mention Fārābī in the same sense that Porphyry or Ṭūsī mention their masters. Second, I question Mehdi's statement that ibn Sīnā's work focuses on an Islamic dimension of philosophy. To begin with, a majority of ibn Sīnā's philosophical work is on technical philosophy written in the style of Aristotle's *Metaphysics*, with very little concern to any religion. Second, unlike Fārābī, ibn Sīnā does not begin with the political philosophy of a religious community, but with analytic metaphysics. However, like Fārābī, ibn Sīnā consciously adopts 'emanation' instead of 'creation.' It is true that many ideas from Fārābī's writings, such as his theory of emanation and logic, were obviously used by ibn Sīnā. These similarities do not imply that ibn Sīnā was a disciple of Fārābī, as there are some sharp differences between them. For example, so far we have no mystical recital attributed to Fārābī. Finally, as it was noted, whereas Fārābī's vision of philosophizing follows Plato's Republic in that philosophy takes place in a *poletia*, ibn Sīnā often proceeds with analytic metaphysics in the manner of Aristotle and Plotinus without any reference to community. It is more reasonable to label him as an original philosopher of 'being' who happened to live and work in an Islamic culture, a culture that is sufficiently fertile to produce thinkers who go beyond Islamic perspectives. Mahdi's account of ibn Sīnā is an accurate search to find Fārābī's influence on ibn Sīnā, but is questionable when considered as an examination of ibn Sīnā's system on its own merits. As Peter Heath mentions, "The purpose of philosophy, according to Avicenna is to 'ascertain the true nature…of all things, in as much as it is possible for human beings to ascertain it.'"[75]

CONCLUSION

This collection proffers that ibn Sīnā is an original philosopher and not a mere follower of either Aristotle or Plotinus; his system is logically incompatible with monotheism; and finally, it is a reasonable interpretation to label his philosophy a 'monistic mysticism,' in the sense used by R. C. Zaehner.

I submit these theses, as well as my criticism of the positions of the aforementioned investigators, in a positive spirit, with the aim of stimulating scholarship on ibn Sīnā's philosophy. Like others, I have learned much from the writings of several investigators whom I have criticized on specific issues, especially from H. A. Wolfson, M. Mahdi, and M. E. Marmura. While I criticize specifics of their works on ibn Sīnā, I still regard that the best contemporary scholarship on ibn Sīnā is found in Marmura's writings, the best work on Fārābī has been completed by Mahdi, and that Wolfson's pioneering investigation on Kalam, Spinoza and Philo will remain classics of research in philosophy.

Al-Ghazālī and ibn Taymiyya were correct in their judgment of the incompatibility of the ibn Sīnian version of Hellenic philosophy with the tenets of monotheism. Counter to their views, I hold that such a divergence is a credit to ibn Sīnā, for the independence of his mind, as well as to Islamic culture for producing thinkers who go beyond the standards of its tradition. Islam is not alone in this distinction. S. Freud and K. Marx are testimonies to the richness of Judaism, as Hume and Nietzsche exemplify the intellectual fertility of the European Christian tradition.

NOTES

1 Maurer, *Medieval Philosophy*, (New York, 1962), p. 94; F. Copleston, *A History of Philosophy*, (New York, 1962), vol. II, pt. 1, p. 215.

2 Y. Mahdavi, *Bibliographie d'Ibn Sina*, (Tehran, 1954); G. C. Anawati, *Essay de bibliographie avicennienne*, (Cairo, 1950).

3 *Al-Shifā' Al-Manṭiq*, ed. I. Madkour, *et al.*, 4 vols, (Cairo, 1960).

4 See Parviz Morewedge, "The Internal Sense of Prehension (*wahm*) in Islamic Philosophy," in *Philosophies of Being and Mind*, ed. James T. H. Martin, (Delmar, 1992), pp. 175-206.

5 Ghazālī, *The Incoherence of the Philosophers*, ed. and trans. Michael E. Marmura, (Provo, 1997), p. xix.

6 H. A. Wolfson, *Studies in the History of Philosophy and Religion*, (Cambridge, 1973), p. 235.

7 Suhrawardī, *The Philosophy of Illumination*, (Provo, 1999), p. xxix.

8 H. Ziai, "The Source and the Nature of Authority: A Study of al-Suhrawardī's Illuminationist Political Doctrine, in *The Philosophical Aspects of Islamic Philosophy, Essays in the Honor of Muhsin S. Mahdi*, ed. C. Butterworth, (Cambridge, 1992), p. 309.

9 J. W. Morris, "The Philosopher-Prophet in Avicenna's Philosophy," in *The Philosophical Aspects of Islamic Philosophy, Essays in the Honor of Muhsin S. Mahdi*, ed. C. Butterworth, (Cambridge, 1992), p. 152.

10 An important case is ibn Sīnā's *Ishārāt wa al-Tanbīhāt*, (Tehran) 1377h.

11 See *The Metaphysics of Ṭūsī*, trans. P. Morewedge, (New York, 1980).

12 Shams Inati, *Ibn Sīnā on Evil: A Study of ibn Sīnā's Theodicy*, (Binghamton, Global Publications, 2000), pp. 169-173.

13 M. Goichon, "The Philosopher of Being," in *Avicenna Commemoration Volume*, ed. V. Courtois, (Calcutta, 1956), p. 108.

14 E. Gilson, *History of Christian Philosophy in the Middle Ages*, (New York, Random House, 1954), p. 206.

15 See *The Metaphysica of Avicenna (Ibn Sīnā), a critical translation-commentary of the fundamental arguments in the Dānish Nama-i 'ala'i* (*The Book of Scientific Knowledge*), Parviz Morewedge, (New York and London, 1973).

16 M. Goichon. *Lexique de la Langue Philosophique d' Ibn Sina* and *Vocabulaires Comparés d'Aristotle et d'Ibn Sina (Avicenne)*, (Paris, Desclée de Brouwer, 1939).

17 *Ibid.*, Morewedge, p. 187.

18 See, for example, *Averroes and the Enlightenment*, M. Whaba and M. Abousenna, (Amherst, NY, 1996).

19 See, for example, ibn Sīnā, *Kitāb al-Ḥudūd*, in *Avicenne Livre Des Définitions*, ed. and trans. A.M. Goichon, (Cairo, Institut Français d'Archéologie Orientale du Caire, 1963).

20 *Fārābī's Kitāb al-Ḥurūf*, ed. M. Mahdi, (Beirut, 1969).

21 See texts such as R. C. Zaehner, *Mysticism, Sacred and Profane*; W. T. Stace, *Philosophy and Mysticism*; and F. Staal, *Experiencing Mysticism*.

22 J. L. Janssens, *An Annotated Bibliography on ibn Sina (1970-1989)*, (Leuven, Belgium: University Press, 1991).

23 See E. Panoussi, *Revue Philosophique de Louvain*, lxvi (1968): 239-66.

24 See J. Finnegan, "Avicenna's Refutation of Porphyrius," in *Avicenna Commemoration Volume*, pp. 187-204.

25 *Ibid.*, *Metaphysics of Ṭūsī*, "Division of Existents," pp. 13-40.

26 See H. A. Wolfson, "Goichon's Three Books on Avicenna's Philosophy," *Muslim World* 31 (1941): 29-38. He states, "Now every student of philosophy knows that none of these topics was invented by Avicenna," p. 31; R. Walzer, *Greek into Arabic*, (Cambridge, Massachusetts, 1962), p. 35.

27 H. A. Wolfson, *Philo: Foundation of Philosophy in Judaism, Christianity and Islam*, 2 vols. (Cambridge, Massachusetts, 1962).

28 *Ibid.*, Gutas, *Encyclopaedia Iranica*, ed. E. Yarshater, (London: Routledge and Kegan Paul, 1989), p. 79.

29 F. Rosenthal, *Knowledge Triumphant: The Concept of Knowledge in Medieval Islam*, (Leiden, 1970), pp. 40, 318.

30 M. Goichon, *La Distinction de l'essence et l'existence d'apres Ibn Sina (Avicenna)*, (Paris, 1937).

31 See the chapter in this collection on Avicenna's notion of the ontological argument as a process of self-realization instead of a formal atemporal proof.

32 *Ibid.*, R. C. Zaehner.

33 G. Jung, *Aion: Research into the Phenomenology of the Self*, trans. R. F. C. Hull. (Princeton, 1959).
34 S. H. Nasr, "Post-Avicennan Philosophy and the Study of Being," in *Philosophies of Existence: Ancient and Medieval*, (New York, 1982), pp. 337-344; H. Corbin, *History of Islamic Philosophy*, trans. L. Sherrard, (London and New York, 1993).
35 P. Morewedge, "Theology," in *The Oxford Encyclopedia of the Islamic World*, ed. J. L. Esposito, (New York and Oxford, 1995), vol. IV, pp. 214-224.
36 *Ibid.* See three senses of 'theology,' philosophical, mystical, and religious.
37 See, for example, H. Corbin, *Avicenna and the Visionary Recital*, trans. W. R. Trask, (New York, 1960).
38 Annemarie Schimmel, *Mystical Dimensions of Islam*, (Chapel Hill, 1975), p. 19.
39 *Ibid.*, H. Corbin, p. 239.
40 Gutas, "Avicenna: Mysticism," in *Encyclopaedia Iranica*, ed. E. Yarshater, (London: Routledge and Kegan Paul, 1989), pp. 79-83.
41 Gutas, *Avicenna and The Aristotelian Tradition; Introduction to Reading Avicenna's Philosophical Works*, (Leiden and New York, 1988), p. 308.
42 H. Reichenbach, *The Rise of Scientific Philosophy*, (Berkeley and Los Angeles, 1951).
43 C. G. Jung, *The Archetypes of the Collective Unconscious*, trans. R. F. C. Hull, (Princeton, 1959).
44 Aristotle's prime mover, 1041 a30, 1049 b 26, *et passim*.
45 Rosenthal, "As-Sayh al-Yunani and the Arabic Plotinus Source," *Orientalia* 21 (1952): 461-492; 22 (1953): 370-400; and 24 (1955): 42-66.
46 M. Fakhry, *A History of Islamic Philosophy*, (New York: Columbia University Press, 1983), pp. 107-163.
47 *Dānish Nāmeh*, p. 100; *al-Ishārāt*, vol. III, p. 279.
48 See J. Finnegan, "Avicenna's Refutation of Porphyrius," in *Avicenna Commemoration Volume*, (Calcutta, 1956), pp. 187-205.
49 L. E. Goodman, *Avicenna*, (London: Routledge, 1992), p. 63. Goodman's statement that ibn Sīnā takes emanation as a "real meaning of creation" is open to two objections. First, ibn Sīnā never stated such a doctrine. Second, the notion cannot be meaningful because "creation" is out of nothing, whereas "emanation" is an overflow of what already exists. This is a typical of Goodman's writing, as he seldom clarifies claims that prima facie appear to be at best confusing, if not nonsense. See also: "creation as a mythical symbol of emanation," (p. 67), "Ar-

istotle analyzed existence in terms of essence," (p. 68), "perhaps the most damaging criticism one can make of ibn Sīnā's epistemic scheme is that it leaves too much to the Active Intellect." (p. 144), *et passim.*

50 Nāṣir Khosrow, *Knowledge and Liberation: A Treatise on Philosophical Psychology*, ed. and trans. Faquir M. Hunzai; introduction by Parviz Morewedge, (London and New York, 1998), pp. 14-18.

51 *Ibid.*, P. Morewedge, "The Internal Sense of Prehension…"

52 N. El-Bizri, *The Quest for Being: Avicenna and Heidegger*, (Binghamton, 2000).

53 See L. Wittgenstein, *Philosophical Investigations*, G. E. Anscombe, Rush Rhees, and G. H. von Wright, ed.; trans. G. E. Anscombe, (Oxford, 1956), sections 202, 272, *et passim.*

54 Kant, *A Critique of Pure Reason*, trans. N. Kemp Smith, (London: Macmillan, 1953), p. 408.

55 P. Morewedge, "Substance and Process Theories of the Self in Islamic Mysticism," in *Essays in Islamic Philosophy, Theology and Mysticism*, (Oneonta, 1955), pp. 183-218.

56 See P. Morewedge, "Mystical Icons in Rūmī's Poetry: Light, the Mediator and the Way," in *Essays in Islamic Philosophy, Theology and Mysticism*, (Oneonta, 1955), pp. 219-266.

57 *Ibid.*, Bizri, *The Quest for Being.*

58 See E. A. Moody, *The Logic of William of Ockham*, (New York, 1965), p. 137.

59 See P. Morewedge, *The Metaphysica of Avicenna (ibn Sīnā)*, p. 313.

60 See M. E. Marmura, *Encyclopaedia Iranica*, pp. 73-79.

61 S. H. Nasr, *Islamic Cosmological Doctrines.* (Cambridge, 1975), pp. 197-98.

62 *Ibid.*, p. 202.

63 Goodman, p. 69.

64 J. H. E. Woodbridge, *Aristotle's Vision of Nature*, ed. with an introduction by J. H. Randall, Jr. (New York, 1965); J. H. Randall, *Aristotle*, (New York, 1962).

65 Goodman, p. 70.

66 Inati, p. 49.

67 M. Cornford, *Plato's Cosmology, the Timaeus*, (London, 1937), pp. 34-35.

68 Inati, p. 169.

69 Alfred L. Ivry, "Maimonides and Neoplatonism: Challenge and Response," in *Neoplatonism and Jewish Thought*, ed. L. E. Goodman, (Albany, 1992), p. 147.

70 *Ibid.*, p. 150.

71 Goodman, p. 108.

72 *Encyclopaedia Iranica*, p. 66.
73 *Ibid.*
74 *Ibid.*, p. 67.
75 Peter Heath, *Allegory and Philosophy in Avicenna (ibn Sina)*, (Philadelphia, 1992), p. 40.

PHILOSOPHICAL ANALYSIS AND IBN SĪNĀ'S ESSENCE-EXISTENCE DISTINCTION*

Ibn Sīnā's "essence-existence" distinction has consistently been misformulated as "Existence is an addition to essence," and "Existence is an accident of essence." In these formulations, the distinction is open to three types of objections: (i) the paradox of the self-referential operation on 'existence;' (ii) the theory that "existence is an attribute;" (iii) a confusion between the analytical nature of metaphysics and the empirical nature of science. We propose to establish a new reformulation by differentiating between 'being' [*hastī*],'essence' [*māhiyya*], and 'existence' [*wujūd*], and by distinguishing between the analytical and empirical domain. While taking account of the three above-mentioned objections, our formulation of ibn Sīnā's distinction is consistent with empiricism, for instead of containing an ontological dualism, it draws a logical distinction between conceptual analysis in languages and existential facts. That this type of distinction is carried out in the spirit of empiricism is illustrated by similar distinctions found in the philosophies of Hume and Carnap. However, in view of ibn Sīnā's doctrines about the self and the Necessary Existent, we wish to recognize the limited extent to which one can reappraise his position as that of consequent, unfaltering empiricism.

I
THE PROBLEM AND ITS SIGNIFICANCE

Ibn Sīnā asserts repeatedly in his texts, for instance, in the *Metaphysics* [*Ilāhiyyāt*] of *al-Shifā,' al-Ishārāt wa al-Tanbihāt,* and the *Dānish Nāmeh 'alāi,* that there is a difference between "essence" [*māhiyya*] and "existence" [*wujūd, anniyya*], which prima facie means that there is a fundamental difference between, for example, the *concept* of "humanity" and a *case* of humanity, such as the existence of Socrates.[1]

In view of its primary historical and philosophical significance, the clarification of his distinction is of major importance to contemporary Near Eastern philosophy, particularly since this distinction has been consistently misunderstood by many philosophers and critics of ibn Sīnā. In this book we shall pursue two goals: to point out some aspects of ibn Sīnā's philosophy that may shed light on this issue and to relate the logic inherent in this controversy to contemporary controversies about the philosophy of logic.

If we turn our attention to the history of this controversy, we shall observe first of all that in their analyses of Near Eastern philosophical texts, contemporary scholars have oftentimes tended to look upon Aristotle as the primary source for the doctrine under consideration.[2] In accordance with this tradition and on the basis of several passages in the *Analytica Posteriora,* 92b3-18, 93a and the *Metaphysica* [iv, 2], Goichon and Rescher advance the claim that the distinction was first formulated by Aristotle.[3] However, not all contemporary scholars agree with such a view. Moody, for instance, in agreement with Ockham, holds the view that Aristotle opposes this distinction in its ibn Sīnian formulation.[4] Rahman takes what may be described as the middle-of-the-road position on this issue when he states that Aristotle's remarks generally concern distinctions in the order of inquiries, whereas ibn Sīnā's key distinction is a logical one.[5] It is his opinion that Aristotle is not to be regarded as the sole source of this distinction. Goichon has pointed to passages of similar content in Platonic dialogues, as in the *Phaedo* and the *Republic.*[6] Rahman, Goichon, and Rescher have reportedly encountered the same distinction in the works of Fārābī.[7] In this book we shall not address ourselves to the problem of ibn Sīnā's indebtedness to his predecessors; but regardless of how one assesses this debt, it appears reasonable to assert in the light of the present state of scholarship that ibn Sīnā was the first to formulate this distinction explicitly and to make it a cardinal theme in his philosophy—cardinal in the sense that his most significant theories, e.g., on universals and substances, can be formulated on the basis of this distinction. However, ibn Sīnā's distinction is important not only because it occupies such a significant place in his own philosophical system, but also because of the role it plays in the philosophical systems of later philosophers, such as ibn Rushd,

Aquinas, and Ockham, who took issue with what they believed to be his formulation of the distinction, and in so doing, centered some of their own significant doctrines around the alleged ibn Sīnian distinction.[8] The topic is of further significance from the philosophic-qua-philosophic point of view. One might even build a case for parallel distinctions in the modern philosophies of Hume, Leibniz, and Kant.[9]

Its deep significance notwithstanding, ibn Sīnā's distinction has been misunderstood by his successors, as well as by many of his interpreters up to the present, even by such distinguished contemporary scholars as Goichon and Gilson. If this misunderstanding had involved nothing but a minor point in ibn Sīnā's philosophy, little damage would have been done. But since this distinction occupies a pivotal position in his philosophy, a misunderstanding of this doctrine can easily lead and has led to a misunderstanding of his entire philosophical system. Rahman has demonstrated that on the grounds of such a misinterpretation philosophers like ibn Rushd and St. Thomas, and even modern scholars like Goichon, Geny, Manser, and Gilson[10] have accused ibn Sīnā of upholding a "fantastic theory," a theory that has become the "official view" of those who would interpret ibn Sīnā's distinction. It is one of the claims of this interpretation that the philosopher subscribes to the view that "essence is an *addition* to existence," or, in Goichon's words, to a view which "did not give existence a higher place than other accidents."[11]

A similar interpretation is offered even by those who generally cautiously avoid making unwarranted conclusions about ibn Sīnā's views. Weinberg, for instance, appears to be reluctant to advance an interpretation about this doctrine. He states, "Now to say that existence is external to essence seems to treat existence as an accident and, therefore, as some sort of attribute. But it is not wholly clear that this is Avicenna's intention. What is meant by existence, then, remains somewhat obscure."[12] But he adds, nevertheless, "It is nonetheless true that Avicenna repeatedly asserts in his various philosophical works that existence is an accidental attribute of essence."[13] For his second assertion Weinberg offers no justification. Similar interpretations of this 'essence-existence' distinction are to be found in other works on the history of philosophy, as, for example, in Maurer's *Medieval Philosophy*[14] and Nasr's *Three Muslim Sages.*[15]

Let us specify the view that has been attributed to ibn Sīnā in terms of propositions expressed by the following sentences:

s. 1. "Existence is an addition to an essence."
s. 2. "Existence is an accident of an essence."

The first sentence expresses the doctrine that in an ontological sense "essence" is prior to existence and is independent of it, implying, therefore, that there can be essences without existence. For instance, when we say that a triangle exists, we mean to say that there is an essence of a particular kind, namely, a closed figure in a Euclidean plane having three straight lines for its sides; such a figure may happen to exist, although it is not compelled to exist. The second sentence expresses the doctrine that in a conceptual sense, "essences" are independent of existence. For example, if all actual triangles should disappear, the essence of the triangle will still exist. Or, in other words, to be a triangle will continue to mean a closed curve in a Euclidean plane having three straight lines as its sides. What is essential, therefore, is not the actual existence of a triangle, but that, which constitutes its essence, namely, having three sides and other related specifications that make up its definition.

It is significant to determine whether or not ibn Sīnā holds the position described above, for whoever holds to such a position will prima facie uphold also the obvious absurdities that follow from it. He who takes such a stance with regard to the essence-existence distinction is committed to three kinds of difficulties: first, the fallacy of self-reference (analogous to Russell's paradox); second, the thesis that existence is a predicate; third, the confusion between the analytical nature of metaphysics and the empirical, contingent nature of science.

The first of these errors may be summarized as follows. Let us assume that the term 'existence' is applicable to whatever is, i.e., to whatever exists, and let us suppose, moreover, that to assert that an essence can be independent of existence is to say that there can be an entity x to which 'existence' is not applicable. But, since x exists, 'existence' must also be applicable to *x*. Hence, we derive the apparent contradiction that 'existence' is and is not applicable to some *x*.

The paradox may be due to the following confusion. 'Existence,' one may argue, is a special term that is applicable to any entity whatsoever, including essences. A feature of any entity is that it exists. Thus, to assert that there is an entity, e.g., an essence, which is independent of existence, is to imply one of the following contradictory propositions: either there is an *x* to which "existence" already applies but in turn does not apply, or we can legitimately use a term which does not name anything, although it has ontological significance. The first alternative is a contradiction. The second alternative entails a category mistake, since *terms* do not exist, but individuals do.[16] Problematic and misleading is the question, "Can existence be applied to *x*?" because a presupposed feature of *x* is its existence; consequently, we must be assuming that 'existence' can be applied to the 'existence' of *x*, which is paradoxical and self-referential.[17] It hardly needs to be mentioned that one can deal with unactualized essences, such as "unicorns," by naming them functors constructed out of individual constants that name individuals that do exist.[18]

The second objection raised does not attempt to reveal an inner consistency in the doctrine that distinguishes essence and existence. Instead, it identifies ibn Sīnā's distinction with another troublesome view that existence is a nonlogical predicate.[19] The argument offered may be delineated as follows. If we suppose that existence is an accident of an essence, then it follows that existence is not a substance, but is one of the nine accidents. On the basis of exhaustive comparisons of these accidents, the conclusion is drawn that existence is a quality that is a predicate. As a consequence, all objections raised by Kant and other philosophers to the doctrine that existence is a predicate are applicable to ibn Sīnā's essence-existence distinction.[20]

The third objection to the essence-existence distinction, as it is formulated by the "official theory" of interpretation, is based on the presupposition of the empiricist concerning what metaphysics should be. The empiricist upholds a sharp distinction between the metaphysics and empirical sciences due to the distinct subject matter of each. While metaphysical analysis deals supposedly with concepts like essences, empirical sciences deal with facts, such as the properties and the relations of individual existents. Accordingly, to equate essences with existents would imply a confusion of metaphysics with empirical sciences. Prima facie, one of the empiricist's objections to the "essence-existence" distinction is therefore based upon the implicit presupposition empiricists hold about the distinction between metaphysics and empirical sciences.[21]

II
RECONSTRUCTION OF THE DISTINCTION

Having mentioned three major difficulties encountered in traditional interpretations of this distinction, let us attempt to solve these obstacles on the basis of ibn Sīnā's writings. Before offering our own construction, let us mention some salient features of Rahman's able defense of ibn Sīnā's position, a defense based on the doctrines expressed in the *Shifā'*.[22] In his article, "Essence and Existence in Avicenna," Rahman defends ibn Sīnā against the misinterpretations of ibn Rushd, St. Thomas, Goichon, Gilson, and Geny by several arguments, of which we shall summarize the most important ones.[23]

1. For ibn Sīnā, "existence" [*wujūd*] is among the most primary concepts accessible to the mind.[24] Hence, those critics who would claim that essence takes precedence over existence in ibn Sīnā's philosophical system misinterpret his views. For example, the philosopher's explicit affirmation of the primacy of existence in the *Ilāhiyyāt* of the *Shifā'* contradicts Goichon's assertion that "he" (ibn Sīnā) did not give existence a higher place than other accidents."[25]
2. Ibn Rushd's objection, that ibn Sīnā violates the definition of 'substance' as something that exists in itself, appears to be unjustified. To understand ibn Sīnā's general position on this topic we should turn to that which is specifically non-Aristotelian in his theory of substance namely, that besides "matter" and "form" another entity is needed to realize an essence, i.e., God. The basic misinterpretation of ibn Sīnā's

doctrine, therefore, is due to confusing a logical distinction with an ontological one. An examination of his doctrines makes evident that he does not assert that 'existence' behaves like another predicate.

3. In connection with this confusion, Rahman argues that ibn Sīnā's distinction is closely related to the distinction between the use of existence as "something" and as "a spatiotemporal entity." The difference between these two expressions can be described as follows: Nothing is gained by asserting the proposition "x is something," whereas the proposition, "an elephant exists" adds something "profitable" to the subject, namely that an instance of an elephant exists. The existence or the "instantiation" of an essence is, therefore, something more than the essence itself. In corroborating ibn Sīnā's position, Rahman points to ibn Sīnā's anti-Platonic theory of universals.

Let us now consider ibn Sīnā's doctrines that appear in texts other than the *Shifā'*, doctrines which may aid us in extending Rahman's formulation, which, although fundamentally satisfactory, is in need of clarification in two of its basic points.[26] The first difficulty lies in the ambiguous use of the term 'existence,' for which ibn Sīnā uses the terms '*wujūd*' and '*anniyya*.'[27] Equally ambiguous is Aristotle's use of '*ousia*,' a term which has given much difficulty to various interpreters of Aristotle.[28] Whether or not Rahman takes a step in the right direction when he recommends "existence" as the translation for Aristotle's '*ousia*,' equating as a consequence '*ousia*' with ibn Sīnā's '*wujūd*' and '*anniyya*,' is a difficult question. At least in one passage ibn Sīnā does use '*jawhar*,' designating substance as the equivalent of Aristotle's '*ousia*.'[29] Therefore, if we translate '*ousia*' as "existence," we would be equating 'existence' with '*jawhar*,' which is incorrect because the second sense of '*jawhar*' is 'essence,' not 'existence.' For this reason we hesitate to accept Rahman's translation of '*ousia*' for 'existence.' Somewhat misleading are certain other uses of "existence," such as Rahman's "is-ness." The confusion resulting from the latter's use of the term is no fault of his scholarship; in the Arabic texts of ibn Sīnā to which Rahman limits himself in his study, the philosopher fails to use any term which stands explicitly for Aristotle's "being-qua-being" in the sense of τὸ ὂν ᾗ ὂν or Ockham's "being" [*ens*].[30] Several obstacles are encountered, therefore, when we attempt to talk about 'existence' and its distinctness from 'essence': a specific logical difficulty arises, for instance, because the formulation lacks another more extensive, all-embracing concept. For this reason we question the possibility of solving the essence-existence problem on a logical basis, and even of being able to formulate it without having recourse to a term which is more extensive than 'existence.' The necessity of using a different term to discuss a specific term is also encountered in the realm of logic where one can talk about propositions in the given language only by means of employing another language, namely a meta-language. For instance, it is necessary to replace the second occurrence of 'existence' with another term in the proposition, "existence has 'existence,'" in order to circumvent a paradox.

A further difficulty concerns the specification of individuals, particulars and concrete entities. Prima facie, the proposed distinction between "is something" and "a spatiotemporal entity" appears to be unsatisfactory, because of an obstacle found in the second concept. Whereas bodies are the only spatiotemporal entities one might argue that ibn Sīnā regards individual souls and intelligences as substances in the primary sense—not as essences. There are some instances where accidents are existents, e.g., the case of blackness, the case of laughter and related instances, in addition to mental predicates, such as "pleasure" and "pain", predicates which are related to substances. Criteria for specifying existents should therefore be established on a logical basis, rather than on the basis of presuppositions of materialistic metaphysics about particulars. Should a philosopher, like Strawson, hold the position that ultimately we must suppose the existence of bodies, then such a position would have to appear as the conclusion of an argument; it could not be embedded in the premises of the argument itself.[31]

In addressing ourselves to these secondary objections, and in broadening the base of Rahman's excellent reconstruction, we shall rely especially on those texts of ibn Sīnā which are not mentioned by either Rahman or Goichon, particularly the *Ilāhiyyāt* and the *Manṭiq* of the *Dānish Nāmeh*.[32]

Let us observe first of all a distinction between being [*hastī*], essence [*huwiyya, dhāt, ma'nā, ḥaqiqa*], and existence [*wujūd, anniyya*], by means of the following explanation. 'Being', the most determinable term, is phenomenologically presupposed in every experience. Although one never experiences being directly, yet a sense that "there is some being", is, as one may say in Kantian terms, a transcendental condition of every experience. Accordingly, any concept, such as essence, is a being. The realm of being includes impossible being [*hastī mumtani'*], such as a round square, improper descriptions like "the present king of France," as well as contingent entities, such as "Socrates" and "humanity."[33]

In determining the specifications of being, we distinguish between two modes of inquiries and their corresponding realms. One is disclosed to us by the intermediacy of sense experience [*ḥissī*], while the other is disclosed to us by conception [*wahmī*].

In the first realm we encounter sensible-movable entities embracing particular bodily substances and some accidents related to them; a mark of these is their divisibility. We are confronted, then, with existents that consist of individual particular bodies and of non-physical attributes related to these. Whatever we experience in this realm must have existence. However, in discussing, defining, and analyzing the existents we experience, we rely on special features expressed by general terms by which we can name individual existents. If we claim to know the essence of an existent, then our knowledge of this essence necessarily presupposes that the existent exists, e.g., if we claim to know that the essence of Socrates is "humanity", then we must necessarily presuppose that the "existent Socrates" exists. As a matter of fact, ibn Sīnā affirms that we cannot attribute properties to entities that do not exist.

In the second realm, which is disclosed to us by the conceptual imagination, we deal merely with concepts, such as "humanity," "triangularity," "unicornness," "being the largest number," or other concepts related to these. The analyses of such concepts involve syntactical and analytical inquiries, yet on the basis of such inquiries we cannot claim that concepts have instances. Ibn Sīnā tells us that such a claim can legitimately be advanced only on the basis of an empirical observation of some subject [*hypokeimenon, mawḍū*].[34] Whatever exists must therefore be related to a subject. A *total* essence of any kind cannot ever exist because essences are common to many entities, whereas existents are particulars. Literally speaking, to affirm that an essence exists is to make a category mistake. Hence, Rahman is quite correct in recommending the use of the term "instantiation" for this particular context in which an essence has an instance but does not exist. Let us depict ibn Sīnā's position succinctly.

A concept can be said to have an instance under one of the following conditions: first, when the concept is an essence of a particular substance, which is the subject of that essence, e.g., Socrates as the subject of humanity, and, second, when a particular substance has a feature that is accidental to it, e.g., the blackness of a man, which is an instance of the concept in question. Ibn Sīnā's basic concern in this issue is not whether or not essences are more or less fundamental than existents; rather, his interest lies in conveying to us the following. If one asserts that an essence has an instance, then one must not only justify this assertion beyond the more conceptual analysis of the essence, but also observe the subject matter in question.[35]

It is a mistake to view ibn Sīnā's doctrine as a non- or even anti-Aristotelian position. In this issue the differences between Aristotle and ibn Sīnā lie not so much in their doctrines as in the kinds of philosophical terrains they investigate. Aristotle is interested only in the domain of actual entities, whereas ibn Sīnā concerns himself with actual entities as well as with the domain of impossible and non-actual concepts. Since their concerns are so different, as is evident from their respective formulations, it is incorrect to distinguish between their doctrines by means of assertions such as the following: Our knowledge of the essence of Socrates, according to Aristotle, depends on Socrates' existence; but, according to ibn Sīnā, the existence of Socrates is a feature added to the latter's essence.

III
A PROPOSED SOLUTION TO THE DIFFICULTIES

In the context of our formulation of the "essence-existence" distinction, let us ask ourselves whether the primary objections raised still hold.

The first objection to ibn Sīnā's distinction we mentioned was the self-referential operation of 'existence' [*wujūd*]. Although Rahman's translation of *wujūd* as "existence" is quite correct within the particular context where he chooses to operate, i.e., the *Shifā',* ibn Sīnā's position can be clarified by means of his Persian vocabulary as it is found in the *Dānish Nāmeh*, where he uses the Persian term '*hastī*', 'being,' and distinguishes it from 'existence' as follows. "Being," he tells us, is more determinable and more extensive than both "existence" and "essence."[36] Although both "existents" and "essences" are beings, not all beings have existence. For instance, some essences are beings, e.g., a round square or a unicorn, even though they do not exist, since no actual subject possesses these attributes. To essence we apply general terms. Since an essence designates many instances, it can never exist *in toto* at a given time. By resorting to the term 'being,' which is more extensive than 'existence,' it becomes possible for us to refer to 'existence' without self-reference and to avoid, therefore, paradoxical expressions, such as, "in its existence an essence is prior to its existence," or Rahman's "is-ness." Hence, the more extensive terminology is useful in that it enables us to avoid the first paradox.

Let us turn to the second problematical objection to the distinction, namely that this distinction carries the implication that 'existence' is a non-logical predicate. In order to meet this objection, we note first of ibn Sīnā divides essences into three kinds of beings: contingencies, impossibilities, and necessities. While 'existence' is neither an essence nor an instance of any entity in his system, it is embedded in the notion 'actual entities,' which are instances of essences. Thus, instead of saying, "an 'essence' exists," strictly speaking, we should state, "an essence has an instance." Ibn Sīnā's system allows the term 'existence' to be used to indicate a correspondence between some essences that are general terms and actual entities. On the basis of such an interpretation, many paradoxical propositions are resolved. For instance, the statement, "some essences do not or cannot exist," would then be taken to mean, "there is nothing in the actual realm which corresponds to these essences." Ibn Sīnā could easily have used 'existence' as a 'predicate', had he wished to do so. But, as a matter of fact, he does not regard 'existence' as essence, except in the case of the Necessary Being [*wājib al-wujūd*], a concept that we have treated elsewhere.[37] In sum, "existence" is not a non-logical predicate for ibn Sīnā, but is a means by which we can relate conceptual essences and actual entities, with the notable exception of the concept of the Necessary Existent.

The third objection to this distinction, we recall, dealt with the supposed confusion between metaphysics and empirical sciences. That such confusion actually does not arise is evident from the following two considerations. In his specification of the sciences, ibn Sīnā is careful to distinguish precisely between physics [*'ilm-i ṭabi'ī*] and metaphysics [*'ilm-i ilāhī*]. The objects of the former are related to bodies by concept [*wahm*] and by definition [*ḥadd*], whereas objects of the latter are not in any way related to bodies.[38] Obviously, ibn Sīnā does not intend to efface the differences between physics and metaphysics, differences that he carefully notes and distinguishes. For the reason that essences, the subject matter of metaphysics, are not analytically related to existents, our metaphysical knowledge of essences cannot give us any information about existents. And because of their abstract nature, essences cannot ever be objects of empirical observation. We must rely on concepts to group existents or to make generalizations about them. If we assume that it is a primary maxim of empiricism that "the existence of facts is known only by the intermediacy of observation," then it is clear that ibn Sīnā's formulation has not violated such a principle. It is entirely possible, therefore, to uphold the distinction he formulates, while subscribing to the view that metaphysics has fundamentally an analytical nature and that sciences have an empirical nature.

IV
DOES THE DISTINCTION ENTAIL AN IRRECONCILABLE DUALISM?

It has been asserted that this distinction leads to an irreconcilable dualism in ibn Sīnā's system, a dualism which separates entities into two realms—that of existences and that of essences. Empiricists who subscribe to the view that there is ultimately only one kind of entity, namely a kind that can be observed, distrust prima facie dualistic positions in metaphysics. Accordingly, we venture the opinion that the intense attack to which the so-called Aristotelians, such as Ibn Rushd and Ockham, subjected Ibn Sīnā can be attributed to such a general presupposed attitude towards empiricism. Should this attitude be the touchstone on the basis of which one rejects or misinterprets Ibn Sīnā's system, then the following objections must be faced.

It should be noted, first of all, that dualisms of various kinds are to be found in the philosophies of the very champions of empiricism, as for instance, David Hume. The dualism in his philosophy will become evident from the consideration of several issues. According to Hume, there are two very distinct kinds of propositions of which we can have knowledge—those belonging to "relations of ideas," and those called "matters of facts." Those in the first category deal with ideas revealed to us in inquiries such as mathematics and logic. From a mere analytical consideration of these ideas in themselves, we cannot legitimately deduce that they are in any way related to some form of existence. Some impression of a subject must be disclosed to us in non-analytical experiences before we can know existential propositions.[39] It is in this Humian sense that our knowledge of ideas corresponds to what we have taken to be, in the ibn Sīnian sense, our knowledge of essences, despite the radical differences between these two philosophers' respective theories of mind.[40] According to Hume, moreover, we do not ever experience abstract ideas by means of impressions we receive from matters of fact.[41] In this realm, therefore, we use our ideas as generalizations derived from past experiences. Turning now to ibn Sīnā, one might say in a similar vein that essences are conceived, but are not observed as unique entities. It is obvious that there are vast differences between a medieval metaphysician-mystic, such as ibn Sīnā, and the modern associationist-psychologist philosopher, such as Hume; yet despite their differences, impressive parallel conclusions about concepts and facts can be noted for both.

Let us also consider the case of the contemporary logician, e.g., Carnap. Like the aforementioned philosophers, Carnap introduces a sharp dualism between the observational and theoretical statements in the sciences, and between synthetic and analytical sentences.[42] He holds the opinion that it is possible to discuss and syntactically analyze concepts, such as force and number, without being obliged to recognize an existential status of these concepts. Of course, this view is by no means common to all modern philosophers. Quine, for instance, unlike Carnap, holds the view that the use of a particular formal syntax does imply an ontological commitment in our part.[43] In sum, it has become evident that Carnap's and Hume's theories offer support for the view that it is possible to uphold a dualism of a special kind without violating empiricism; such a dualism, moreover, does not need to be restricted to a differentiation of two kinds of entities, for it concerns the linguistic-conceptual realm and the empirical realm. The apparent dualism is not in the world, but rather, in the language and in that which this language designates.

If, so far, our analysis is correct, then we are now in a position to make a hypothetical judgement. If ibn Sīnā's distinctions can be interpreted syntactically and logically as we have attempted to do in this paper, then the accusations aimed at this distinction appear spurious, if not completely unjust. However, if ibn Sīnā does not imply by his distinction a distinction between syntax and non-conceptual facts, then his theory is indeed confusing. Evidence from texts touching on this issue substantiates the view that his theory can be used in a manner that is consistent with a correct methodological distinction. But, on the other hand, in order to evaluate the situation fairly, we should acknowledge that ibn Sīnā's system contains many exceptions to this rule. One is his theory of the Necessary Existent whose essence is existence.[44] Another deals with his attitude towards the necessary knowledge the soul [*nafs, ψυχή, anima, ravān, jān*] can possess.[45] Yet despite these two rather significant theories, we ultimately agree with Rahman that ibn Sīnā's effort to establish a distinction deserves a better evaluation than it has hitherto received from ibn Rushd, Aquinas, and Ockham, not to mention some of the more contemporary commentators.

NOTES

* A version of this paper was delivered at the Third Annual Meeting of the Middle East Studies Association of North America at the University of Toronto, Canada, November 14-15, 1969.

1 Allusions to this distinction appear in many different passages in ibn Sīnā's works, for instance, (a) *Al-Shifā': Al-Ilāhiyyāt* (*La Métaphysique*), ed. G. Anawati, M.Y. Moussa, S. Dunya, and S. Zayed, 2 vols. (Cairo, 1960), II, 344, *'anniyya'* ("existence") and *'māhiyya'* ("essence"); II, 347, *'wujūd'* and *'māhiyya'* are used for "existence" and "essence" respectively. (b) *Al-Ishārāt wa al-Tanbīhāt* ed. S. Dunya, 3 vols. (Cairo, 1960). In III, 15 [*Metaphysics*], a procedural differentiation is carried out between the *ma'nā* ("idea", "intention") of a triangle and its *wujūd* ("existence"). In I, 219-27 [*Logic*], a clear analysis of *'māhiyya'* ("essence") is given, while the nature of *'wujūd'* ("existence") is discussed in the first section of the *Metaphysics*, III, 1-57. (c) The *Dānish Nāmeh 'alāī* (*Ilāhiyyāt*), ed. M. Mo'in (Tehran, 1952) [quotations are taken from my own as yet unpublished translation of this work]. See chaps. 11, 22, 24-5; *'anniyyat'* and *'māhiyyat'* are used for "existence" and "essence" respectively.

2 See P. Morewedge, "Contemporary Scholarship on Near Eastern Philosophy," forthcoming in *Philosophical Forum.*

3 See, e.g., N. Rescher, *Studies in the History of Arabic Logic* (Pittsburgh, 1963), p. 41; A. M. Goichon, *La Distinction de l'essence et l'existence d'après Ibn Sīnā* (Avicenne) (Paris, 1937), p. 132, note 1.

4 E. A. Moody, *The Logic of William of Ockham* (New York, 1965), p. 263. Moody mentions Aristotle's *Analytica Postériora*, 93 a, 18-20, 27-28, and 90 a 14.

5 F. Rahman, "Essence and Existence in Avicenna," *Mediaeval and Renaissance Studies*, IV (1958), 1-16.

6 Goichon, *La Distinction. . .*, p. 132. Mention is made of passages such as *Phaedo* 74 a, *Republic* 509 b, *Timaeus* 50 c. Plato's position on this topic can be established only with great difficulty. See, for instance, J. Ackrill's criticism of Conford's interpretation of Plato's 'existence' in "Plato and the Copula: *Sophist* 251-259," in *Studies in Plato's Metaphysics*, ed. R. E. Allen (New York, 1965), p. 218. Since, apparently, prima facie no one clear interpretation can be given to Plato's use of those terms that are central to the "essence-existence" distinction, it would seem that the attempt to trace the theory to Platonic dialogues would only increase the difficulty of our inquiry.

7 In *La Distinction. . .*, pp.132, 134, Goichon refers to several passages in the *Fuṣūṣ*, which she attributes to Fārābī. Rescher [*Studies,* p. 41] observes that Fārābī preserves this distinction in his *Risālah fī jawāb masā'il su'ila 'anhā* ("Treatise on Answers to Questions asked of him"). Rahman, "Essence. . .," p. 2, mentions that in the *Fuṣūṣ* Fārābī formulates the distinction on an elementary level; it is likely that the *Fuṣūṣ* is the work of ibn Sīnā.

8 See, for instance, ibn Rushd in Averroes' *Arabic Commentary on Aristotle's Metaphysics* (Beirut, n.d.), part I, 313, part II, 557, cited in Rahman's "Essence. . ."; ibn Rushd's *Tahāfut al-Tahāfut in Averroes' Tahāfut al-Tahāfut*, tr. S. Van Den Bergh (London, 1954), I, p. 236. Ibn Rushd advances the thesis that the existence of an entity is prior to its essence, and that Sīnā's view, or rather, what he takes to be ibn Sīnā's view, is incorrect. See further, St. Thomas Aquinas, *Commentary on the Metaphysics of Aristotle*, trans. J. P. Rowen (Chicago, 1961), I, 223. St. Thomas accuses ibn Sīnā of claiming that the term being, or existence, signifies existence itself, and that it cannot, therefore, be derived from its substance or essence, as is the case with other entities. Hence existence, or being, must be something that is added to essence. See, finally, Ockham, who presents a formulation of the problem of essence (*entitas*) and existence (*existentia*) such that a distinction between them would very likely have to be denied. He asserts that these terms do not signify two distinct things, but rather, one and the same 'thing' (*res*) and one 'to be' (*esse*). It is interesting that both the noun and the verb signify the same thing [*Summa Totius Logicae*, I, c. xxxviii, and III, II, c. xxviii]. Ockham, in effect, interprets Aristotle in such a way as to deny this distinction, while he forces an anti-Aristotelian interpretation on ibn Sīnā's formulation. For an excellent treatment of Ockham, see Moody, *Logic.* A translation of the texts cited appears in T. Boehner, *Ockham's Philosophical Writings* (New York, 1957).

9 As shall become evident, a few themes recur in the distinctions drawn by ibn Sīnā and modern philosophers, e.g., that statements of logic and statements about empirical facts are classified separately. "Relations of ideas," "truths of reason," and "analytic a priori sentences" are, according to Hume, Leibniz, and Kant, classes which contain sentences of logic, whereas corresponding types of sentences, such as "matters of fact," "truths of fact," and "synthetic a posteriori types of sentences," are groups under which observations are classified. These philosophers affirm, moreover, that the possession of knowledge about logic does not reveal to us any information about the existence of particulars. From

these two features common to ibn Sīnā and the European philosophers, some similarities can be observed between ibn Sīnā's distinction and what may be called "a family of distinctions" held by some European philosophers. Obviously, the task of setting up a causal relation between the Near Eastern philosopher and these European philosophers, especially Hume and Kant, is rather difficult on account of a lack of references by them to ibn Sīnā. For Leibniz, such data would be even more difficult to obtain, in view of the unavailability of his texts.

10 Rahman cites the following: Goichon, *La Distinction. . .*, p. 136; P. Geny, "Le problème métaphysique de la limitation de l'acte," *Rev. de philosophie* (1919), pp. 138-39; E. Gilson, *Le Thomisme: Introduction à la philosophie de saint Thomas d'Aquin* (Paris, 1948), p. 56, note; Manser, *Das Wesen des Thomismus*, p. 519.

11 Rahman, p. 3.

12 J. Weinberg, *A Short History of Medieval Philosophy* (Princeton, 1964), p. 114.

13 *Ibid.*

14 Maurer, *Medieval Philosophy* (New York, 1964), p. 98.

15 H. Nasr, *Three Muslim Sages* (Cambridge, 1964), p. 26.

16 The term "category mistake" is employed here in the sense in which it is used by G. Ryle in "Categories," in *Logic and Language*, ed. A. G. N. Flew, Sec. Ser. (New York, 1965), pp. 281-98; see also G. Ryle, "Systematically Misleading Expressions," *Ibid.*, First Ser., pp. 13-40.

17 For problems concerning the self-reference paradox, see A. Fraenkel and Y. Bar-Hillel, *Foundations of Set Theory* (Amsterdam, 1958), chap.1.

18 With regard to the notion "functor," see R. Carnap, *Introduction to Symbolic Logic and Its Application* (New York, 1957), section 18. In an informal manner one could specify a non-actualized essence, e.g., "being a unicorn," as the thought of some actual person. In this situation only the person who thinks of "unicornness" is an actual existent; his humanity is an actualized essence. If he were to draw a picture of a unicorn x, then this x would be an instance of the idea of the unicorn in the person's mind. The instance of a non-actualized essence can therefore be realized by means of the mediacy of an instance of an actualized essence.

19 Many objections have been raised against the view that "existence is a non-logical predicate." This view received its classical formulation from I. Kant, *Critique of Pure Reason*, trans. N. Kemp Smith (London, 1929), pp. 502-03. For an unusual objection to this view, see W. A. Alston,

"The Ontological Argument Revisited," in *Philosophical Review*, LXIX (1960), 452-74.

20 Opposed to Kant's view is, for instance, Descartes', as is evident from his assertion in the second Meditation:

> I now know that even bodies are not really perceived by the senses or the imaginative faculty, but only by intellect; that they are perceived, not by being touched or seen, but by being understood; I thus clearly recognise that nothing is more easily or manifestly perceptible to me than my own mind. But because the habit of old opinion is not to be laid aside so quickly, I will stop here, so that by long meditation I may imprint this new knowledge deep in my memory.

Descartes, *Philosophical Writings*, ed. E. Anscombe and P. T. Geach (London, New York, Toronto, 1963), p. 75. Descartes takes a non-empirical position when he claims that some synthetic truths about bodies are known independently of any observation. For a paradigm of an empirical position, see subsequent quotations from Hume.

21 For an example of such an objection, see Moody's succinct formulation of Ockham's position, in *Logic*, p. 265.

22 Rahman bases his analysis on the *Ilāhiyyāt* of *al-Shifā'*, bk. 1, chap. 5.

23 Our summary omits some of the interesting points Rahman introduces about universals and particulars as well as several penetrating remarks on various misunderstandings of ibn Sīnā.

24 Other concepts of primary importance to ibn Sīnā's philosophy are: "thing" and "necessity". That ibn Sīnā uses '*wujūd*' in a different sense than the Persian term '*hastī*' ("being") is obvious, for he states in his *Dānish Nāmeh*, chap. 3, that "being" (*hastī*) is the most primary concept; he does not place it on a par with any other concept in his system.

25 Rahman, p. 3.

26 In the light of the following considerations, great caution should be exercised by those who claim to have found ibn Sīnā's fundamental philosophical doctrine contained in the *Ilāhiyyāt of al-Shifā.'* (i) In this work, as in his other Arabic texts, ibn Sīnā does not use *'hastī'* (being), a pure Persian term, which is more extensive than *'wujūd'* or *'anniyya'* ("existence"). (ii) Some doctrines which appear in *al-Shifā,'* e.g., punishment and reward after death, are not upheld elsewhere, and, as a matter of fact, are even retracted in other works (see *Risālat al-Qadar* in George F. Hourani, "Ibn

Sīnā's 'Essay on the Secret of Destiny,'" *BSOAS*, XXIX (1966, 25-48). In comparison with his other works, he places greater emphasis in the *Shifā'* on some doctrines, e.g., prophecy, than in other works, such as the *Dānish Nāmeh* or the *Ishārāt*, where hardly any mention is made of this doctrine. (iii) In his *Manṭiq al-mashriqiyyīn* (Cairo, 1910), pp. 2-4, ibn Sīnā himself describes *al-Shifā'* as a popular work in which his secret doctrines are not to be found.

27 The difficulty arises chiefly for the reason that ordinarily there are many different senses of 'is,' e.g., identity, predication, and existential assertion, in addition to "being-qua-being." For the nature of the Arabic sense of "is," see Fadlou Shehadi, "Arabic and 'to be,'" in *The Verb 'Be' and Its Synonyms*, ed. J. W. M. Verhaar, (New York, 1969), IV, 112-25.

28 While R. Hope, translator of Aristotle's *Metaphysics*, (Ann Arbor, 1966), renders '*ousia*' as "primary being," omitting "substance," almost every other translator has relied on "substance." Different approaches to Aristotle's doctrine have been taken by many scholars. One approach has been to bring out a particular interpretation of Aristotle by comparing his doctrines with those held by another philosopher, e.g. Frege or Ockham. Moody, for instance, presents a very precise and clear, but thoroughly nominalistic interpretation of Aristotle's analytic and metaphysical doctrines [*Logic*]. An alternative approach has been taken by coining a new name, or superimposing a system upon Aristotle's work, as, for instance, the word "entity," by which means J. Owens, *The Doctrine of Being in the Aristotelian 'Metaphysics': A Study in the Greek Background of Medieval Thought* (Toronto, 1951) has attempted to clarify the Aristotelian doctrine.

29 See S. Afnan [*Philosophical Terminology in Persian* (Leiden, 1964), pp. 26, 99-100], who claims that '*jawhar*,' used both in Arabic and Persian, is derived from the Middle Persian *gaw*, meaning "to grow." Ibn Sīnā uses *gawhar* (a Persian term) and *jawhar* synonymously in his Persian text, e.g. the *Dānish Nāmeh*, chap. 4. But, both before and after ibn Sīnā, others have employed this term for substance. Al-Kindī, for instance, mentions it in *Fī'l-sabab alladhī (lahu) nasabat al-qudamā' al-khamsah ilā 'l-usṭuqussāt*, see Rescher, *Studies in Arabic Philosophy*, (Pittsburgh, 1967), p. 29; Fārābī discusses it in his *Kitāb Ārā' Ahl Al Madīna Al Fāḍila*, ed. A. N. Nadir (Beirut, 1968), p. 47; Suhrawardī mentions it in many of his works, such as in *Ḥikmat al-Ishrāq*, ed. H. Corbin (Tehran, 1952), p. 115; and F. Rāzī refers to it in *Al-Risāla al-Kamāliyya fi'l taḥqīq al-ilāhī*, ed. M. Sabziwārī, (Tehran, 1957), p. 78.

30 For Aristotle's use of the term, see *Metaphysica* bk. 4, chap. 1, where "being" is presented as the subject matter of metaphysics, the most abstract science. Ibn Sīnā regards Aristotle's '*ousia*' as the equivalent of his '*jawhar*,' as is evident from his acknowledgement of Aristotle's use of '*ousia*' as substance in definition 15 of his *Fīl-ḥudūd* in *Tis'rasā'il* (Cairo, 1908). For a clarification of Ockham's use of the term "being" in his previously quoted text [see above, note 8], see Moody [*Logic*, p. 118], who links the positions of Ockham and Aristotle.

31 Many references in his works point to non-material existents, e.g., *al-Shifā'*, p. 93, bk. 9, chap. 2; *Fīl-ḥudūd* in *Tis'rasā'il* (Cairo, 1908), defs. 3, 4; *Ishārāt*, II, 343-450; *Dānish Nāmeh*, chaps. 3, 47, 55. Many passages in these texts deal with the substantiality of the soul, e.g., *al-Nafa* of *al-Shifā'*, in Avicenna's *De Anima* (Arabic text), ed. F. Rahman (London, 1959); *Risāla-i Nafs*, ed. M. 'Amid (Tehran, 1952). Our position should not be taken to mean that ibn Sīnā's "essence-existence" distinction implies a specific ontology. In contemporary philosophy we find a view opposed to that of ibn Sīnā, e.g., that held by P. F. Strawson, *Individuals, An Essay in Metaphysics* (London, 1959), p. 291, that we must suppose the existence of spatiotemporal particulars (material objects). He derives his conclusions apparently independently of observing particulars—in pursuit of his aim to avoid solipsism and to adhere to the proper use of language. J. Kaminsky, *Language and Ontology* (Carbondale, 1969), chap. 3, presents a succinct exposition of Strawson's position. Ibn Sīnā's view differs from that of Strawson, for the Near Eastern philosopher would claim that pure analytical inquiries are concerned solely with essences and do not inform us about the world of actual particulars.

32 Among the very few who have taken cognizance of ibn Sīnā's Persian works is N. Rescher, who refers to the *Ṭabī'iyyāt* of the *Dānish Nāmeh* in explicating ibn Sīnā's assertion that only names which designate individuals in the actual domain can primarily be predicted by genuine predicates. "Existence in Arabic Logic and Philosophy," in *Studies in Arabic Philosophy*, (Pittsburgh, 1966), pp. 72-73.

33 For a lucid discussion of various theories on how to handle improper descriptions in a formal language, see, R. Carnap, *Meaning and Necessity* (Chicago, 1947), section 8: "Frege's Method for Description."

34 *Dānish Nāmeh*, chap. 25. Although analysis alone enables us to know the meaning of a second substance (*deutera ousia*), such as a species, knowledge of a first substance (*prōtē ousia*) is possible only if we know that there is a subject that corresponds to the substance.

35 When we assert that "an essence has an instance", it is significant to recognize that we are involved in a twofold type of inquiry, concerning (i) the analysis of the essence in question, and (ii) the observation of some subject in the empirically accessible realm that is related to bodies. Instead of saying, "existence is an addition to an essence," we should say that the justification of the existence of an instance of an essence requires more than the mere conceptual analysis of that essence. The order in which essences and existences are arranged as being "prior" or "posterior" to each other is a problem that is not encountered in ibn Sīnā's philosophy.

36 Dānish Nāmeh, chap. 3.

37 P. Morewedge, "Ibn Sīnā's Concept of the Self," forthcoming in *Philosophical Forum.*

38 Ibn Sīnā draws the same distinction in several texts in the framework of discussing the various sciences, e.g., *al-Shifā'*, bk. 1, chaps. 1-4; *'Uyūn al-ḥikmah*, ed. A. Badawi (Cairo, 1954), p.17; *Fī aqsām al-'ulūm al-'aqliyya* in *Tis'rasā'il* (Cairo, 1908), pp. 104-11; *Dānish Nāmeh*, chaps. 1-2.

39 This view has been expressed in Hume's *Enquiries Concerning the Human Understanding* and *Concerning the Principles of Morals*, ed. L. A. Selby-Bigge (London, 1957).

> All the objects of human reason or enquiry may naturally be divided into two kinds, to wit, *Relations of Ideas*, and *Matters of Fact.* Of this first kind are the sciences of Geometry, Algebra, and Arithmetic; and in short, every affirmation which is either intuitively or demonstratively certain. *That the square of the hypotenuse is equal to the square of the two sides* is a proposition which expresses a relation between these figures. *That three times five is equal to the half of thirty* expresses a relation between these numbers. Propositions of this kind are discoverable by the mere operation of thought, without dependence on what is anywhere existent in the universe. Though there never were a circle or triangle in nature, the truths demonstrated by Euclid would forever retain their certainty and evidence. [p. 25]

Sentences concerning relations of ideas are, therefore, discoverable by operations of mind, though by themselves they tell us nothing about the world. For a relevant quotation from his *Treatise*, see note 41.

40 One radical difference is to be found in the Humian associationistic psychological explanation of abstract ideas and ibn Sīnā's doctrine of universal being, according to which objects of intelligent perception are derived from the active intelligence. The latter believes, moreover, that even God does not perceive particulars by means of intelligible perception.

41 In his work, *A Treatise of Human Nature*, Hume mentions the distinction philosophers have drawn between "substance" and "accident." In this context he uses the term "substance" in its second sense, namely as "essence;" to illustrate this sense he cites the example of "humanity," a species. Hume flatly refuses to subscribe to the view that we actually have a simple impression of "substance," as is evident from the following: "The idea of a substance as well as that of a mode, is nothing but a collection of simple ideas, that are united by the imagination, and have a particular name assigned to them, by which we are able to recall, either to ourselves or others, that collection" (*A Treatise*... p. 16). According to Hume, we do not experience an impression of a substance (in the sense of an essence). Ibn Sīnā's position is similar to Hume's when the former claims that in the empirical realm we do not experience essences, such as substance (in the second sense). With regard to this issue, the chief difference between Hume and ibn Sīnā is obviously to be found in their respective theories of the imagination.

42 Carnap rejects the position which assumes that the choice of a particular language implies ontological assertions about the world; he states, for instance:

> In contrast to this view, we take the position that the introduction of the new ways of speaking does not need any theoretical justification because it does not imply any assertion of reality. We may still speak (and have done so) of "the acceptance of the framework" or "the acceptance of the new entities" since this form of speech is customary; but one must keep in mind that these phrases do not mean for us anything more than acceptance of the new linguistic forms (R. Carnap, "Empiricism, Semantics, and Ontology," in *Semantics and the Philosophy of Language*, ed. L. Linsky (Urbana, Ill., 1952), p. 219.

43 In contrast to Carnap, Quine holds the view that the form of language, specifically that kind of sign by which quantification is permitted, implies

an ontological commitment. Here Quine's position is linked to his refusal to recognize the sharp distinction Carnap draws between semantics and syntax. We could translate the medieval controversy into modern terminology by means of the following formulation. According to the Quine-type of meta-theory of languages, the use of essences in a theoretical language commits us to an ontology. From such a theory one may deduce this: If we quantify over essences, then we are ontologically committed to the existence of essences. According to the Carnapian theory of language, the use of those terms which designate essences commits us in no way to the ontological position that there are individual essences because essences can be considered as part of the framework of a theory; they do not have to designate individuals. With regard to W. V. Quine, see *The Ways of Paradox* (New York, 1966); *Selected Logic Papers* (New York, 1966). For additional information on Carnap's position in this controversy, see *The Philosophy of Rudolph Carnap*, ed. P. A. Schlipp (Chicago, 1963).

44 *Dānish Nāmeh*, chap. 25. For an analysis of his position, see P. Morewedge, "Ibn Sīnā (Avicenna), Malcolm and the Ontological Argument," *Monist*, II, ii (April, 1970).

45 A constructive interpretation of ibn Sīnā's view about the self appears in P. Morewedge, "Ibn Sīnā's Concept of the Self," forthcoming in *Philosophical Forum*, and "The Logic of Emanationism and Ṣūfism in Ibn Sīnā," in *Journal of the American Oriental Society*, Part one: 91 (1971), 467-476; Part two: 92 (1972), 1-18.

THE LOGIC OF EMANATIONISM AND ṢŪFISM IN THE PHILOSOPHY OF IBN SĪNĀ (AVICENNA)*

One of the most controversial problems in contemporary scholarship on ibn Sīnā concerns the nature of the relationship between his philosophy and Ṣūfism. A comparative analysis of five approaches taken to this problem demonstrates the need for a clarification of the argument by means of conceptual analysis. This study attempts to clarify concepts related to one aspect of this problem: the relationship of persons and the ultimate being. In this context explicit distinctions are drawn between (1) creation, co-eternity and emanation; (2) harmony, connection and (mystical) union; and (3) religious (Qur'ānic), philosophical (Aristotelian) and mystical (Ṣūfic) systems. On the basis of these distinctions and selected passages from ibn Sīnā's texts, a hypothetical argument is advanced which confirms an affinity between ibn Sīnā's views and Ṣūfism. Some limitations and merits of this procedure are outlined at the end of this study.

I
PROBLEM AND AIM

The purpose of this inquiry is to clarify the logic of one of the most controversial problems in contemporary scholarship on ibn Sīnā, namely the relationship between ibn Sīnā and Ṣūfism, the mysticism among the Muslims. Since mysticism is a salient feature of many Near Eastern philosophies, we hope that the results of our analysis will be of value at least insofar as they illustrate a method of analyzing similar problems, as well as in clarifying the language of the controversy on a crucial point in ibn Sīnā's philosophy.

FIVE CONFLICTING VIEWS ON THE RELATIONSHIP BETWEEN THE PHILOSOPHY OF IBN SĪNĀ AND ṢŪFISM

There are few topics in contemporary scholarship on ibn Sīnā on which one finds a greater diversity of opinion among scholars than on the relationship between ibn Sīnā's philosophy and Ṣūfism. We shall cite a number of diverse, representative positions and opinions taken with regard to this problematical issue prior to offering our own views.

1

The first view: ibn Sīnā's philosophy and Ṣūfism are similar since both are basically "Islamic"

Many scholars are of the opinion that there is an affinity between Islamic doctrines and the most fundamental mystical doctrines. This affinity is regarded either as a direct historical one, initiated by Muḥammad, a Ṣūfī par excellence, or as an indirect affinity in which Islam is seen as being receptive to mystical points of view, for it would be the wish of a Muslim Ṣūfī, for instance, to follow the example of Muḥammad. A predilection for certain topics that tend to support such an affinity can be found among proponents of this position. Topics most often cited by them include the following: (i) The doctrine of the unity of being (*waḥdat al-wujūd*) or a modification of it, which stresses the theme of an affinity between man and God; (ii) The personality of Muḥammad, which is described in terms of his existence as a man as well as a human ideal; (iii) The development of personality cults in *Shi'ism* where Imams such as 'Alī and Ḥusain are treated as mediators between persons and God, and form, therefore, a "continuum" between man and God. (iv) Finally, there is a wealth of literature on the topic of mystical union in the Islamic world, which can be singled out as a representative element in the Islamic culture.

If we keep this hypothesis in mind, then the discovery of an affinity between the doctrines of ibn Sīnā and the Ṣūfīs, both part of the same Islamic culture, comes as no surprise to us. Even if some differences should be found between the doctrines of ibn Sīnā and

Ṣūfīs on one hand and Islam on the other hand, we can ascribe these differences to different methods, rather than to different basic aims, for it is only natural that the topic of the unity between man and God should be treated differently by philosophers relying on the tools of logical analysis, mystics expressing themselves in the figurative language of poetry relying on intuition, and orthodox religious dogmatists recognizing only the authority of the scriptures. In his study, *The Idea of Personality in Sūfism*, R. Nicholson describes this unity (as "an absolute unity") and the transcendent nature of the divine. Strong personal relations, which bind the Ṣūfīs to each other, to the Prophetic Mediator, and to God, seem to reach their climax, according to Nicholson, in this unity, which excludes all alienating relations. He compares this unity to the raindrop that disappears in the ocean and to the moth which is consumed in the flame. To explain this unity as "pantheism" is unsatisfactory, in his opinion. In order to attempt an explanation one would have to advance from the Muslim conception of personality. God, rather than man, is the measure of all things in Islam, and "the Perfect Man, who is identified with Muḥammad, represents the idea of the Divinity revealing itself in man rather than the ideal of humanity realizing itself in the personal life of God."[1] With regard to ibn Sīnā, Nicholson suggests that numerous similarities can be observed between the doctrine of ibn Sīnā and that of many Ṣūfīs concerning the immortality of the individual soul and its union, though not its total unification, with the World Spirit, a union which constitutes the "blessedness of the good."[2] "Others, again," he affirms, "seem to regard 'absorption in the Deity, the merging of the individual soul of the saint in the Universal Soul of God,' as the ideal which, though temporarily attainable in this life, only receives permanent realisation in another state of existence."[3] The union of the individual soul that Nicholson mentions, or the way in which an individual mystic relates to God, is the pivot, in his opinion, of ibn Sīnā's notion of mystic union.

In Ṣūfī literature, this union is often achieved by means of a mediator between man and God whose God-like aspirations relates an aspect of man's "soul" (*'aql-i qudsī*) to God. This figure is encountered not only in the writings of mystics, but also in Islamic literature, where figures resembling mediators are personified by

Muḥammad and the Imams. In his study, *Medieval Islam*,[4] von Grunebaum describes the Ṣūfic conception of "the unity of absolute being." He asserts that Ṣūfīs attempted to reach an emotional understanding of the "essence of the One" while theologians and philosophers made efforts to "define and rationalize the absolute unity of the divine being." That Ṣūfīs attributed reality to God alone von Grunebaum ascribes to the Neo-Platonic ideas. He continues,

> Man participates in reality only inasmuch as he has attained to identification with the divinity. An elaborate path, *tarîqa*, of spiritual perfection leads to the gnosis *ma'rifa*, of the divine Unity and to the bridging of the gap between the creature and its Creator when the soul transcends the confines of personality by losing itself in the intuition of the One. The mere attribution of the reality to any entity beside the One is polytheism, *shirk*. The finite soul views the Infinite with love. Love implies longing. And longing makes man renounce the world for the beatific vision in which no distinction is felt any more between himself and the Most High, in whom the individual mind has become completely absorbed.[5]

Von Grunebaum points out that this unity to which the Ṣūfīs aspire is not alien to Islam, but that it is achieved in Islam by means of mediators between man and God which are personified by religious figures, such, as Muḥammad, for example. Such a mediator, or Perfect Man, is portrayed by von Grunebaum as a cosmic power that unites the One and the many, a power upon which the continued existence of the universe depends. He is the microcosm of a high order who reflects the forces of nature as well as the divine powers. The Perfect Man, who is shown as an Islamic Logos, is an "outward manifestation of the essence of Muḥammad," an ideal type of humanity, and "a copy of God," according to von Grunebaum.[6] Moreover,

> The beauty of this world is borrowed from him and subsists through his Light. This pre-existent Light that had been revealed in all the prophets from Adam to Jesus con-

> tinues to affect the world through the saints who commune with Mohammed in the oneness won by love.[7]

The Christ-like role of the mediator between God and man is attributed not only to the Prophet, but also to Ḥusain and other Imams. Von Grunebaum suggests even that basic *Shi'a* doctrines show a resemblance to the doctrine of the mediator. In explaining this resemblance, he singles out some possible historical influences:

> The idea that a personality of metaphysical significance is temporarily removed from this world, . . . to introduce the millennium by his reappearance is anchored in the Judeo-Christian milieu and corroborated by Zoroastrian eschatology. Sunnite Islam, too, has been receptive to messianic hopes. The Muslim masses . . . cherished the belief in the Mahdhi, the absolutely guided (by Allah), who would when the end of the world was at hand bring about a short period of perfection.[8]

There are striking parallels between Ḥusain and Christ, particularly in the nature of their deaths. Von Grunebaum observes this resemblance in *Muḥammadan Festivals*.[9] After describing the ritual at *Ta 'ziya*, he interprets the incident of Kerbela " . . . as an action of cosmic significance. As a Passion play, it is strongly reminiscent of the death of Christ."[10]

It is evident, then, that according to this point of view (which we have called "the first view") similar conceptions of a topic like mystical union are expressed in Islamic religion, philosophy, and mysticism. Minor differences found in the respective descriptions of mystical union can generally be attributed to the different methods by means of which religious, philosophical, and mystical doctrines are expressed. But even if this interpretation should be correct in its claim that there is a relationship between Ṣūfism and a philosopher like ibn Sīnā, the mere recognition of such a relationship does not diminish our chief tasks—to make explicit those presuppositions which support the view that ibn Sīnā's position has an affinity with Ṣūfism and to present one clear version of this problem. Before we concern ourselves with this problem, we should observe that not all commentators on Islamic culture agree with the position that ibn Sīnā's doctrines correspond to the Islamic doctrines. It is this alternative view to which we shall address ourselves next.

2

The second view: ibn Sīnā's philosophy is regarded as being non-Islamic although the doctrines of many Ṣūfīs are viewed as being Islamic.

J. J. Houben is one of the commentators who has undertaken a careful investigation of ibn Sīnā's particular version of mysticism from the religious point of view and has found his mysticism to be different from that of several "Islamic" Ṣūfīs as well as from orthodox Islamic doctrines. In describing the nature of this difference between ibn Sīnā and other Muslim mystics, he claims that the latter, unlike ibn Sīnā, "took the reality of God's transcendental being as the starting point for their mystical life and for the teaching about it."[11] The reason for this contrast between ibn Sīnā and the Ṣūfīs who were genuine Muslims Houben attributes to ibn Sīnā's "natural knowledge of God" through which it is possible for him to obtain direct knowledge of God because he upholds "a monistic order of being," and on the basis of such a "monistic order of being" a logical philosopher like ibn Sīnā cannot make a distinction between the natural and supernatural.[12] Among the non-Islamic features of ibn Sīnā's doctrines Houben lists the necessity of emanation and the naturalness of the relationship that man has to God.[13] In accordance with his interpretation he translates *wājib al-wujūd* as "God." It is his opinion that ibn Sīnā's emanationistic doctrine of an "ontological descent from God by necessary emanation" and the "ascent of the creature in a movement of love towards God" could lead to the highest spiritual doctrine. Ibn Sīnā falls short of this height, however, according to Houben, because his inherent monism "falsifies his doctrine."[14] In documenting his particular interpretation of this union of the creature with "God" Houben refers to ibn Sīnā's own description of the last stage of mystical union:

> Then he [the gnostic] passes away from himself and contemplates only the Divine Glory and if he looks upon himself, it is only as the one contemplating, and when he has come to this, he has attained complete union with God.[15]

Although he recognizes ibn Sīnā's achievements as a philosopher, Houben is critical of ibn Sīnā's mystical teaching for the very reason that it represents the philosopher's approach to God, rather than that of the devout, and, moreover, the approach of a philosopher "who has cut himself adrift from this belief in the transcendental God and therefore form the reality of things."[16] We assume Houben's position to be representative of the majority of those readers of ibn Sīnā who believe in God as a transcendent entity. It may be helpful to examine how this particular religious point of view approaches the doctrine of mysticism.

According to this view, Ṣūfism can be described as follows. Many Ṣūfīs expressed the desire for a mystical union or a relationship with the transcendent being in their emotional and aesthetic modes of expressions. Two kinds of mysticism are generally differentiated by this religious interpretation: a "natural mysticism" which is secular and hence illegitimate, and a "supernatural mysticism" which is regarded as being legitimate. Adherents to the religious position claim that these "natural mystics" should never have alluded to the possibility of reaching an identity with God, a possibility that, according to them, cannot even be achieved in the realm of religion or "supernatural mysticism." Judged by their standards, ibn Sīnā is mistaken on the grounds that his "union with God" is an impossible path. It is obvious that this interpretation presupposes the truth of religion and judges ibn Sīnā's doctrine according to the extent to which it has departed from the yardstick of religion. Houben's stance is peculiar in that he attempts to identify the "good Ṣūfīs" with Christians because the Islamic system does not measure up to the Christian system, for it fails to explain the mystery of God as a mystery of love and as a consequence cannot explain sin adequately (in his opinion) because it denies original sin and, hence, Christ's redemption of man from sin. Houben finds, however, that some mystics (but definitely not ibn

Sīnā) come close to the Christian mystics in their love to God and their detachment from everything, even from themselves. As an example of such mystics, "the good Ṣūfīs," he cites Ḥallāj, whom he quotes as saying:

> Thou Spirit has little by little mixed itself with my spirit
> and now I am Thyself; Thy existence is mine.[17]

Our approach differs from that of Houben in the sense that we do not intend to discuss the truth or the falsehood of ibn Sīnā's doctrines; we are interested in clarifying the latter's doctrines, in ascertaining their consistency, and in correlating these with the doctrines of other philosophers. Obviously, a devoted Christian could not uphold the Islamic doctrine as the true one. Hence he might well attempt to identify or correlate the doctrines of Ṣūfīs admired by him with corresponding Christian doctrines. To such a believer, ibn Sīnā's "natural" doctrine of love, as Houben names it, can hardly be acceptable, whereas a "mystery of love" and a notion of a "transcendent being" on the other hand could be acceptable. We observe also that in his interpretation of ibn Sīnā's doctrines Houben fails to question their inner consistency but objects to them from the Christian position. He demonstrates this: If one assumes the Christian doctrine to be true, then ibn Sīnā's views, failing to correspond to this doctrine, could not be correct. Houben's views are not generally acclaimed by Christian commentators of ibn Sīnā, for a different view of the relationship between ibn Sīnā and Islam is taken by other able scholars like A. M. Goichon and E. Gilson whose positions we shall examine next.

3

The third view: ibn Sīnā's doctrine is interpreted as a religious non-mystical philosophy.

Some Christian scholars have taken the following stand on ibn Sīnā's doctrine: The notion of his Necessary Existent represents a highly religious attitude, which finds its expression in his particular use of his philosophical tools. Gilson supports this religious interpretation when he suggests that ibn Sīnā should be regarded as a representative of the Jewish tradition,

> ... for, his God, whom he calls strictly and absolutely the First, is not the first in the universe; He is first in relation to the being of the universe, prior to that being, and consequently also outside it.[18]

Goichon corroborates Gilson's description of ibn Sīnā's Necessary Existent, but adds that love is the very basis of ibn Sīnā's monotheistic system (herein she differs sharply from Houben). For support of her view that the essence of the Necessary Existent is love and intelligence, and that ibn Sīnā could hardly have reached greater heights as a philosopher, Goichon cites his *Najāt*:

> The Necessary Being is thus 'He Himself for Himself the greatest Lover and the greatest Beloved, the One who enjoys the greatest bliss and is the greatest object of bliss.' 'His love for his essence is therefore the most perfect, the most faithful, love. And since the divine attributes are not essentially distinguished in essence, love is truly *essence* and *being*—i.e., in the Pure Good.'[19]

In sum, the essence of God, according to Goichon, is intelligence, love, and life.[20]

Believing the core of his philosophy to be contained in his systematic works, such as *al-Shifā'*,[21] Goichon regards ibn Sīnā's so-called Ṣūfī tendencies as being of only minor importance. Accordingly, she reacts to his mystical works, such as *Ḥayy ibn Yaqẓān*[22] by recasting the entire language into the terminology of *al-Shifā'* which she holds to be his scholastic work. In her study, *Le Récit de Ḥayy ibn Yaqẓān commenté par des textes d'Avicenne*,[23] she takes the position that ibn Sīnā's most substantial work is to be found in *al-Shifā'* and that his *Dānish Nāmeh 'alāī* (*Ilāhiyyāt*)[24] is to be considered as a mere summary of *al-Shifā'*. We shall take issue only with this point.

Whereas Goichon has advanced the claim that *al-Najāt* constitutes a summary of *al-Shifā'*, she has not demonstrated that the

Dānish Nāmeh is a summary of the latter work. We object to her tendency to force an a priori interpretation on all of ibn Sīnā's writings, even on those which are generally regarded as being mystical in nature, but which she regards as being either religious or of only minor importance.

But in spite of our objection, we find it difficult to agree with Wickens's somewhat flagrant claim that Goichon rejects the possibility of hidden meanings in ibn Sīnā's works, apparently because her devotion to her subject takes precedence over her common sense, for she cannot accept the fact that a writer may resort to intentional ambiguity in his works "while surrounded by, and participating in, all the . . . confusion of his companions."[25] Nevertheless, we do wish to question her interpretation by pointing to some evidence with which she does not deal in a satisfactory manner in our opinion. (i) Why should we consider *al-Shifā'*, as being of greater importance than his mystical works? This question, in particular must be answered, for ibn Sīnā himself disclaims *al-Shifā'*, as a work which does not contain his true doctrines. (ii) Even if one were to dismiss the mystical themes in his allegorical recitals, it is difficult to disregard the text of *al-Ishārāt wa al-Tanbīhāt*[26] in which both mystical and classical doctrines are discussed extensively. (iii) Finally, we note the explicit references to a mystical union with the Necessary Existent in the *Ilāhiyyāt* and in the *Ṭabī'iyyāt*[27] of the *Dānish Nāmeh*, as well as references in the latter work to the prophetic soul, references which do not relate this soul to the personality of Muḥammad.

In order to prevent a possible confusion about the true nature of ibn Sīnā's doctrines on the one hand and the definition of "religion" and "mysticism" on the other hand, we propose to introduce a distinction which should be rather obvious, but is often overlooked for that very reason. Assuming that the definitions of our respective arguments are justified, how can we properly relate ibn Sīnā's doctrines to religion and to mysticism? Unless an understanding is reached between Goichon and ourselves, for instance, on the basic terms of this controversy (i.e., as to whether she should call "religious" what we call "mystic") the controversy will not be avoided, even though we might be in basic agreement on ibn Sīnā's doctrines.

4

The fourth view: ibn Sīnā's doctrine is viewed as philosophical mysticism although ibn Sīnā himself is not regarded as a Ṣūfī.

It should be mentioned that all scholars who believe in the existence of a harmonious relationship between ibn Sīnā's philosophy and the doctrines of Islam do not express an antagonism to Ṣūfism or to other forms of mysticism. For instance, G. C. Anawati, who has contributed extensively to the scholarship on ibn Sīnā, holds the view that many Ṣūfīs actually borrowed doctrines from ibn Sīnā, though he rejects the notion that ibn Sīnā was a Ṣūfī. In basic agreement on ibn Sīnā's position on Ṣūfism are Anawati and L. Gardet.[28] Gardet views ibn Sīnā's philosophy as a monistic existentialism, or as a religious mysticism which is a component of every great philosophy.[29] Like Anawati and Gardet, B. Fūrūzānfar denies that ibn Sīnā was a Ṣūfī and contends that the latter's attention to topics related to Ṣūfism is due to their Islamic nature, which is expressed in themes such as the appearance of the prophet or in asceticism. He stresses ibn Sīnā's personal experiences, such as his famous meeting with Abū Saʿīd, in which the mystic is said to have said, "All he knows I see," and ibn Sīnā is said to have replied, "All he sees I know." On the basis of biographical data, secular works, and political activities, Fūrūzānfar affirms that ibn Sīnā was not a Ṣūfī.[30]

5

The fifth view: Zoroastrianism had an influence on ibn Sīnā and on other Ṣūfīs.

Mention should also be made of another interpretation of ibn Sīnā's texts, which traces his Ṣūfī doctrines to Zoroastrianism, even though such an historical inquiry into ibn Sīnā's Zoroastrian heritage is beset by many difficulties. Several scholars have suggested that the Persian-Zoroastrian influences on ibn Sīnā should be regarded as indigenous "casual" influences on him, or at least as being essential to a proper understanding of his works. For instance, H. Corbin has been very successful in discovering Zoroastrian influences on Suhrawardī as well as on ibn Sīnā. Great insight into this issue is gained through his studies. In *Avicenna and the Visionary Recital*[31] he points, for instance, to the relationship between Zurvanism and ibn Sīnā's cosmology and makes specific references to the affinity between the ibn Sīnian theory of intelligences and Zoroastrian angelology. He cites the seventeenth-century commentator of ibn Sīnā, the Sayyid Aḥmad 'Alawī as one who amplified ibn Sīnā's cosmology in the framework of a reformed Zurvanism "in the spirit of Suhrawardī's work."[32]

Among the possible sources for Ṣūfism other than Islam, Neo-Platonism, and independent origins, E. G. Browne mentions those who view Ṣūfism either as a Persian or an Indian reaction against the Semitic religion.[33] From a similar historical (but also sociological) approach, Wickens reaches the conclusion that there are many similarities between ibn Sīnā and Manichaeism of which there always remained a trace in Iran. Among such similarities he lists first of all the doctrine of the relationship between the soul and the body, and secondly the Manichaean conception of the eternity of matter and ibn Sīnā's notion of God's remoteness from this world and his direct action which is restricted to the First Universal Spirit. Ibn Sīnā's view of "determinist materialism" Wickens finds, then, to be similar to the heresy of Zurvanism where even God is subject to fate, or, as ibn Sīnā would say, where God is bound by his own nature.[34]

S. M. Afnan, like Wickens, turns to the indigenous sources of ibn Sīnā's mysticism as well as to the Neo-Platonic ones. He contends, "what is known as Ṣūfism was in its essentials a distinctive contribution of the Persian mind."[35] Among the Iranian studies of ibn Sīnā one finds numerous references to the so-called non-Islamic sources of ibn Sīnā's philosophy. For example, S. Naficy not only singles out some of the non-Islamic tendencies that were present in ibn Sīnā's time, but he refers also to the attempts of non-Sunnī sects to minimize the influence of the Arabs on Iranian culture.[36] Recently, more inquiries have been undertaken into the alleged Iranization of ibn Sīnā's thought. For instance, in his article, "La théosophie iranienne source d'Avicenne?"[37] Panoussi points to the resemblance between many themes that found their expression in the *Avesta* and in the later "Twilight" stage of Zoroastrianism. Panoussi is chiefly concerned with the controversy over what ibn Sīnā means by "oriental" philosophy. After pointing to the different positions taken with regard to this topic and summarizing them, Panoussi concludes that the controversy has not been settled decisively.[38] His view casts some doubts on the widely accepted controversial theory of Pines who holds the opinion that ibn Sīnā regarded the peripatetic Christians of Baghdad as his adversaries.[39] According to Panoussi, Pines rejects the distinctness of the school of Gundīshāpūr and the continuous development in science and philosophy of pre-Islamic Zoroastrian thought. Pines arrives, therefore, at his position without having taken into account the rich indigenous background which played an important role in the development of ibn Sīnā's theories. Panoussi claims to have found many Zoroastrian doctrines within the corpus of ibn Sīnā's works, and in particular doctrines which are related to "participation," "illumination," and the division of the world. On the basis of the linguistic, historical and philosophical observations he has made, Panoussi recommends a close study of the doctrine of participation in Zoroastrianism and investigation of the possible influence of this doctrine on ibn Sīnā's metaphysics, an inquiry which may shed light on the issue of his "oriental" philosophy.[40]

Having discussed the relationship between ibn Sīnā, and Ṣūfism from the point of view of those scholars who claim to have discovered definite Zoroastrian sources or themes in ibn Sīnā's philosophy, let us evaluate briefly some of the claims of this interpretation. An inquiry into the particular aspects of ibn Sīnā's background and his cultural heritage is justified by the abundant data available in this area; moreover, such an inquiry seems to be promising in the sense that it will assist us in clarifying some issues within ibn Sīnā's philosophical system, particularly the relationship between ibn Sīnā's thought and Ṣūfism. Let us anticipate some possible results and directions of such a study.

(i) In his works on Suhrawardī, especially in *Les motifs zoroastriens dans la philosophie de Sohrawardî*,[41] Corbin has singled out Ṣūfīs who came after ibn Sīnā, who were conscious of Zoroastrian themes and gave expression to these themes in their works. Now, if Zoroastrian theological works, written for the greater part at least a century before ibn Sīnā's birth, were still used extensively by philosophers a century after ibn Sīnā's death, then it appears likely that these texts were also available to ibn Sīnā who, spending his entire life in Iran, probably had easy access to them. (ii) It has been pointed out that there are affinities between the doctrines of ibn Sīnā and those of various Zoroastrian sects. Whether or not he expressed a preference for these doctrines over the Islamic ones because they were part of his Persian heritage is an extremely difficult hypothesis to justify. An examination of his metaphysical text in Persian, the *Dānish Nāmeh (Ilāhiyyāt)* reveals that he is conscious of using Persian terms as equivalents for Arabic terms and that he does so in order to develop what might be called a Persian philosophical vocabulary. From his autobiography one receives the prima facie impression that ibn Sīnā was politically active and patriotic (to his prince). Although an interest in reviving an anti-Islamic school cannot be attested for him, he could well have taken the familiar Zoroastrian doctrines into serious consideration. The same cannot be asserted of ibn Rushd, for example, who lived in Spain. Since Manichaeism and other Zoroastrian sects affected St. Augustine and Plotinus in North Africa, however, it is unlikely that Zoroastrian doctrines were ignored by those philosophers who were born and who lived in the very areas where Zoroastrianism had flourished. Ibn Sīnā's own texts show evidence not only of his familiarity with Pahlavi and Zoroastrian vocabulary, but they show also that he made active use of it. For instance, in *Mazdaism and Persian Literature,* M. Mo'in points out that ibn Sīnā uses *warj*, "the heavenly power," as it was used consistently in the *Avesta* and in Pahlavi texts.[42] We find it significant that he employs this term in referring to the "intelligence-stage" of persons contemplating the best of all possible world orders. Moreover, since he mentions the doctrine of the Magi on the difference between the body and the soul in his *Risāla Aḍḥawiyya fī Amr al-Ma'ād,*[43] he must have studied Zoroastrian doctrines and must not have regarded them exclusively from the religious point of view.

In expounding the last view (the fifth), a view which we tend to support, it has been our aim to show that there is some justification for investigating the Zoroastrian tradition which had a direct bearing on ibn Sīnā's works, as well as for examining the relationship between ibn Sīnā and Ṣūfism, at least from the Zoroastrian viewpoint. Several immediate tasks of such an investigation are obvious—thematic studies of Zoroastrian texts and appraisals of the actual availability and popularity of these texts in ibn Sīnā's time. That this labor is momentous hardly needs mention, for only isolated evidence is available to us on ibn Sīnā's direct contact with Zoroastrianism. We know very little of this matter apart from the fact that one of his students was a Zoroastrian. Hence, establishing a causal relation between ibn Sīnā and Zoroastrianism will be an extremely difficult task, if only on account of the scarcity of the source material.

It should be evident from the preceding discussion that wide disagreement exists among scholars on whether or not ibn Sīnā's views correspond to Ṣūfī doctrines. We have demonstrated that the evidence cited by those who support and those who reject either position is strikingly different. While some would place both ibn Sīnā and Ṣūfīs into the Islamic tradition, others would have them in the Zoroastrian tradition. Whereas some interpreters have taken the position that ibn Sīnā's doctrine is not mystical but the highest of religious achievements, others have claimed that it is a philosophical theory directed against Ṣūfism and Islam. The views are many, but for the sake of brevity it will suffice to recall this and earlier discussions.

II
ON THE METHODOLOGY OF OUR ANALYSIS

Any attempt which aims to solve this complex problem in its entirety must investigate many issues, such as (i) the themes of creation-emanation, salvation-immortality, and various other doctrines of Islam, classical Zoroastrianism, Manichaeism, and other similar religious sects; (ii) the doctrines of persons, mystical union, steps of the mystical ascent, types of mystical knowledge, and related topics found in the vast body of Ṣūfī literature; and, perhaps, (iii) the life of ibn Sīnā and the conditions of Iran during his life. Obviously, since we cannot address ourselves to all of these issues, a conclusive solution to the problem is beyond the compass of this paper. Instead, we shall concentrate only on what we regard as being of philosophical and primary importance—namely, a clarification of the problem and some of its ramifications. What is meant by "Ṣūfism"? On what grounds can we decide whether or not Ṣūfism is related to the doctrines of ibn Sīnā, and, if such a relationship is discovered, how can it be described? In our attempt to answer the question "What is Ṣūfism?" we shall, unfortunately have to restrict ourselves even further to a conceptual type of inquiry. We shall refer only to some significant topics in Ṣūfism since it is impossible for us to cover the entire body of concepts expressed in Ṣūfī literature. Moreover, since Ṣūfism has been defined in many different ways, we shall restrict our interpretation to a limited sense of Ṣūfism, namely to "Ṣūfism" as the mysticism of the Muslims.

If we ask what is meant by "mysticism," we are faced with many diverse opinions centering mainly on the relationship between mysticism and religion. Many have advanced the claim that mysticism is either religious, or there are at least religious (supernatural) and secular (natural) types of mysticism. A well-known spokesman for this particular school of opinion is R.C. Zaehner who has completed important research on Zoroastrian and Indian mysticism. In his classical study, *Mysticism, Sacred and Profane,*[44] Zaehner declares openly that he considers the problem of mysticism from a Roman Catholic point of view. In his conclusion to this book he mentions the complexity of mysticism: " . . . Our investigations have led to the tentative conclusion that what goes by the name of mysticism, so far from being an identical expression of the selfsame Universal Spirit falls into three distinct categories."[45] Zaehner views it as his aim to distinguish between what he calls "nature mysticism" and a different type of mysticism that is acceptable to religion. He objects to the first and to the confusion which results, in his opinion, from failing to distinguish between these two types, for such confusion tends to throw the latter into disrepute. He attaches great importance to such a differentiation because of his recognition that a failure to differentiate between these two types leads to the conclusion that God is merely another term for nature. But, since nature is ignorant of morality, charity, and common decency, God would then be reduced to the sum total of natural impulses in which the terms "good" and "evil" are meaningless.[46] In another study, *Hindu and Muslim Mysticism*,[47] Zaehner distinguishes between three basic types of mysticism. Though he establishes them with reference to the Hindu tradition, they are applicable to other traditions as well.[48]

Not all investigators of this subject agree with Zaehner's thesis that there is an affinity between religion and mysticism. W. T. Stace holds the opposite view, for example, in his study, *The Teaching of the Mystics*.[49] He insists that mystical experience is not, in itself, a religious phenomenon, but that a connection between the two is to be regarded as subsequent and circumstantial.[50]

In our attempt to explain mysticism and to discover its relationship to religion, we view the crucial issue as the portrayal of the relationship between the transcendent being and persons. Inherent in the dogmata of monotheistic religions is the explicit assumption that God is the ultimate being, and that a true union between God and man cannot ever take place. The mystics, on the other hand, refer constantly to such a union which they tend to express in terms of "union with" the One, or "becoming identified" with this One. Although for this very reason many hesitate to identify mysticism with religion, they tend also at the same time to relate the two because many features are common to both. The serious devotion to the ultimate being and the intimate relation with it which is characterized on the one hand by mystical practices and the union a mystic feels with the world and on the other hand by God's grace or by the prayer of the believer are examples of this phenomenon. In short, there is an evident confusion concerning the relationship between mystical and religious experiences. It is also evident that the portrayal of the relationship between the ultimate being and persons—the core of this confusion—is of supreme significance to our problem.

We should discover also in our investigation what place or role has been assigned to the ultimate being in philosophical systems relevant to ibn Sīnā's philosophy, for as a philosopher ibn Sīnā approached this issue from a philosophical viewpoint. Therefore, the mystical portrayal of the relationship between the ultimate being and man should be compared not only with its religious depiction but also with the pertinent philosophical formulations of this relation. Accordingly, in our analysis of this topic we shall adopt the following procedure:

1. We shall examine one relation that is pivotal to this topic, namely the relationship between persons and the ultimate being.
2. We shall distinguish between the two aspects of this relationship in ibn Sīnā's system, the one being the bond coming from the ultimate being to persons, and the other being that relation which is directed from persons to the ultimate being.
3. We shall assume that there are three traditional theories by means of which the relationship from the ultimate being towards persons has been depicted in the context of the relationship between God and the world: creation, emanation, and co-eternity.
4. We shall also assume that the basic theory about the relationship from persons to the ultimate being has traditionally been expressed in three different ways by means of the following relationships: by harmony (*ittiḥād*), connection (*ittiṣāl*), and union (*ḥulūl*).

On the basis of these clear distinctions it will be possible to construct informal schemata that will enable us to distinguish between religious, philosophical, and mystical kinds of theories. In the context of such distinctions, we shall be able to determine whether or not ibn Sīnā was a Ṣūfī. While we shall not claim categorical conclusiveness for our answer, we do claim hypothetical validity for it on the basis of the suppositions we have stated. Perhaps ultimately such schemata as the ones we are about to construct have chiefly a methodological value, for they can become models whose precise distinctions can serve as the prelude to future studies on this issue.

III
THE ULTIMATE BEING AND PERSONS

As the most crucial issue of our inquiry we have singled out the relationship between the ultimate being and persons. The "ultimate being" designates the God of religions, the One of the mystics, and the Necessary Existent of ibn Sīnā. We have mentioned the two basic aspects of this relation. The one is directed from the ultimate being toward persons, while the other is directed from each person toward the ultimate being. Let us now consider the first aspect of this relation.

THE RELATIONSHIP DIRECTED FROM THE ULTIMATE BEING TOWARD PERSONS

We have cited three basic types of ways in which the ultimate being is thought to be related to the world: creation, co-eternity, and emanation. Ibn Sīnā, who accepts the emanation theory, rejects the first two. It shall be our first task to examine the significant features of the theories he rejects.

Creation

The widely acclaimed creation theory is advocated by every monotheistic religion. Its lasting popularity, which extends beyond religion into mythology, has been attested historically. Without fear of contradiction, we can safely assert that monotheistic religions, such as Judaism, Christianity, and Islam hold the following dogmata: (i) That the ultimate being is God, and (ii) that the relationship from the ultimate being to the world is represented as a creation of the world *ex nihilo*. Man's existence is ascribed to an act of creation.

The *Qur'ān* offers many specific illustrations of this theory. Though we do not intend to enter into the arena of theological disputes by attempting an exegesis of Qur'ānic passages, we shall cite some quotations from this work to support our contention that the religious doctrine upholds creation.
It is written in the *Qur'ān*:

To Him is due
The Primal origin
Of the heavens and the earth:
When He decreeth a matter,
He saith to it: "Be,"
And it is. (S.II.117)

And again it is written:

Verily your Lord is God,
Who created the heavens
And the earth in six days . . . (S.X.3)

One cannot fail to observe the striking correspondence between the Qur'ānic and the Biblical accounts of the creation of the world. The relationship between God and man (persons) is also characterized in numerous passages in the *Qur'ān*. Of these we shall quote only one:

He has created man:
He has taught him speech
(And Intelligence). (S.LV.3-4)

The doctrine of creation has also been held by many philosophers. Even though they have at times expressed some reservations about it, which may have given rise to their peculiar versions of the creation theory, they accepted it as revelation. For instance, notwithstanding the fact that Ghazālī (the mystic-skeptic), an adherent to the creation theory, "refutes the Belief [of philosophers] in the Eternity of the World," in his *Tahāfut al-Falāsifah*,[51] he affirms that he does not wish to present a doctrine of his own:

> However, in this book we have undertaken only an attack on their doctrines [of the philosophers] and a refutation of their arguments. It is not our business to support a particular point of view.[52]

In another section of the same text, however, he does present the creation theory without any criticism:

> They [any set of events observed to be connected together] are connected as the result of the Decree of God . . . , which preceded their existence. If one follows the other, it is because He has created them in that fashion, not because the connection in itself is necessary and indissoluble. He has the power to create . . . the survival of life when the head has been cut off, or any other thing from among the connected things [independently of what is supposed to be its cause].[53]

From the tenor of his discussion we infer that he, like many other philosophers, accepts the creation theory on the basis of divine revelation. It is well known that many philosophers have offered sophisticated theories of creation, from the Muslim Kindī to the Jew Maimonides and the Christian Aquinas. We shall not enumerate these theories but shall merely list some logical features of a system of the creation theory and compare this system with ibn Sīnā's doctrine of emanation. We regard the following features as the essential marks of the creation theory: (i) The ultimate being is the God of monotheistic religions. (ii) God has created the world *ex nihilo;* nothing is co-eternal with Him. (iii) God is logically independent of the world; hence, it is possible for the world not to exist while God exists. (iv) In one sense or another God is "conscious" by being aware of the thoughts of persons. For instance, He can be aware of our motives and intentions and can sit in judgment of them if He wishes to do so. (v) God can intervene in man's life (having knowledge of man's thoughts) in the sense, for example, that He can affect man's future by means of some divine plan or miracle. (vi) There is nothing in God's nature that is also an essential constituent of man's nature. For instance, while man may suffer pain and while his soul may be tormented eternally, God feels no pain. Keeping in mind these major features of the creation theory, let us compare and contrast ibn Sīnā's doctrine with this theory.

Since S. H. Nasr's exposition of ibn Sīnā's doctrine[54] is representative of those who claim to find a marked affinity between the creation theory and ibn Sīnā's doctrine, we shall outline what seem to be the major steps of Nasr's position before we examine specific features of it. He interprets all uses of *iḥdāth, ibdā', khalq,* and *takwīn* to mean "creation" (different senses of "production") in ibn Sīnā's philosophy. Creation itself he takes to refer to God's intellection (*ta'aqqul*) of His own essence, which, in conjunction with the knowledge (*'ilm*) of His own essence brings about the existence of all things. "The act of intellection is eternal (*lā yatanāhā*) and the manifestation of the Universe is God's eternal knowledge of Himself." Since creation is the giving of Being by God as well as the radiation of intelligence, each being is, therefore, related to God by its being as well as by its intelligence. Ibn Sīnā has even identified God with the source (*al-manba'*) of overflowing light (*fayḍan al-nūr*) in some of his less well-known works. For this reason creation can be construed to mean "the realization of the intelligible essences and existence the theophany (*tajallī*) of these essences, so that being and light are ultimately the same. To give existence to creatures is to illuminate them with the Divine Light which is the same as His Being."[55] It is also Nasr's opinion that Muslim philosophers like ibn Sīnā, who held the emanation theory actually attempted to adhere to the religious doctrine creation as it is presented in the *Qur'ān*. Accordingly, these thinkers offered their views as a rejection of Aristotelian co-eternity theory and supported the Islamic doctrine of creation. Creation, according Nasr, is like emanation. In his opinion, ibn Sīnā does not step out of the Islamic perspective in his vision of the cosmos or in the doctrine of divine intellection, although he diverges somewhat from orthodox Islamic doctrines in viewing the power of God as existing in a predetermined logical structure and in the lesser sense of awe with which the creature, in his system, approaches God. In the Islamic doctrine God is absolute determination as well as absolute freedom, for He is the source of all qualities. Hence His will cannot be limited to finite systems. It is Nasr's belief that philosophers like ibn Sīnā, particularly in following the Neoplatonists, started out from profound metaphysical intuition which resulted to a lesser or greater extent from applying the first *Shahāda* of Islam.[56]

Let us criticize Nasr's position briefly in our attempt to clarify the meaning of emanation and creation. The key word in Nasr's description of God's creation of the world is "production." In disagreement with Nasr, we wish to point out that there is a difference between "producing something out of nothing" and "producing something by emanation out of one's thought." In the latter case, there is a resemblance between the agent and the product; this resemblance is not to be found in the first case. Whereas the Islamic God produces the world *ex nihilo,* in ibn Sīnā's philosophy we find the explicit assertion that the Necessary Existent does not produce the world in such a manner, but that It emanates (*padīd āmadan*) the first intelligence. Consequently, the view that ibn Sīnā upholds the creation theory is open to serious objection.

Ibn Sīnā affirms that the will of the Necessary Existent cannot in any sense be changed by consciousness, choice, or deliberation (*DAI* chap. 33). This will is equated with His knowledge of the good universal world order, or of the general laws that best regulate the order of the universe (*DAI* chap. 33). In this sense it follows, therefore, that the Necessary Existent is governed by the physical-moral laws of the universe. Moreover, since the Necessary Existent cannot act in an arbitrary manner (by intervening, for example, in this order) and remain at the same time necessarily good (perfect), it follows also that the structure of the laws governing the universe is independent of the will of the Necessary Existent. In this sense ibn Sīnā's view of the Necessary Existent resembles Leibniz's view that the righteousness of God's acts is not due to the fact that God performs them, while it differs from Descartes' view that any act of God is analytically right. For this reason we can raise those objections to ibn Sīnā's doctrine which Arnauld raises to Leibniz's doctrine in which the latter attempts to retain overtones of religion in a deterministic metaphysics.

Though the analogy of the sun and its rays (an analogy often cited by mystics) gives insight into a part of the emanation process, it does not portray accurately the relationship between the Necessary Existent and the world as ibn Sīnā himself confirms, because the sun is a substance having a subject matter while the Necessary Existent is not a substance (*DAI* chap. 28). The very fact that ibn Sīnā does not regard the Necessary Existent as a substance forces us to recognize his theory as a non-creation type of theory, for a creation theory assumes the existence of a substance which is separated from other substances and exists independently.

We question Nasr's view that the problematical controversy between the Islamic and the ibn Sīnian view arises not out of a different interpretation of intellection, but over the issue of a determinism. The argument, in our opinion, results not from a quarrel over whether or not there is intellection; it results from different views on whether or not this intellection is determined. Within ibn Sīnā's metaphysical system the intellection itself is determined by the quality of the absolute perfection attributed to the Necessary Existent. The determinism, therefore, by means of which the Necessary Existent is chiefly explained includes intellection. It is our opinion that as a result of such determinism the Necessary Existent cannot be said to have created the world. And herein we differ rather strongly with Nasr's interpretation of ibn Sīnā's doctrine, for ibn Sīnā's Necessary Existent does not satisfy our criteria for the creation theory, particularly with regard to criterion (iii), God's logical independence of the world, and criterion (vi), God's constitution which differs totally from that of man.

At odds, moreover, with the religious dogma of creation is ibn Sīnā's doctrine that the Necessary Existent is not directly related to persons and the world, but that It acts only through intermediaries. When it is compared to the criteria we have listed for the creation theory, ibn Sīnā's position conflicts explicitly with criterion (iv), [God is conscious of Himself and His creation] and criterion (v), [God has the ability to intervene in the order of the world], criteria which are assumed by our interpretation of a creation theory.

The dissimilarity between the Necessary Existent and the Islamic God is accentuated by other non-Islamic theories held by ibn Sīnā, such as the non-resurrection of the body and the lack of punishment and reward after death. On the basis of the foregoing, we take the following position: If one relationship between the ultimate being towards persons can be expressed as a creation theory in the manner we have described it and as the quotations cited from the *Qur'ān* confirm it, then ibn Sīnā's doctrine conflicts with the theory of creation.

Co-eternity

Another alternative to the creation theory is the doctrine of co-eternity, which states that the ultimate being and the world are co-eternal. In a prefatory way we wish to point out that the chief difference between this theory and the emanation theory lies not in any "temporal" feature of emanation, for emanation, which can be atemporal, need not take place at a specified time. Although there are many differences between the co-eternity theory on the one hand and the creation theory and the emanation theory on the other hand, we shall mention only some of the more significant ways in which the former differs from the other two theories. (i) According to the co-eternity theory, matter exists and has always existed independently of the ultimate being. Even though the ultimate being may "move" the material realm, matter is neither created by it nor emanated from it. (ii) The ultimate being is regarded as a substance that is absolutely independent of the rest of the world. Whereas the creation theory usually does not attribute any descriptive feature to the ultimate being, which is regarded as a transcendent being and is therefore not reduced to the same category of other entities (by being placed into such a category), in the co-eternity theory the ultimate being is considered as another substance whose special attributes are usually described as physical operations rather than as special "moral" attributes. Finally, (iii) on account of the peculiar nature of the ultimate being, it is absurd to speak of a mystical union with it in the context of the co-eternity theory. Having singled out same features of the ultimate being by which it is described in the co-eternity theory, let us now examine and clarify this theory further.

It should be mentioned that the co-eternity theory, which explains supposedly how the ultimate being relates to the world, has been popular among the philosophers and has customarily been designated as the "philosophical theory." Ghazālī, for instance, expounds this theory and assesses its position among the philosophers in his *Tahāfut.* Although he notes the disagreement among philosophers as to the eternity of the world, he finds that most of them agree that it always co-existed with God in time, as an effect can be said to be concurrent with its cause. God's priority to the world he describes as the priority of the cause to the effect, i.e., priority according to essence and rank rather than to time.[57] Another difference between the theories of creation and co-eternity is suggested by Ghazālī's assertion that philosophers have generally taken the position that whatever has a beginning proceeds from the eternal by means of an intermediary.[58] In the creation theory the ultimate being is related directly to individuals. It can create them, can interfere in their order by means of miracles, but can also destroy them. In the case of the co-eternity theory, however, the ultimate being acts through a series of intermediaries. Since we have dealt with this topic so far only in schematic terms, let us now turn to a philosophical system that is closely related to the co-eternity schema.

Telling similarities can be observed between the co-eternity theory and the Aristotelian doctrine. In the Aristotelian system of the universe, the generation of all substances is caused by substances having the same form. About coming into being, Aristotle asserts:

> We note next that neither the material nor the form of a thing comes into being [when the thing comes into being]; and I mean this even of the matter and form closest to things. For everything that changes is something that is changed by something into something. That by which it is changed is its first mover; what is changed is its material; and that into which it is changed is its form. . . . We note next that all primary beings (both those generated naturally and otherwise) come into being out of something with the same name. (*Metaphysics* 1070 a)

That Aristotle's doctrine is different from the creation theory, such as the one held by Christianity, is confirmed by Gilson's comparison of Aristotle and Aquinas and by some of the following differences he observes between them. Aristotle's God is "one of the causes and one of the principles of all things, but not the cause nor the principle of all things," according to Gilson, for He fails to account for matter in the Aristotelian domain of being. As a consequence it is impossible to reduce Aristotle's metaphysics to unqualified unity. In the system of St. Thomas, however, God is the cause of everything, even of matter. Hence, the notion of metaphysics itself is modified by the doctrine of creation, for a first cause is introduced into the realm of being and from this cause everything comes into being.[59]

A comparison of some features of the ibn Sīnian theory of emanation and the Aristotelian version of the co-eternity theory and a depiction of how both theories treat three different issues that have a bearing on them will enable us to establish the differences between these two theories. (i) Aristotle considers the ultimate being as God (θεῖοσ), a non-sensible eternal substance (οὐσία), whereas ibn Sīnā names the ultimate being not God, but the Necessary Existent (*al-Wājib al-Wujūd*) which, according to his explicit assertion, is not a substance (*jawhar nīst*) (*DAI* chap. 25). (ii) We notice, furthermore, that Aristotle views matter as being eternal, rather than as an effusion from the ultimate being, even though it is related to the ultimate being only through motion. According to ibn Sīnā, on the other hand, matter is an effusion from the Necessary Existent by way of the thought of the first intelligence, which first emanated from the Necessary Existent. (iii) Finally, we observe that substances, according to Aristotle, are generated out of the same substances where the form is transmitted, whereas in ibn Sīnā's system, an intelligence generates a (heavenly) body (*DAI* chap. 39). Consequently, the entity that generates another entity is not like that which is generated. In the light of these differences it is obvious that it is possible to construct a theory of the co-eternity of the world that differs not only from the ibn Sīnian emanation theory, but also from the creation theory upheld by monotheistic religions. Moreover, it is evident that such a theory of co-eternity is supported by the Aristotelian doctrine.

THE RELATIONSHIP DIRECTED FROM PERSONS TO THE ULTIMATE BEING

Having discussed that aspect of the relationship between the ultimate being and persons which is directed from this ultimate being to man, we shall now turn to the other side of this relationship, namely the relationship which is directed from persons to the ultimate being. Three major theories have been advanced which take account of the direction of this movement: the theories of harmony, connection, and (mystical) union. At first glance it appears to be the case that the wording of ibn Sīnā's texts supports all three. However a detailed examination of his doctrine reveals that he actually supports the third formulation of this relation more than the first two versions listed. Let us begin our analysis of this relationship by examining its first portrayal, namely the harmony theory.

Harmony

The central thesis of the harmony theory states that man can at best hope to live a life that is in harmony with the order ordained by the ultimate being, a being which is usually described as God. Let us now list some of the significant features of this theory on the basis of which it can explicitly be distinguished from the other two theories. (i) Man cannot ever become God, nor can he ever hope to share a God-like existence. The highest state to which he can attain can be reached by abiding by the rules laid down by God. Michelangelo's famous painting on the ceiling of the Sistine chapel depicts this separation of man from God by portraying how God almost—but not actually—touches the hand of man. (ii) The relationship between God and man is affected by mediators standing between them who have direct access to prescriptive rules governing man's behavior. These mediators are not independent of God. For instance, Muḥammad denies that he has the power to change the Word of God, but claims that God's Word was given to him, and that he must obey and accept it (S.X.15). (iii) In this relationship man is pictured as being completely helpless and dependent on God. For instance, Job, the good man, could not bargain with God nor importune justice from him. In the *Qur'ān* a similar point of view is expressed. Though God breathes his spirit (*rūḥ*) into man (S.XV.29), He can also burn him by means of fire or destroy him by causing him constant suffering (S.LXIX.31).

When we speak of the harmony theory, then, we mean the theory that satisfies the three criteria cited regarding the way in which man can relate to the ultimate being. Whereas it can be concluded that the Islamic doctrine supports this view, it is disputable whether ibn Sīnā's doctrines would support such a harmony relation; the evidence available from his works seems to deny support to such a view. Several passages (e.g., *DAI* chap. 37) contain explicit mention of his view that the Necessary Existent is that entity with which persons should become united in a state of mystical union (*paīvand*). Since it is possible, according to ibn Sīnā, for persons to attain the highest state, i.e., to become one with the Necessary Existent, ibn Sīnā's doctrine cannot satisfy the first criterion of the harmony relation—that man cannot become like the ultimate being.

We should also take into consideration the last two chapters of *al-Ishārāt* in which ibn Sīnā, designates the stages of mystical union and differentiates, in addition, between the mystic (*'ābid*) and the believer (*zāhid*). The mystic he describes as someone to whom no specific object, e.g., a cross, or the Star of David, is sacred in itself. An object acquires value only insofar as it helps the mystic to advance in his path towards realization. Rejecting the rituals that were imposed by "institutionalized religions" has involved Ṣūfīs often in serious difficulties. In his study, *Muḥammadan Festivals,* von Grunebaum cites the case of Ḥallāj (executed 922) as an instance of such behavior and mentions that Ḥallāj was accused of heresy as a consequence of his alleged abrogation of the obligation to undertake the pilgrimage to Mecca.[60] Subsequently, von Grunebaum relates the mystical attitude of Ḥallāj to that of other Ṣūfīs and specifically to ibn al-'Arabī's (d. 1240), who asserted "that the true *Ka'ba* was nothing but our own being."[61] In sum, there seems to be some strong evidence as the basis for rejecting the view that ibn Sīnā and some Ṣūfīs held a position similar to the second criterion we mentioned for the harmony theory, namely that some particular rituals (considered mandatory by all religions) must be practiced by him who wishes to live according to the order established by the ultimate being. According to ibn Sīnā and the Ṣūfīs, man can reach mystical union by means of introspection alone without undergoing fixed rituals.

The third criterion, man's complete helplessness and dependence upon God, finds no support in ibn Sīnā's system. With regard to this criterion it should be observed that man cannot depend totally on God's mercy if there is neither punishment nor reward after death. G. Hourard has established the latter position for ibn Sīnā.[62] Moreover, Houben[63] has affirmed that the mystical stages in the *Ishārāt* and the stages of love in the *Risāla fī al-'ishq*[64] are dependent on the human endeavor. But ibn Sīnā's system contains still another "natural" aspect, for the prophetic soul (*'aql-i qudsī*) is a constituent of every soul and is not regarded as being peculiar to Muḥammad. In this sense, his view approaches what may be called a "natural mysticism." In ibn Sīnā's determined system, the Necessary Existent can only act through the supra-lunary mediators; it lacks the ability to intervene in particular events. Ultimately, its power and ability are described in terms of its knowledge of the best of all possible worlds. M. Marmura has shown that ibn Sīnā's Necessary Existent differs from the Islamic God in lacking knowledge of particulars which are capable of generation and corruption.[65] For these reasons, man is definitely not at the mercy of the Necessary Existent, particularly since he can approach It and become one with It. As a consequence, the third criterion of the harmony relation is repudiated by evidence gleaned from ibn Sīnā's texts. On grounds such as those cited, ibn Sīnā's view of the relation of harmony, if this relationship is formulated within a religious framework.

Connection

Obviously, the position of the mystics who advocate a "complete union" with the ultimate being is opposed to and, perhaps, even at the opposite pole of the harmony theory. Whereas the mystics claim that the unity of persons with God is not only possible, but that it represents the "return" of the person to its origin, adherents to the harmony theory would reject such a view as being blasphemous, for in a religious version of the harmony theory the acceptance of a specific scripture (as the word of God) and a certain prophet on the basis of revelation are firmly established religious tenets. The phenomenological introspective "ways" of the mystics as well as their claims to a direct relationship with the ultimate being differ strongly from the mandatory activities of "institutionalized religions."

In the present context we wish to construct a theory that occupies an intermediate position between these two extreme views, a theory which we propose to call a "connection theory." We shall demonstrate that such a theory resembles the views of some philosophers, though definitely not the views of ibn Sīnā. In order to clarify the features of the connection theory, let us enumerate and describe the conditions on the basis of which we shall be able to decide whether or not the name "connection theory" should be assigned to a relationship directed from persons to the ultimate being. (i) According to this theory, persons cannot ever become the ultimate being (or God). But it is possible for persons to participate in God-like activities by means of being active in certain kinds of experiences. The nature of this first condition is clarified by means of the following two conditions. (ii) There are entities, such as "eternal truths," "universals," "moral directives," and other similar entities, which are "experienced" primarily by God. Nonetheless, either through grace, work, or other methods, persons can experience these entities and thereby establish a "connection" with the ultimate being. (iii) The capacity possessed by a person for God-like experiences may be due to some "divine-like" constituent in him, such as "active intelligence," or "the light of reason." Some have gone so far as to say that God may have implanted this attribute into persons, or that this capacity is to be ascribed to the effect of the stars on the formation of man's soul at birth.

Let us now specify how this particular theory is to be differentiated from the "harmony" theory as well as from what may be called the theory of "(mystical) union." According to the harmony theory, there is no realm common to both man and the ultimate being that they can share. The connection theory, on the other hand, assumes that there is a realm of intellectual experiences shared by both, a realm in which man can have a "God-like" experience. Consequently, there is a divergence between the harmony theory and the connection theory.

The connection theory departs also from the (mystical) union theory in the following way. Though man can have "God-like" experiences, he can never become identical with God, for the ultimate being, which is regarded as an immaterial substance by this type of reasoning, cannot be equated with the material part of this world in which man's body is included. And even if persons are regarded as immortal souls, it is still impossible for man to become identical with the ultimate being, for the reason that both the soul and the ultimate being belong to the category of substance; substances, however, do not "blend" into one another. The views of ibn Sīnā, and many Ṣūfīs differ sharply from this position. In their discourses on the self we find an emphasis on the "stages" of the ascent and a view of the person not as a fixed substance but as a "process" of development whose final stage consists in a union with the ultimate being. And this view, that a person is to be regarded as a "process" rather than as a "thing" permits a union to take place between the person and the ultimate being. Such a person who can be united with God or the One is, therefore, capable of having a much stronger relationship with the ultimate being than a relation of either harmony or connection.

Having enumerated and clarified some features of the connection theory, let us examine whether it resembles the doctrines of those philosophers who are of concern to us. In this connection we might recall a famous passage from Aristotle in which he asserts that the activity of God is contemplation, and that the best activity in which man can engage is also, therefore, contemplation:

> But that perfect happiness is a contemplative activity will appear from the following consideration as well . . .. Therefore the activity of God, which surpasses all others in blessedness, must be contemplative; and of human activities, therefore, that which is most akin to this must be most of the nature of happiness.
>
> (*Nichomachean Ethics* 1178 b 8-10)

Aristotle regards the highest activity as being of a contemplative nature since this activity is akin to God's activity, and is therefore God-like. Similar in tenor are the last passages of Socrates' speech on love in the *Symposium* where the view is expressed that man experiences supposedly the highest vision when he has the experience of beauty. Of this experience Plato states:

> But what if man had eyes to see the true beauty—the divine beauty, I mean, pure and clear and unalloyed, not clogged with the pollutions of mortality and all the colours and vanities of human life—thither looking, and holding converse with the true beauty simple and divine?
>
> (*Symposium* 212 A)

Plato continues in this vein by relating that in this experience, a person, confronted not by "images" but by "realities," will "become the friend of God and be immortal, if mortal man may. Would that be an ignoble life?"

We shall now turn to the general topic: Can Aristotle's philosophy be related to the connection theory? And if so, in what manner? It is difficult to justify the assertion that Aristotle actually upheld the theory of a connection, particularly since his concept of νοῦς is highly ambiguous. A consideration of its ambiguity is significant to our study because νοῦς is the very aspect of persons that is eternal and God-like, according to the famous passage found in the third book of *De Anima* (430a 3-25). In addition to these celebrated passages, we take into consideration some remarks Aristotle makes on this subject in his *Generation of Animals*. In chapter two of this work Aristotle expresses his uncertainty about the origin of νοῦς in the context of questioning when animals receive reason νοῦς.

> That is why it is a very great puzzle to answer another question, concerning Reason. At what moment, and in what manner, do those creatures which have this principle of Reason acquire their share in it, and where does it come from? This is a very difficult problem which we must endeavor to solve, so far as it may be solved, to the best of our power.
>
> (*Gen. of An.* 736b)

Subsequently Aristotle advances a solution to this puzzling issue:

> It remains, then, that Reason alone enters in as an additional factor, from outside, and that it alone is divine, because physical activity has nothing whatever to do with the activity of Reason.
>
> (*Gen. of An.* 736b 25)

Aristotle's theory, expressed in these passages, approaches our view of the connection theory in the sense that there may be an aspect of each person which is "divine-like." Moreover, Aristotle also seems to point to a "divine-like" activity, namely contemplation. Notwithstanding his ability to contemplate, man is nevertheless not identifiable with God because man is made from matter as well as form, whereas God is nonmaterial in being a pure actuality as Aristotle confirms when he states, "It is clear then that there is a substance which is eternal and immovable and separate from sensible things." (*Metaphysics* 1073a 3-5) Having quoted some passages from Aristotle's works to establish what we regard as an affinity between Aristotle's point of view and what we regard as the connection theory, let us observe how ibn Sīnā's own theory differs from the connection theory and how it appears in its Aristotelian modification.

A person, according to ibn Sīnā possesses not only a body (*māddat*) and a soul (*nafs*), but also intelligence (*'aql*) [(*'aql*) being an aspect of the soul]. Being immortal, the soul is transformed in one sense or another into *'aql* after the death of the body. The mystical union, ibn Sīnā tells us, takes place when the intelligence receives the Necessary Existent. The "entire" person, having lost its former physical constituents, can then be said to be *united* (*paīvand*), and not just *connected* with the Necessary Existent. This view, that a person can be identified with the ultimate being (which is the prime mover, according to Aristotle) is an anti-Aristotelian position. For this reason, our discussion of this philosophical view describing how a person relates to the ultimate being by a "connection" relation brings out the differences between ibn Sīnā's position and Aristotle's typically philosophical stand on this issue.

IV
EMANATIONISM AND ṢŪFISM IN IBN SĪNĀ'S PHILOSOPHY

In our attempt to establish the nature of the relationship between ibn Sīnā's philosophy and Ṣūfism, we have observed many confused and conflicting views in the treatment of this subject. Often this confusion is not due to the mistakes of the able scholars treating the subject, but is due to many other factors, such as: (i) the complexity and the interrelatedness of many different aspects of the subject matter in Near Eastern texts which are a blend of religious, mystical, and philosophical themes; (ii) different presuppositions, aims, and methodological approaches of the contemporary scholars who treat this subject, and most of all, (iii) the lack of agreement on the standard meaning and use of key concepts, such as "mysticism" and "religion" for instance, which are used in the discussions of these texts.

The last factor, namely the lack of preciseness in the use of these concepts, is especially significant as the following example illustrates. If two scholars who disagree on the meaning of a key term such as "Ṣūfism" should read a certain passage in ibn Sīnā's texts about whose meaning and content they agree, they could argue indefinitely over whether or not the particular passage supports or denies the view that ibn Sīnā's philosophy has an affinity with Ṣūfism. Consequently, a clarification of terms is called for in order to prevent such confusion. By their very nature, however, precise conceptual clarifications have only a restricted application. This restriction applies particularly to this rich domain of texts relevant to the problem of this inquiry. Recognizing this limitation, we nonetheless wish to make use of the theoretical distinctions we have drawn in the context of our problem. Let us specify these limitations further.

In our discussion we assume one relation to be primary: namely the relationship between persons and the ultimate being. We assume also that one of the major confusions is due to a failure to distinguish the religious, philosophical and mystical features of this problem. In the context of our subsequent analysis, we shall illustrate how this particular confusion can be solved. But let us first attend briefly to the "religious" and "philosophical" systems in which this relationship between a person and the ultimate being is expressed in order to differentiate these systems from ibn Sīnā's "mystical" system, which we intend to examine in detail.

The Religious System

Let us assume the following distinguishing marks for this relationship within the context of a "religious system": (a) the relationship from the ultimate being to a person is described as a *creation,* and (b) the other side of this relationship from a person to the ultimate being is said to be one of *harmony.*

The Philosophical-Intellectual System

Let the characteristic marks of a "philosophical-intellectual" system be the following: (a) the ultimate being is related to the world by a *co-eternity* relationship, and (b) a person relates to the ultimate being in terms of a *connection.* We call this a "philosophical-intellectual" approach in order to emphasize that the ultimate being and a person can have a relationship by means of sharing the "intellectual" realm. We do not claim, however, that all philosophers hold this view.

The Ibn Sīnian Version of the Mystical System

The major distinguishing marks of a "mystical system" can be constructed as follows: (a) The ultimate being is related to a person by the *emanation* of the contingent realm, a realm which includes each person, and (b) it is possible for a person to relate to the ultimate being by means of a (mystical) *union.*

In the context of these schemata we shall investigate how ibn Sīnā's views are related to the mystical system. And in view of this objective we shall outline first of all some of the general features of his doctrine. The ultimate being in the ibn Sīnian system is the Necessary Existent (*al-Wājib al-Wujūd*), from which the world has emanated in a "flow" or a descent. But in the very process of mystical union (*paīvand*), there is a return of what he calls "persons" to the Necessary Existent. The latter is not portrayed as a substance (*jawhar*), but as the beholder (*dāranda*) of the world. In this sense, the Necessary Existent is not separated from the realm of contingent beings, but constitutes the ground for their actualization. In addition, more detailed aspects of ibn Sīnā's doctrines that are related to this view should also be mentioned.

On the basis of some of his texts, it is possible to interpret his views on this issue in such a manner that their close correspondence with the mystical system we have depicted will become evident. Among the doctrines that support such an interpretation we would include the following: (i) The view (which is an implicit premise of his philosophy) that there is a multiplicity of substances in the contingent world.[66] (ii) It is possible to arrange these substances and the Necessary Existent according to a ranking system where rank is determined by criteria of value.[67] The amount of actuality entities possess and their type of motion or lack of motion are the two explicit criteria mentioned by ibn Sīnā on the basis of which entities are assigned a certain rank. Accordingly, that which possesses a greater amount of actuality receives a higher rank than that with a lesser amount of actuality. The motion of entities is a co-incidental feature of this grading system. Whatever is composed of elements that move in a straight line is accorded a lower rank than that which moves in a circular motion, and whatever does not move at all is better than that which moves.[68] (iii) There are two aspects to every contingent being, one of necessity with respect to its cause, and another of contingency with respect to itself. By the latter ibn Sīnā means that it is possible to conceive of a world in which the entity in question is not realized.[69] (iv) In the process of emanation only some entity must be emanated from the Necessary Existent, for the absolute perfection of the latter implies that some being had to emanate from It. Since It is a unity, however, at most one being can be emanated from It. Therefore, exactly one entity emanated from It.[70] (v) In one sense or another, ibn Sīnā regards the process of emanation as thought. It is possible that he adopted this view from Neoplatonism and possibly even from another earlier source, namely from the Persian Zoroastrian sects, e.g., Zurvanism. Followers of Zurvan, for instance, believed that Zurvan (eternal time) emanated various kinds of beings by the act of thought alone.[71] (vi) Every entity desires to "return" to its cause, which is portrayed as being "better" than that entity.[72] On the basis of these premises and the basic distinctions we have drawn, it is possible to construct the following model of the ibn Sīnian emanation theory.

A flow of emanation (*padīd āmadan, faid*) effuses from the Necessary Existent toward the world. In this flow, exactly one entity, namely the first intelligence, emanates from the Necessary Existent. This intelligence is described as having two aspects—one of necessity when it is regarded with respect to its source, and one of contingency when it is regarded with respect to itself. Accordingly, two emanations are thought to take place. Considered from the aspect of contingency, a body emanates from the intelligence, whereas another intelligence emanates from the aspect of the necessity of this intelligence. The initial emanations are followed by similar series of emanations in which intelligences and heavenly bodies are generated.[73] In some texts ibn Sīnā asserts that the emanation of the heavenly substances terminates when that heavenly intelligence is generated from which no heavenly body can emanate.[74] On some occasions he refers to this last heavenly intelligence specifically as "the active intelligence."[75] Moreover, he identifies the heavens with the stars and the moon with the lowest of these. The sub-lunary realm, therefore, is that realm which comprises elements receptive to both generation and corruption.[76] Since it is not able to generate a heavenly body, the active intelligence, or the last intelligence of the heavenly realm, emanates the substratum-matter. From these differences four kinds of primary, simple bodies are derived which are capable of composition: fire, air, water, and earth. The active intelligence emanates three different kinds of souls: the vegetative soul, the animal soul, and the rational soul. No other kind of entity can be emanated after the emanation of the rational soul.[77]

In the preceding section we have summarized some salient features of relationship, which is directed from the ultimate being to persons, but we have yet to examine the other side of this relationship, which is directed from persons to the ultimate being. In portraying the second relationship, we refer only to those works of ibn Sīnā in which this "ascent" towards a mystical union is emphasized.[78]

Every entity, according to ibn Sīnā, has a desire to reach its perfection (*kamāl*, ἀρετή), a desire that is expressed in the form of love for this perfection. In the *Risāla fī al-'ishq'*, this desire is expressed in terms of *'ishq*, or "love." Discussions of the nature and function of love appear in many other writings of ibn Sīnā.[79] But with regard to persons, our present concern, this desire is depicted best in his description of the activities of the intelligence aspect of a person, i.e., that aspect of the soul which he calls *'aql*. Two implicit arguments are presented in support of this point.[80] (i) Since the intelligence (*'aql*) is originally implanted in the body of the person, and, since the embodiment of this intelligence is necessary to its development, the desire of the intelligence toward a "higher realm" represents a longing to return to its source.[81] (ii) For the reason that the intelligence finds its highest pleasure in the act of receiving the greatest of intelligibles, namely the Necessary Existent, this "ascent" can be explained on the basis of the "pleasure principle."[82]

The foregoing discussion has exhibited the complexity of ibn Sīnā's philosophy of persons. His texts suggest that he identifies persons first of all with a composite of "body and soul," thereafter with a "disembodied soul," still later with an "intelligence," and finally with that entity which is united with the Necessary Existent.[83] The notes of explanation he offers with regard to this topic may help to clarify it at least to some extent. The intelligence aspect of the person can be considered as "a relation" (*πρός τι, iḍāfa, ad aliquid*) when it is embodied; when it is in a disembodied state, however, it is called a substance (οὐσία, *substantia, jawhar, gauhar*).[84] In another work he mentions that the functions of the soul that had been related to the body disappear during the last stages after its disembodiment. It should be observed that many powers of the soul are related to bodily functions and disappear, therefore, with these functions. The intelligence (*'aql*), however, persists after its separation from the soul, and, since it is that aspect which can be separated from the soul, it seems to participate in the mystical union. In the *Ṭabī'iyyāt* of the *Dānish Nāmeh*, in which ibn Sīnā describes the soul as a substance, he states, for instance:

> Subsequent to its realization, the soul remains a substance and continues to be the fundamental source of the person's substantiality. And when the body, the soul's instrument, is destroyed, the soul is not destroyed. As its instrument is destroyed, its instrumental [physical] powers, such as sensation, memory imagination (*taḥayyul*), lust, anger, and whatever resembles these, are also destroyed and separated from it.[85]

Since ibn Sīnā's accounts of an "afterlife" contain significant variations and appear, moreover, in some as yet unedited texts, one should be especially cautious and avoid sweeping generalizations about it. For this reason, our explanations are limited in scope, being based only on those texts in which this topic is emphasized. With this note of caution in mind, let us examine his doctrine of persons.

In several texts we find the assertion that persons are ultimately to be united with the Necessary Existent Itself. He states, accordingly, in the *Dānish Nāmeh*:

> The greatest pleasure and the highest happiness and fortune are found in union (*paīvand*) with the Necessary Existent, although most people imagine other states to be more pleasant.[86]

In several other texts he restricts this intimate relation to a relationship between the mystic (*'ārif*) and the Necessary Existent. This restriction is confirmed in the *Ishārāt* where he describes the nature of the Necessary Existent, or "the First."

> The First has no parallel; it has no contrary; it has no genus; it has no differentia; it cannot be indicated except by pure mystical intelligence (*bi-ṣarīḥ al-'irfān al-'aqlī*).[87]

In the *Risāla fī Ma'rifat al-Nafs* ibn Sīnā, asserts that persons can "ascend" (*yartaqū*) to the world of intelligence and divine making and can immerse themselves (*yangamisū*) in the true pleasure which is beyond description.[88] In still other texts the intelligence is described as being united with the active intelligence (*'aql fā'il*) after the death of the body.[89] We should not fail to observe, however, that in some works, for instance in *al-Shifā'*, the emphasis is placed on the doctrine of prophecy, while little is made of the notion of mystical union.[90]

From some of his texts, then, it appears that ibn Sīnā's depiction of the relationship between the ultimate being and persons corresponds to what we have described as the mystical system but differs from the religious system typified by the Qur'ānic doctrines as well as from the philosophical system which we have linked to the doctrines of Aristotle. It is our opinion, therefore, that ibn Sīnā's views can be said to be mystical with regard to this crucial issue.

V
CONCLUDING REMARKS

In order to avoid unwarranted generalizations, certain explicit limitations have been recognized in this inquiry. Although it has been demonstrated that the term "Ṣūfism" has been used vaguely in the various positions taken in this controversy, and is, therefore, in need of clarification, we have left aside the vast field of Ṣūfī literature which forms an important part of the Ṣūfic tradition, for we regard this significant task as being beyond the scope of this investigation which emphasizes the conceptual analysis of themes in ibn Sīnā's philosophy. In our attempt to be both brief and precise, we have concentrated on those sections of ibn Sīnā's philosophy that accentuate the differences between mystical, religious, and philosophical systems. Since Ṣūfism has traditionally been regarded as "mysticism among the Muslims," there has been a tendency among writers on this subject to regard it as being basically religious. It has been pointed out in this paper, however, that objections can be raised to such an interpretation of Ṣūfism.

As a type of mysticism (which we take to be its primary distinguishing mark), Ṣūfism can be interpreted differently from religious as well as from philosophical points of view, at least with regard to the important topic of the relationship between the ultimate being and persons. The construction of these systems in this paper has strongly emphasized the differences in the respective points of view. And should the construction that has been attempted prove to be applicable, then it can safely be concluded that ibn Sīnā's views parallel the mystical doctrines of the Ṣūfis in the significant context of this particular relationship.

Another note of caution should be introduced at this point. A different approach to this topic has been taken by many scholars who have tended to stress those aspects of Ṣūfism that would move it into closer rapport with Islam. By advancing from premises that differ from ours, they have obviously come to conclusions that depart from ours. Examples of such approaches can be found in the excellent works of Gardet and Anawati[91] whose approaches differ from ours chiefly in their premises and in the greater emphasis that is placed on the religious features of ibn Sīnā's doctrines. The divergence between such writers on this subject and ourselves, however, is not totally confined to an emphasis on our part of those nonreligious and mystical works of ibn Sīnā in which we find frequent mention of the determinism of the Necessary Existent, lack of punishment and reward after death, and mystical union; the differences concern also the interpretation of ibn Sīnā's texts.

In this paper, ibn Sīnā's emanationism has not been interpreted as a version of the creation theory as this theory is portrayed in the *Qur'ān*.[92] Unlike our position is the stand taken by that school of opinion which finds that ibn Sīnā's philosophy occupies the middle ground between Islamic doctrine and the Aristotelian position. The cursory reader might even see ibn Sīnā in the role of a St. Thomas, attempting to establish a harmony between religion and philosophy, even though Gardet would dissuade him from such a position.[93] The interpretation taken of ibn Sīnā's doctrines in this paper favors the view that his emanationistic doctrine is theoretically in agreement with mysticism, and perhaps even with a mysticism of the kind that was present in the pre-Islamic Zoroastrian tradition. Though such an interpretation is at best hypothetical, it is presented if only to show that the religious interpretation of ibn Sīnā's emanationism and related concepts is by no means the only logical possibility. It cannot, therefore, be accepted prima facie or on the basis of an argument from analogy which might attempt to link his philosophy with the development of Western Scholastic philosophy.[94]

There are other considerations which have a bearing on our attempt to connect ibn Sīnā's philosophy with Ṣūfism and to demonstrate that in certain respects both are at odds with the orthodox Islamic point of view. (i) Many Ṣūfīs have suffered under adverse conditions for the very reason that they were Ṣūfīs. Some renowned Ṣūfīs like Ḥallāj and Suhrawardī were even killed by orthodox Muslims for their apparently heretical practices and beliefs. Regardless of what stand contemporary scholarship may choose to take with regard to these events (e.g., Massignon's masterful effort to establish Ḥallāj's allegiance to Islam[95]), it remains a fact that Muslims themselves viewed Ṣūfīs as being detrimental to Islam. (ii) It is well known that ibn Sīnā was attacked by Ghazālī and later Muslim philosophers for holding anti-Islamic views. (iii) Mention has been made of those writers on mysticism who distinguish between "natural" (secular) and "spiritual" (religious) mysticism and favor, moreover, the recognition of the distinctness of mysticism and religion.[96] (iv) The "unity of being," in which all alienating differences between man and God disappear, has oftentimes been recognized as a basic theme of mysticism. This feature of mysticism accords with the version of mysticism presented in this paper, as well as with the passages cited from the works of ibn Sīnā. According to this view of mysticism, persons are emanated from the ultimate being by means of intermediaries and return to it by way of mystical union.[97] In view of the foregoing, we consider our depiction of a nonreligious mysticism as which we regard the mysticism of ibn Sīnā and Ṣūfism to be more than a mere logical gimmick, notwithstanding the fact that our interpretation may not be supported by some interpreters of ibn Sīnā's philosophy and Ṣūfism.

But there is another fundamental difficulty that has encumbered our investigation and has placed severe limits on the scope of our conclusions: the availability and the nature of the sources. Unfortunately, there are relatively few critical editions of ibn Sīnā's texts upon which the investigator can rely.[98] M. Watt, therefore, observes correctly that any generalization about a Near Eastern philosopher may be subject to revision as more data become available from newly edited or newly discovered texts.[99] It is for this very reason that we have confined ourselves to those texts of ibn Sīnā which we have quoted, yet even among these marked differences of emphasis and doctrine have been discovered.[100] The interpretation of his doctrine depends not only on the emphasis the interpreter places on particular parts of his works, an emphasis that is also influenced by the preconceptions with which the interpreter approaches the work, but also on the translation of key concepts.[101] Hence, our interpretation and our conclusions do not apply to ibn Sīnā's philosophy in toto, but only to his philosophy as it is expressed in the texts to which we referred.

Another problematic issue involves the notion of ibn Sīnā's Necessary Existent, the ultimate being in his system. In some passages he contends explicitly that It is neither a substance nor an accident, whereas he merely suggests this position in other passages.[102] He asserts, for instance, that whatever exists must be either a primary substance (*jawhar-i ḥaṣ*, πρώτη οὐσία) or an accident.[103] The nature of his Necessary Existent is, therefore, highly paradoxical. Since we have discussed this topic elsewhere,[104] we shall not pursue it in this study. We do wish to mention, however, that one plausible reconstruction of the Necessary Existent that can shed some light on Its nature is Its portrayal by ibn Sīnā as "the principle of sufficient reason," "the cause of the completion of persons," and "the cause" of the world in the sense that It is its beholder or the necessary explanation for its existence. By failing to lend to the Necessary Existent the metaphysical status of an individual in his system, ibn Sīnā makes it possible for persons to attain to the final stage of their development by being united with It in a mystical union. Such a union between persons and the ultimate being would be an impossibility in the Aristotelian system (with the prime mover) as well as in the religious system (with the God of Islam), since the use of "substance" precludes such a union.[105]

In sum, despite its obvious restrictions, our investigation has attempted to contribute in two ways to the problematical issue of the relationship between ibn Sīnā, and Ṣūfism. It has made precise distinctions between concepts that have occupied a central position in the controversy and have frequently been confused. It has argued hypothetically (in a semi-deductive fashion) that ibn Sīnā's doctrine has a definite affinity with Ṣūfism. The argument it has advanced is hypothetical, since it is based on premises such as (i) our view about the nature of Ṣūfism, and (ii) the emphasis we have placed on certain texts of ibn Sīnā. It is our opinion that general analyses leading to categorical statements about ibn Sīnā's philosophy must wait until further substantial research has been completed in this field. Such research should address itself to (i) additional critical editions of ibn Sīnā's Arabic and Persian works so that more of the corpus of his works will become available; (ii) investigations of his possible authorship of several important texts which have traditionally been attributed to him; and (iii) content-analyses of his metaphysical texts in order to establish guidelines and variables by means of which it will be possible to assess the relative significance of his mystical doctrines in contrast to the classical ones as they are stated in the *Shifā'*, for instance. The scope of such tasks becomes evident from the extensive bibliographies Anawati and Mahdavī have prepared on the works of ibn Sīnā.[106]

We hope, then, that this paper will be of some value to the research we have advocated, particularly with regard to its methodology. Furthermore, it is our hope that our investigation has illustrated a method by means of which the concepts involved in these problems can be clarified and has provided some insight into the general problem of how, and in what sense, we can relate ibn Sīnā's doctrines to Ṣūfism. From the preceding analysis, the existence of problems of an even greater magnitude has become evident—the need to establish distinctions between the concepts of "religion," "philosophy," and "mysticism" in contexts more extensive than the realm to which we have limited ourselves: a depiction of the relationship between persons and the ultimate being.

NOTES

* A version of the first part of this paper was delivered at the one hundred and seventy-ninth meeting of the American Oriental Society held at New York City, March 25-27, 1969.

1 Reynold A. Nicholson, *The Idea of Personality in Ṣūfism* (Lahore, 1964), pp. 100-101.

2 *Ibid.*

3 *Ibid.*

4 Gustave E. von Grunebaum, *Medieval Islam: A Study in Cultural Orientation* (Chicago and London, 1966).

5 *Ibid.*, p. 133.

6 *Ibid.*, p. 141.

7 *Ibid.*

8 *Ibid.*, pp.193-94.

9 Gustave E. von Grunebaum, *Muḥammadan Festivals* (New York, 1951).

10 *Ibid.*, p. 92.

11 "Avicenna and Mysticism," in *Avicenna Commemoration Volume*, ed. V. Courtois, (Calcutta, 1956), p. 221.

12 *Ibid.*, p. 220.

13 These two points are often very significant in establishing a "religious" cosmology. If God's "generation" of the world is necessary, then He is not free and hence not omnipotent. Furthermore, if man has a "natural" relationship to the ultimate being, rather than a "supernatural" one (e.g., "being saved by grace"), then it will be difficult to arrive at a transcendent feature of God.

14 Houben, *op. cit.*, p. 217.

15 *Ibid.*, p. 219.

16 *Ibid.*, p. 220.

17 *Ibid.*, p. 221.

18 Etienne Gilson, *The Spirit of Medieval Philosophy* (New York, 1936), p. 80.

19 M. Goichon, "The Philosopher of Being," in *Avicenna Commemoration Volume*, (Calcutta, 1956), pp. 116-17.

20 *Ibid.*, p. 117.

21 Ibn Sīnā, *al-Shifā'*, ed. G. C. Anawati and S. Zāyed (Cairo, 1960). Subsequent references to the *Shifā'* refer to this edition. Goichon's position is surprising in view of (i) ibn Sīnā's assertion that he is not a blind follower of the Greek philosophers and (ii) his acknowledgment that the *Shifā'* was written for the general populace [*Manṭiq al-mashriqiyyin* (Cairo, 1910), pp. 2-4.

22 Ibn Sīnā, Ḥayy ibn Yaqẓān in H. Corbin, *Avicenne et le récit visionnaire* (Tehran, 1952).

23 A. M. Goichon, *Vocabulaires Comparés d'Aristote et d'Ibn Sina (Avicenne)*, (Paris, Desclée de Brouwer, 1939). For a summary and a comparison of her position with that of H. Corbin, see G. C. Anawati, "Gnose et philosophie," *Cahiers de Civilisation Médiévale*, VI, 2 (1963), 159-73.

24 Ibn Sīnā, *Dānish Nāmeh 'Alāi (Ilāhiyyāt)*, ed. M. Mo'in (Tehran, 1952). Subsequent references will be made to the abbreviated title, *DAI*. Mention of the text will be made by the short title, *Dānish Nāmeh*. Quotations are taken from my as yet unpublished translation of this text.

25 G. M. Wickens, "Some Aspects of Avicenna's Work," in *Avicenna: Scientist and Philosopher*, ed. G. M. Wickens (London, 1952), p. 58.

26 Ibn Sīnā, *al-Ishārāt wa al-Tanbīhāt*, ed. Sulaiman Dunya, 3 vols. (Cairo, 1960). Subsequent abbreviation: *Ishārāt*. Various notes to her excellent translation of this text confirm her position [*Livre des Directives et Remarques* (Beyrouth and Paris, 1951)]. She translates *'ārifūn*, for instance, as "savent," although it is generally translated as "mystic" (p. 483); *'irfān* she renders as "science mystique" (p. 497). It is our interpretation that she underplays the mystical content of this text in her translation; it is well

known, for instance, that *ārif* means "mystic" rather than "wise." Only in very few instances does *'ilm* refer to the "science of mysticism," as she translates it consistently; *'irfān,* in our opinion, could just as well be translated as "the way of mysticism." That she does not ignore the ṣūfic point of view altogether is evident from her essay, "Le sirr 'l'intime du coeur' dans la doctrine Avicennienne de la connaissance," in *Studia Semitica Philologica necnon philosophica Ioanni Bakoš dicata,* ed. S. Segert (Bratislava, 1965), pp. 119-26. For a critical review of her translation, see G. Vajda, "Récentes études avicenniennes," *JA,* 240 (1952), 219-30.

27 Ibn Sīnā. *Dānish Nāmeh 'Alāi (Ṭabi'iyyāt),* ed. Sayyid Muḥammad Mishhkat (Tehran, 1952). Abbr.: *Ṭabi'iyyāt*

28 G. C. Anawati and L. Gardet, Mystique Musulmane: Aspects et Tendances—Expériences et Techniques (Paris, 1961).

29 L. Gardet, *La Pensée religieuse d'Avicenne* (Paris, 1951), chap. 5. Gardet acknowledges the significance of mystical elements in ibn Sīnā's system to the extent that it could not be comprehended without these elements. Making use of the "natural-supernatural" distinction, he brings many factors to bear on the problem of ibn Sīnā's mysticism, e.g., the strong influence of the Greek and Islamic traditions. He stresses the spiritual nature of ibn Sīnā's ultimate being, identifying it with the Islamic God and differentiating it from the phenomenological God of the Ṣūfis.

30 "Abū Alī Sīnā wa Taṣawwuf" in *Le Livre du Millenaire d'Avicenne* (Tehran, 1955), pp. 183-97.

31 H. Corbin, *Avicenna and the Visionary Recital,* trans. W. R. Trask (New York, 1960).

32 *Ibid.,* p. 120.

33 E. G. Brown, *A Literary History of Persia* (Cambridge, 1964), I, p. 419.

34 Wickens, *op. cit.* (see note 25, above), p. 62.

35 Soheil M. Afnan, *Avicenna: His Life and His Works* (London, 1958), p. 188.

36 *Avicenna: His Life, Works, Thought and Time* (Tehran, 1954), p. 101. For a history of the development of philosophy in Iran prior to Islam, see Z. Ṣafā, *Tāriḥ-i adabiyyā dar* Iran, I (Tehran, 1963); *idem, Tāriḥ-i 'ūlūm-i 'aqli dar tamaddun-i Islām* (Tehran, 1952), pp. 17-27. Looking at history from an Iranian point of view, Ṣafā stresses the direct contact between the Greeks and Persians prior to the rise of Islam as well as the Zoroastrian heritage of Iran.

37 Estipahn Panoussi, "La théosophie iranienne source d'Avicenne," *Revue Philosophique de Louvain,* lxvi (1968): 239-66.

38 *Ibid.,* p. 256.

39 S. Pines, "La philosophie orientale d'Avicenne et sa polemique contre les bagdadiens," Extract from *Archives d'histoire doctrinale et littéraire du moyen âge* (Paris, 1953), pp. 5-37. For a brief summary of this problem and an updated list of sources, see F. E. Peters, *Aristotles Arabus: The Oriental Translations and Commentaries on the Aristotelian 'Corpus'* (Leiden, 1968), pp. 72-74.

40 Panoussi, p. 266.

41 Les motifs zoroastriens dans la philosophie de Sohrawardî Shaykh-ol-Ishrâq (Tehran, 1946); Idem, Oeuvres philosophiques et mystiques de Shihabaddin Yahya Sohrawardî, Opera Metaphysica et Mystics, II (Tehran and Paris, 1952).

42 Mohammad Mo'in, *Mazdaism and Persian Literature* (Tehran, 1959), p. 424.

43 Ibn Sīnā, *Riṣāla Adḥawiyya fi Amr al-Ma'ād* (Cairo, 1949), pp. 40. Subsequent abbr.: *Ma'ād*. For additional examples of "pure Persian" terms in ibn Sīnā's works, see H. Massé, "Termes philosophiques de langue persane employes par Avicenne," *Le Livre du Millenaire d'Avicenne*, IV (Tehran, 1956) [from conference of 1954], 35-41; M. Mo'in, "Lugat-i Fārsi-i ibn Sīnā wa ta'sir-i 'an dar adabiyyāt," *Le Livre du Millenaire d'Avicenne*, II (Tehran, 1955) [from conference of 1954, 329-341. But cf. also, S. H. Nasr, "The Persian Works of Shaykh al-Ishrāq Shihāb al-Dīn Suhrawardī," IQ, XII (1968), 3-8.

44 R. C. Zaehner, *Mysticism, Sacred and Profane* (Oxford and London, 1967).

45 *Ibid.*, p. 198.

46 *Ibid.*, p. 200.

47 London, 1960.

48 *Ibid.*, p. 19. "The types are (i) the pantheistic or panenhenic in which the human personality seems to comprise all existence, the 'I am this All' of the Upanisads; (ii) the realization of undifferentiated unity, however philosophically interpreted; and (ii) the loving dialogue with God which results in transforming union, to use the Christian phrase."

49 W. T. Stace, *Idem*, p. 341, *Mysticism and Philosophy* (New York and Philadelphia, 1960).

50 W. T. Stace, *Teaching*, p. 23.

51 *Tahāfut al-Falāsifah (Incoherence of the Philosophers)*, trans. Sabih Aḥmad Kamāli (Lahore, 1963). Abbr. as Tahāfut.

52 *Ibid.*, p. 53.

53 *Ibid.*, p. 185.

54 Seyyed Hossein Nasr, *An Introduction to Islamic Cosmological Doctrine* (Cambridge, Mass., 1964). See pp. 212-13 for a detailed representation of this

doctrine, of which we present only a brief summary. As his chief sources Nasr cites Gardet, *La Pensée*, p. 65; and A. M. Goichon's *La Distinction de l'essence et l'existence d'après Ibn Sina* (*Avicenne*) (Paris, 1937), pp. 249-55.

55 *Ibid.*, p. 213.

56 *Ibid.*, p. 214.

57 *Tahāfut*, p. 13.

58 *Ibid.*

59 Etienne Gilson, *Being and Some Philosophers* (Toronto, 1952), p. 156. The identical view is expressed *Posterior Analytics* (Oxford, 1965), p. 80. ". . . the formal cause is not a distinct cause over and above the final or efficient cause or the eternal ground, but is one of these when considered as forming the definition of the thing in question. The one type of cause that can never be identical with the formal cause is the material, and hence the material cause is silently omitted from the present passage."

60 Von Grunebaum, *Muhammadan Festivals*, p. 48.

61 *Ibid.*

62 G. F. Hourani, "Ibn Sina's 'Essay on the secret of destiny'," *BSOAS*, XXIX (1966), 25-48.

63 Houben, *op cit.* (above, note 11), pp. 216-217. See, e.g., "It will become clear that this fruition [of the mystical experience, the *ma'rifat Allāh*] is not a gratuitous gift from God, but is solely dependent on the human endeavor and secondly that what the mystics grasp in the encounter with the Truth is God only in so far as He is the truth of their own being." (p. 217).

64 Ibn Sīnā, Risāla fī al-'ishq, ed. M. A. F. von Mehren in Traités mystiques d'Abou Ali al-Hosain b. Abdallah b. Sīnā ou d'Avicenne; texte arabe avec l'explication en français, III (Leiden, 1894). Subsequent abbr.: 'Ishq.

65 "Some Aspects of Avicenna's Theory of God's Knowledge of Particulars," *JAOS*, LXXXII (1962), 299-312.

66 That ibn Sīnā assumes the existence of different kinds of entities is evident from the following passage. "It was (analytically) discovered that in the first realm of the realization of existents only one existent can come from the Necessary Existent. Here in this world, however, we observe many existents." (*DAI*, p. 112) From his discussion of the classification of the sciences it is obvious that he assumes the existence of different kinds of subject matters, for he assigns to each kind a special science, which corresponds to it. [*DAI*, chap. 1; *Shifā'* (*Ilāhiyyāt*), bk. 1, chaps. 1-2;] He follows the same procedure in other texts on the nature of the sciences, e.g., *Fī aqsām al-'ulūm al-'aqlīyya* in *Tis'rasā'il* (Cairo, 1908); *'Uyūn al-ḥikmah*, ed. A. Badawī (Cairo, 1954).

67 Entities are divided into levels in several ways according to some criterion of value. For instance, entities can be classified by being into *supremely perfect* entities (those which are both self-sufficient and constitute a source of other entities), *sufficient* entities (those who persist being self-sufficient), *deficient* entities (those lacking a feature that has yet to be realized), and absolutely *deficient* entities (those in need of an external entity in order to persist). The supremely perfect entity (*fauq al-tamām*) is recognized as the Necessary Existent, explicitly in the *Shifā'* (bk. 8, sec. 6) and implicitly in the *Dānish Nāmeh* (chap. 41). Another classification can be undertaken on the basis of the "goodness" or the "evil" of entities. *Absolutely good* is that entity from which only good can come; *predominantly good* is that from which more good comes than evil; and *predominantly evil* is that from which more evil comes than good. The second classification is not extensional because evil is a by-product of this actual world and a consequence of emanation; hence, the question "What is absolutely good?" has not been answered. The classification is not intentional, however, because it fails to consider the logical possibility of the absolutely bad. For a discussion of this and related topics, see *Shifā'*, bk. 9, sec. 6; *DAI*, chap. 42; Hourani, *supra*, note 62. The grading to which we refer in this premise is directly related to the ranking system mentioned above. More direct grading systems will be taken up in subsequent discussions.

68 Ibn Sīnā states that it is better for "a being" to be actualized, (i.e., to be an existent than not to exist, or to be a mere essence) (*DAI*, p. 164). An entity, such as a body (a material substance made of form and substratum-matter [*DAI*, chap. 8; *Ishārāt*, II, 207; III, 183; *Shifā'*, bk. 1, p. 72], is actualized due to its form. The latter corresponds to its actuality, while its substratum-matter corresponds to its potentiality. (*DAI*, p. 115; *Ishārāt*, II, 214; *'Ishq*, pp. 6-7) Whatever is actualized is necessary due to its cause; hence, its actuality is responsible for the realization of an existent. Thus, actuality is better than potentiality. The second part of this premise deals with movements. Various existents in the world can be viewed as belonging to one of these three realms: to the realm of the Necessary Existent [*DAI*, chaps. 19-38, 55; *Ishārāt*, III, 231-41; *Shifā'*, bk. 1, chap. 1; bk. 6, chap. 2; bk. 8, chaps. 2-7; bk. 9, chap. 1], to that of the heavens [*DAI* chaps. 46-55; *Ishārāt*, III, 185; *Shifā'*, bk. 9, chaps. 2-5], or to the sub-lunary realm, which consists of substances receptive to generation and to corruption, in addition to intelligence aspects of the human soul. (*DAI*, chap. 55; *Ishārāt*, II; *Shifā'*, bk. 2, chaps. 2-3) Subsequent discussion will clarify that the first realm emanates the second, and that

the second emanates the third. The first, therefore, is better than the second, and the second is better than the third on the grounds of one of the following arguments: (1) Whereas the first realm is pure actuality, the second consists of both substratum-matter and form, where the substratum-matter is inseparable from the form, and the third consists of substratum-matter and form, where the substratum-matter is separable from the form. Since form is related to actuality, and matter to potentiality, and, since the former is better than the latter, the first is better than the second, and the second is better than the third. Since "better" designates a transitive relation, the first is therefore better than the third. (2) Relevant to the issue are Proclus' propositions (i) "Every productive cause is superior to that which it produces" [*Elements of Theology*, ed. and trans. by E. R. Dodds, (Oxford, 1963), p. 9], and (ii) "All that is produced by secondary beings is in a greater measure produced from those prior and more determinative principles from which the secondary were themselves derived." (*Ibid.*, p. 55) Since the first realm is a cause of the second, and the second is the cause of the third, and, moreover, since "being the cause of" is a transitive relation, the first is therefore better than the second, and the second is better than the third. Now, the first realm does not move [*DAI*, p. 76], and the second realm moves in circular motion on account of its love of the first realm [*DAI*, chaps. 51-55; *Ishārāt*, III, 442-49; *Shifā'*, bk. 9, chap. 2], while those elements constituting bodies in the first realm move in straight motion (*DAI*, chap. 45). From these considerations it follows that whatever does not move is better than that which moves, and that which moves voluntarily in circular motion is better than that which is composed of constituents which cause it to move in a straight line. It is not claimed that ibn Sīnā relies on these particular arguments when he writes about this issue. But his frequent recognition of a hierarchy of being from "the most noble" to the "substratum-matter" [e.g., *Ishārāt*, III, 240-49], could well be based on arguments similar to the ones presented in this note, arguments which are present in his works and in those of his predecessors.

69 Ibn Sīnā uses "causality" to describe relationships between events and individuals. Traditionally, "individuals" designate substances, whereas "events" designate properties of substances and relationships among substances. Accordingly, "causality" has been used as a relationship between events, while the corresponding relationship between individuals has been designated by the expressions "agent" and "patient," attributes ascribed to individuals. Even though ibn Sīnā does not make such distinctions consistently, his treatment of causality and problems related to

causality shows that he is aware of these distinctions. Since no confusion results from his use of these distinctions, we shall make use of them in our paper.

That each contingent entity is a contingency with respect to itself and a necessity with respect to its cause is mentioned, for instance, in the *Dānish Nāmeh*, chap. 39; *Ishārāt,* III, 19*; Shifā'* bk. 1, p. 29.

70 *DAI*, p. 111-12; *Ishārāt*, III, 214.

71 We hesitate to express an agreement with those who would place ibn Sīnā's philosophy into the tradition of the Neoplatonists, particularly when the claim has even been advanced that not only ibn Sīnā but Near Eastern philosophy *in toto* "derived from" Neoplatonism. Though he does not make such a claim, F. E. Peters states, for instance, "It was Neoplatonism that finally emerged victorious in the philosophical skirmishing of the final days of pagan antiquity; but not before it had absorbed into itself many of the elements of Aristotelianism" (*Aristotle and the Arabs: The Aristotelian Tradition in Islam* [New York and London, 1968], p. 14). We shall not pursue this issue here, for we have treated it elsewhere, ["Contemporary Scholarship on Near Eastern Philosophy," forthcoming in *Philosophical Forum*] but we shall list several clear distinctions between Neoplatonism and ibn Sīnā's philosophy. (i) The latter bases his entire metaphysical theses in the *Shifā'* and the *Dānish Nāmeh* on the language of the Aristotelian categories. His treatment of the categories in the sections on metaphysics in these texts, however, is far more extensive than Aristotle's own use of them. Plotinus, on the other hand, rejects the Aristotelian categories (*Enneads* VI 1 [I-24]). Thus, the two philosophers cannot be said to have made use of the same language on many important issues related to the categories. (ii) Ibn Sīnā's Necessary Existent is conscious of Itself (*DAI*, p. 100; *Ishārāt*, III, 279). In the works of Plotinus, however, there are many passages in which the One, Plotinus' ultimate being, is not described as being conscious of itself [e.g., *Enneads* VI 9[9], chap. 6 III 9[13], chaps. 7, 9]. Plotinus even attacks Aristotle for making the One conscious of itself (*Ibid.*, V 1[9]). Numerous passages in the works of Aristotle confirm that the non-sensible eternal substance is conscious (see for instance, *Metaphysics* 1074 b 15-1075 a 10). (iii) The separation Neoplatonists make between the realm of intelligibles and sensibles is not made by ibn Sīnā. Whereas Plotinus holds what might generally be called a "realistic theory" of universals, ibn Sīnā rejects this position (*DAI*, chap. 12; *Shifā'*, bk. 5, chaps. 1-2). The view Neoplatonists and ibn Sīnā take of numbers illustrates this point. The latter regards them as 'accidents' [*DAI*, chap. 101 and follows

Aristotle in this position [*Categories* 4 b 31]. Plotinus, on the other hand, calls numbers 'substantials' and associates them with the soul (*Enneads* VI [9] 5). (iv) There is a striking difference between ibn Sīnā's portrayal of the relationship between the philosopher and his community and Plotinus' depiction of the philosopher as someone who is remote from practical life [*Shifā'*, bk. 10, chaps. 2-5; E. I. J. Rosenthal, *Political Thought in Medieval Islam* (Cambridge, 1962), pp. 143-157]. (v) Ibn Sīnā is not at all receptive to the doctrine of Porphyry, who is considered to be a Neoplatonist. For ibn Sīnā's rejection of Porphyry, see J. Finnegan, "Avicenna's Refutation of Porphyrius," in *Avicenna Commemoration Volume*, ed. V. Courtois, (Calcutta, 1956), pp. 146-78. On one key issue, namely the nature of "being-qua-being," ibn Sīnā's views are opposed to those of Proclus, another Neoplatonist, and perhaps different from those of Plotinus, depending on how we interpret the position of Plotinus. In his Persian texts, e.g., the *Dānish Nāmeh*, ibn Sīnā states that *hastī* is the most determinable sign in his language of metaphysics (*DAI*, chap. 3). He distinguishes between *hastī* ("being") and *wujūd* ("existence") and equates *anniyya* with *wujūd*. For other versions of this problem in the context of his Arabic texts, see M. T. d'Alverny, "Anniyya-Anitas," *Mélanges offerts à Etienne Gilson* (Toronto and Paris, 1959), pp. 59-91; I. Madkur's list of Latin equivalents for *anniyya* which includes *esse, qui est,* and *anitas* in his "*Introduction à la Métaphysique du Shifā'*," *MIDEO*, VI (1959-61), 281-234; A. M. Goichon's *Lexique de la Langue Philosophique d'Ibn Sīnā* (*Avicenne*) (Paris, 1938), p. 9. Ibn Sīnā regards every existent, including the Necessary Existent, as an explicit determination of "being-qua-being." L. Gardet arrives at a similar observation on the basis of examining ibn Sīnā's commentary on the pseudo-theology of Aristotle ["En l'honneur du Millénaire d'Avicenne, "*Revue Thomiste*, LI (1951), 335]. By contrast, Proclus places the One and even God above being, ὑπερούσιος (*Elements*, p. 101). Even if one should translate ὑπερούσιος as "*supra*-being", his doctrine would still diverge from that of ibn Sīnā. Plotinus' view is rather vague on this topic. In the *Enneads* V 2, he asserts that the One generates being. But compare the different translations of this passage by S. MacKenna, *The Enneads* (London, 1962), p. 380, where τὸ ὄν is rendered as "being" and γεννητή as "generates," and by P. Henry and H.-R. Schwyzer, *Plotini Opera*, II (Paris and Bruxelles, 1959), p. 291, who use "things" for the former and "gush" for the latter. But regardless of how we choose to interpret this crucial passage, the difference between ibn Sīnā and the Neoplatonists cannot be obliterated. According to ibn Sīnā, "nothing" is "beyond being" and "nothing" "generates being," whereas the Neoplatonists view the One not as a determination of "being," but as something that transcends it in some sense. For Zoroastrian examples of the "emanation from thought" principle, see for instance, R. C. Zaehner, *The Dawn and Twilight of Zorastrianism* (New York, 1961), pp. 207-08; for a list of other sources, consult Zaehner's *Zurvan: A Zoroastrian Dilemma* (Oxford, 1955), pp. 419-29.

72 The desire of persons "to return" is mentioned repeatedly by ibn Sīnā [*'Ishq*, p. 5; *Ishārāt*, IV, 47]. The argument which is implied corresponds usually either to (1) or to (2). (1) Since the higher realm is the cause of the completion (or the final cause) of an entity in the lower realm, the return, being the last stage in the development of the person, is interpreted as his fulfillment. (2) Since the necessity of actualizing entities in the lower realm belongs to entities in the higher realm, the desire of the intelligence to return to its source is a return to "the active intelligence." This doctrine is in accord with a general theory held by Neoplatonists, which is expressed by Proclus as a "reversion of effects to their causes" [Elements, propositions 31-5].

73 The doctrine that exactly one entity can be emanated from the Necessary Existent appears in several passages, e.g., *DAI*, p. 111-12; *Ishārāt*, III, 213-31. There are two aspects to this doctrine. (1) Being simple, the Necessary Existent cannot concurrently contain two causes for two distinct effects, and (2), according to Proclus [*Elements*, p. 47] whatever is self-constituted is without part and is therefore simple. Thus, the "simplicity" of the Necessary Existent implies "having only one effect," but Its "simplicity" is derived from "not being caused externally." Since It is "the most perfect being," the Necessary Existent must be the source of some other entity. As a consequence, Its emanation is determined. (For the concept of the "most perfect being," see above, note 67). The doctrine of the generation of intelligences is found in many works of ibn Sīnā, e.g., *DAI*, chap. 55; *Shifā'*, bk. 9, chap. 4; *Ishārāt*, III, 229-31.

74 *Ishārāt*, Ill, 214; III, 229-31.

75 A Persian opusculum attributed to ibn Sīnā, *Risāla dar ḥaqīqat wa kaifiyyāt-i silsilah-i mawjūdāt wa tasalsul-i asbāb wa musabbabāt*, ed. Mūsā, 'Amīd (Tehran, 1952), contains a more elaborate argument and a rather dialectical treatment of the generation of the elements out of one another. Fire, for instance, falls to its antithesis, earth; air and water are generated later as intermediaries between the two extreme elements (extreme in dryness and wetness, coldness and heat). Y. Mahdavī questions ibn Sīnā's authorship of this text on the basis of its stylistic difference from

the *Dānish Nāmeh* and for the reason that no mention of this text is made in any one of ibn Sīnā's texts [*Bibliographie d' Ibn Sīnā* (Tehran, 1954)]. The doctrine, however, he regards definitely as ibn Sīnian, concluding that either ibn Sīnā wrote this work, or someone else close to him summarized his views in this text. Anawati does not list this text in his bibliography [*Essai de Bibliographie Avicennienne* (Cairo, 1950)].

76 In his *Shifā'*, II, 393-94, ibn Sīnā mentions that it is the sub-lunary realm which contains entities receptive to generation and to corruption. Several references appear in the *Ṭabī'iyyāt* of the *Dānish Nāmeh* [e.g., p. 68] to the effect of the moon on other entities, e.g., causing the fruit to ripen, increasing seeds, and moving the waters of the sea.

77 *Ishārāt*, III, 231-40.

78 Not all of ibn Sīnā's texts mention the doctrine of the mystical return. In the *Shifā'* the doctrine of prophecy is stressed instead of the return, while the latter is emphasized in other works, e.g., the *Ishārāt* (see the last three chapters of vol. IV), and the *Dānish Nāmeh* (see chap. 37 of the *Ilāhiyyāt*). In these two texts prophecy fails to occupy the important position it has in *al-Shifā'*. For notes on the return, see also ibn Sīnā's opuscula, e.g., *'Ishq; Risāla fī Ma'rifat al-Nafs al-Nāṭiqa wa Aḥwālihā*, in *Aḥwāl al-Nafs*, ed. F. El-Ehwany (Cairo, 1952), pp. 191-92; *Risālat al-Ṭair*, [*le traité mystique al-Thair*] in *Traités mystiques*, ed. Mehren [*op. cit.*, see above, note 64], II (1891), pp. 42-8 *Ḥayy ibn Yaqẓān*, in Corbin [*op. cit.*, see above, note 22].

79 References to love recur throughout this text. Ibn Sīnā refers to a similar conception of *'Ishq* in *DAI*, chap. 54, for instance, where the Necessary Existent is mentioned as "the common beloved of the intelligences." In this context he explains that the intelligences are in voluntary motion for the sake of imitating the Necessary Existent. A similar view of love as a force explaining motion is expressed in *Shifā'*, II, 392; *Ishārāt*, III, 195. In *Ishārāt*, IV, 40-5, he mentions that man's soul has reached its highest stage when it is in love with the greatest beloved, namely the Necessary Existent.

80 *DAI*, p. 106; *Ishārāt*, III, 241.

81 *Ishārāt*, III, 244; DAI, p. 107. The second reference reiterates the Platonic doctrine that the body causes the soul to forget its "true" mission, and that the soul takes its ascent at the time of the disembodiment. (*Phaedo* 81 b-e) But ibn Sīnā does not follow Plato in one crucial point. According to ibn Sīnā, the soul does not exist prior to the body as an individual, whereas Plato upholds such a doctrine. Because of the complexity of ibn Sīnā's theory of the soul (a theory which contains elabo-

rate epistemology and medical terminology), it is difficult to draw extensive comparisons between him and Plato.

82 *DAI*, pp. 102-106. The argument runs like this: Pleasure is felt by the receiver of something when he receives something that is considered pleasant because it is agreeable to him. Pleasures are of two kinds: sensible and intelligible pleasures. In the first case, the degree of pleasure that can be experienced is limited, since the senses can be destroyed by strong sensations, e.g., the eye is blinded by a strong light. But intelligences can receive unlimited pleasure, since an intelligence is not destroyed by the intelligible. A similar but less extensive version of this argument is presented in *Ishārāt*, IV, 7-10.

83 Ibn Sīnā presents three arguments for the immortality of the soul in *Ma'rifat al-Nafs* [*op. cit.*, see above, note 78]. After its separation from the body, the intelligence is said to receive immobile substances. (*DAI*, p.106) The ultimate happiness of persons lies in being united with the Necessary Existent. (*DAI*, p. 102)

84 Ibn Sīnā, *Ma'rifat al-Nafs*, p. 185.

85 *Ṭabī'iyyāt*, *op. cit.* (see above, note 27), chap. 43.

86 *DAI*, p. 102; *Ishārāt*, IV, 20-6. Subsequent to its union with the active intelligence, the intelligence seeks whatever is "thereafter"; accordingly, the "union" does not terminate with the active intelligence.

87 *Ishārāt*, III, 53.

88 Ma'rifat al-Nafs, p. 192.

89 Ishārāt, III, 270; see also, P. Merlan, Monopsychism, Mysticism, Metaconsciousness: Problems of the Soul in the Neoaristotelian and Neoplatonic Tradition (The Hague, 1963), pp. 27-30.

90 *Shifā'* bk. 10, chaps. 2-5.

91 L. Gardet, *La Pensée*, *op. cit.*, (see above, note 29); Anawati and Gardet, *Mystique Musulmane*, *op. cit.*, (see above, note 28).

92 Despite the differences he notes between the two theories, L. Gardet [La *Pensée*, p. 45] calls ibn Sīnā's emanationism "creation." He refers consistently to ibn Sīnā's Necessary Existent as "God" ("Dieu"). Even though he makes frequent use of "*Allāh*" and "*khalq*" ("creation") in the *Shifā'*, ibn Sīnā rarely uses terms with religious connotations, such as "God" or "creation", in the *Ishārāt* or the *Dānish Nāmeh* (the last text is not mentioned by Gardet). In these last two texts "*ibdā'*," "*faiḍ*," and "*padīd*" are found, terms which are closer in meaning to emanation than to creation. In his translation of the *Shifā'*, M. Horton [*Die Metaphysik Avicennas: Das Buch der Genesung der Seele* (Frankfurt, 1960)] refers to the

Necessary Existent as "*Gott*", a term by which he refers occasionally also to ibn Sīnā's *al-Wājib al-Wujūd*; see pp. 542-650 for examples.

93 Gardet affirms that ibn Sīnā's philosophy cannot be called "an Islamic philosophy" in the sense St. Thomas's philosophy is called "a Christian philosophy." (*La Pensée,* pp. 202-03) Compare this view with R. Walzer's statement that ibn Sīnā was primarily interested in philosophy as a "religious way of life" and that he wanted Islam to conform to philosophy without risking the basic tenets of Islam [*Greek into Arabic: Essays on Islamic Philosophy* (Cambridge, 1962), pp. 248-49]. Walzer claims that ibn Sīnā and Islamic philosophy on the whole owe a heavy debt to Greek philosophy. "Islamic philosophy," he asserts [*Ibid.*, p. 35], "is Greek philosophy, but it is not Greek philosophy studied for scholarly reasons nor for the satisfaction of scholarly curiosity. It is meant primarily to serve the needs of the new religion of Islam: it is an attempt at a Muslim natural theology, and the greatest representatives of this theistic Islamic philosophy went so far as to see the only valid interpretation of Islam in following the ways of the philosophers."

94 There is a strong tendency among historians of philosophy familiar with Medieval Western philosophy to carry over formulae that may be valid in the Western tradition to the Near Eastern context, as for instance, the view that philosophers discovered the works of Aristotle and attempted to harmonize their religious views with Greek philosophy. Obviously, many Near Eastern philosophers were concerned with the problem of the harmony of philosophy and religion [e.g., ibn Rushd (Averroes), *Kitāb faṣl al-maqāl*, ed. G. F. Hourani (Leiden, 1959)], but one should not prima facie regard this particular interest of philosophers as a characteristic of the entire field of Near Eastern philosophy. The same consideration applies to the interpretation of ibn Sīnā's works. In a study of his *opera*, special attention should be paid to the renaissance of Persian works in ibn Sīnā's time, a time in which works, such as Firdūsī's "nationalistic" epic were composed and mystical poetry experienced a new upsurge. In view of such developments, ibn Sīnā's works need not be interpreted as works whose primary interest is religious. An approach to his works that seems to be promising is to examine or to reconstruct his system as a rationalistic metaphysics, a metaphysics that is to form the basis of mystical experience. He seems to establish the ground for such a system at least in the last chapters of the *Ishārāt,* where he specifies a "way" for the mystic that is closed off to the believer. This nonreligious view of mysticism in particular deserves the undivided attention of scholars because it is presented in one of his last works.

95 L. Massignon, *La Passion d'al-Ḥosayn ibn Mansoūr al-Ḥallāj, martyr mystique de l'Islam*, 2 vols. (Paris, 1922). It is noteworthy that certain themes that recur in the works of ibn Sīnā and the Ṣūfīs are also found in other sources which exhibit a predilection for mystical themes. Persian poetry is a case in point. We cite only a few lines in order to illustrate the presence and the continuity of themes like the "return" or ascent of the person [soul], mystical union of God and persons, the unity of God and man—where man is part of God as a wave is part of the ocean, and to illustrate the lack of a duality or alienation.

> Since all sacred souls [heavenly intelligences] are waiting for you, why do you not [O heart] become like life and leap [aim] towards the source of life? / Awaiting you is a station on the moon; it is sacrilegious that you should look here and elsewhere.
>
> J. Rūmī, in *Kūlliyyāt shams*, ed. B. Fūrūzānfar, VI (Tehran, 1961), p. 155, no. 2874.

> My search shall not cease until my perfection is reached / Until [my] life is connected with the source of life or [this] life [soul] is disembodied.
>
> Ḥāfiẓ, in *Dīvān-i Ḥāji Ḥāfiẓ-i Shīrāzī*, ed. A. Anjavī(Tehran, 1967), p. 71.

> Thy being [God's] (*hastī*) is the form [cause] of the union (*paīvand*) / Thou art in persons [like them, persisting in them] and persons are in Thee [like, persisting in Thee].
>
> Niẓāmi, in *Kulliyyāt-i Hamsi-i Ḥakīm Niẓāmī-i Gajiyī*, A. Kabir edn. (Tehran, 1966), p. 13.

> From wave to wave is the path of the intelligence / For the mystic there is no being but God.
>
> Sa'dī, in *Kulliyyāt-i Shaiyḥ Sa'dī*, ed. M. Furūqī (Tehran, 1960).

> Totality is a unity; there is no duality / Here is no "I-ness" nor [distinct] "Thou-ness."
>
> Aṭṭār, in *Manṭiq al-Ṭair* (Tehran, 1963)

> The [actual] agent (*fā'il*) is the (*Ḥaqq*) [God, Truth, reality]; others a mere instrument. Existence, being the effect of *Ḥaqq*), is a unity; / Any other [the apparent duality] is a mere image and conjecture.
>
> Jāmī, in *Dīvān-i Kāmil-i Jāmī*, ed. H. Riḍā (Tehran, 1962), p. 816.

96 Stace, *Teaching, op. cit.*, (above, note 49), p. 14.
97 *DAI*, p. 106, p. 156.
98 Even though Mahdavī lists two hundred and forty-four titles for works by ibn Sīnā [*loc. cit.*, above, note 75], and Anawati mentions two hundred and seventy-six titles [*loc. cit.*, above, note 75], there are only a few critical editions of ibn Sīnā's texts, such as Anawati and Zāyed's *Shifā'* [*op. cit.*, (above, note 21)]; *De Anima*, ed. F. Raḥman (London, New York and Toronto, 1959); *Psychologie d'Ibn Sīnā (Avicenne) d'après son oeuvre 'Aš-Shifā', ed. Jan Bakoš, 2 vols. (Prague, 1956); Persian texts: in vols.* X-XXV *of Silsia-i Intišarāt-i Anjumani-i Àsāri Millī (*Tehran, 1951).
99 M. Watt, *Islamic Philosophy and Theology* (Edinburg, 1964). The author recommends caution to anyone writing about Islamic philosophy and philosophers, "for all kinds of things may happen which make his wider statements false. The text of a crucial passage may be proved to be erroneous; a new work by the author in question may be discovered; or a work supposed to be his may be shown to be by someone else. Thus most of the general statements about Islamic philosophy made at the present time must be regarded as in part provisional" (p. xi).
100 For instance, the emphasis on prophecy we have observed in the *Shifā'* and the lack of such emphasis in the *Dānish Nāmeh* and the *Ishārāt* (see also above, note 78); the extensive description of mysticism in the *Ishārāt* and the absence of such description in the *Shifā'*; the affirmation of the theory of the survival of the body after the occurrence of death in the *Shifā'* and the rejection of this doctrine in the *Ma'ād* (*op. cit.*, above, note 43) as well as the denial of reward and punishment in the "afterlife" (Hourani, *op. cit.*, above, note 62).
101 See above, note 92; see also Nasr, *Introduction op. cit.*, (above, note 54), pp. 212-213 on "production."
102 See, for instance, *DAI*, p. 77, where he demonstrates "that the Necessary Existent is neither a substance nor an accident." That the Necessary Existent is neither is also indirectly indicated in his assertion that It has neither genus nor differentia [*Shifā'*, II, 348; *Ishārāt*, III, 53].

103 *DAI*, p. 9.

104 P. Morewedge, "Ibn Sīnā (Avicenna), Malcom and the Ontological Argument," *Monist* LIV, No. 2 (1970); *idem*, "Ibn Sīnā's Concept of the Self," forthcoming in *Philosophical Forum.*

105 In the Aristotelian scheme substances undergo only one type of change in being "generated" or "destroyed." (*Metaphysics* 1069 b 7) The notion that a substance (such as ibn Sīnā's notion of the person as *'aql*) can blend (*paīvand*) into something like his Necessary Existent is, therefore, purely non-Aristotelian doctrine. Aristotle rejects the theory that depicts the universe as a mere succession of episodes of substances in which one substance is generated after another (*Metaphysics* 1075 37-1076 b 5). Ibn Sīnā departs in his theory from Aristotle, for an intelligence-substance emanates a body in his system, and such a kind of emanation can continue in series. If we decide to use "substance" in its Aristotelian sense, the ibn Sīnā's different use of this term will present a paradox. However, if ibn Sīnā's system is interpreted in the "process" language, rather than in the "substance-event" language, the apparent paradox in his system can be avoided. (See also above, note 104.)

106 See above, note 75.

A THIRD VERSION OF THE ONTOLOGICAL ARGUMENT IN THE IBN SĪNIAN METAPHYSICS*

INTRODUCTION

In this inquiry we shall evaluate the philosophical significance of the concept of the Necessary Existent in the context of ibn Sīnā's ontological argument for the existence of God. We shall focus especially on the so-called "mystical" aspects of the ultimate being, which are important for contemporary philosophical theology, as exemplified in the works of H. D. Lewis, R. C. Zaehner, and others. The outline of our argument follows a fivefold division, presenting: (I) a clarification of two versions of the ontological argument, (II) ibn Sīnā's support of the second version of this argument, (III) the pragmatics of the experimental features of the concept of the Necessary Existent which figure in religious experience, but are not fully accounted for in the first two versions of the ontological argument, (IV) the development of a third version of this argument within ibn Sīnā's writings, a version for which analogues will be cited from the doctrines of western philosophers such as Descartes, Augustine and others, and finally (V) an assessment of the philosophical significance of our inquiry, which points out the difficulties embedded in all ontological arguments encountered as well as in the experiential approach to the concept of the Necessary Existent in religious experience.

THE TWO VERSIONS OF THE ONTOLOGICAL ARGUMENT

Recently interest has mounted concerning the philosophical significance of the ontological argument for the existence of God—an argument traditionally associated with St. Anselm's *Proslogion.* Accordingly, in a collection of articles exclusively devoted to this argument, Hick and McGill note, "Recent decades have seen a great and growing interest in the ontological argument for the existence of God, and a considerable twentieth-century literature has grown up around it," and, moreover, "There has been an intense and many-sided investigation of the meaning of this argument for the man who first proposed it, St. Anselm of Canterbury."[1] In another collection, also devoted to this argument, R. Taylor holds that, "This argument has had a profound fascination for men since it was first so thoroughly and beautifully formulated by St. Anselm of Canterbury in the eleventh century."[2] Numerous studies relate this argument to Anselm, calling, for example, Anselm's formulation "The classical version,"[3] or naming the argument itself "his [Anselm's] proof for God's existence."[4]

Perhaps the contemporary revival of interest in this argument may have been stimulated by an essay titled "Anselm's Ontological Argument" by a major contemporary philosopher, Norman Malcolm, who uses the following strategy to "save" the ontological argument.[5] To begin with, he distinguishes between two different versions of the same argument of Anselm, stating, "I believe that in Anselm's *Proslogion and Responsio editoris* there are two different pieces of reasoning which he did not distinguish from one another, and that a good deal of light may be shed on the philosophical problem of 'the ontological argument' if we do distinguish them."[6] Malcolm then agrees with the critiques of the argument, recognizing that one version is inadequate, and attempts to "prove" the so-called second version of the argument.[7] This striking attempt by a major contemporary philosopher to prove the existence of God by an a priori argument has caused an uproar in contemporary philosophy. In a recent essay, we too attempted to criticize Malcolm's "proof" in the context of our study of ibn Sīnā's philosophy, by showing that: (i) prior to Anselm (1033 -1109), ibn Sīnā (980 -1037) held a second version of the ontological argument, (ii) the analysis of ibn Sīnā's argument unearths some new objections to Malcolm's version, and (iii) the ibn Sīnian version is not logically adequate.[8]

Let us briefly present a formulation of these two versions, since it will be necessary to refer to them in subsequent discussions.

The formulation below displays some of the key features of the first version:

(V1P1) By "God I mean the most perfect being.
(The "most perfect be meaning that entity which has all positive properties to the maximum degree, e.g., it loves maximally).[9]

(V1P2) "Existence" is a perfection.
(This assumes that existence is a property and furthermore, that it is a positive property. A legitimate subject of which existence would be predicated would supposedly be a concept or an idea).[10]

∴ God exists. (For every perfection Φ, God has Φ to the maximum degree; since existence is a Φ, it follows that, but the rule of Universal instantiation, God has existence, which is interpreted as God exists).

In brief, the three types of objections to this version are the following:

(Leibniz 1) "(V1P1)" may not describe a possible entity.[11]
(Naming a concept does not assure that a concept in question can be realized in any possible world).

(Kant 1) We should reject (V1P2), since "Existence is not a predicate."[12]

(Hume 1) The entire machinery of the argument is inadequate. If the conclusion of any argument is a matter-of-fact statement, then at least one of its premises must also be a matter-of-fact statement. Since in this argument the conclusion is a matter-of-fact statement and the premises are all relations-of-ideas statements, the implication is not legitimate.[13]

(Hume 2) "(V1P1)" is inadequate, since it attempts to describe an actual entity purely by analysis of ideas. The only legitimate basis we may have for talking

> about an actual entity is on the basis of impressions rather than ideas.[14]

If one accepts this objection (Hume 2), then (Leibniz 1) becomes superfluous since, as will become evident, the Humean objection would not enable us to claim legitimately that it is conceivable for an entity such as God to be "necessary."

Malcolm places the first version of the ontological argument into *Proslogion 2* and rejects it in accordance with (Kant 1) as follows:

> Anselm's ontological proof of *Proslogion 2* is fallacious because it rests on the false doctrine that existence is a real perfection (and therefore that existence is a "real predicate"). It would be desirable to have a rigorous refutation of the doctrine but I have not been able to provide one. I am compelled to leave the matter at the more or less intuitive level of Kant's observations.[15]

However, Malcolm attempts to prove or to support what he regards as a second variation of Anselm's argument, a version which does not assert that existence is a perfection, but rather that the "Necessary Existence" is a perfection. He affirms: "*Necessary Existence* is a property of God in the *same sense* that *necessary omnipotence and necessary omniscience* are His properties."[16] The second argument may be formulated as follows:

(Malcolm 1) The Necessary Being (existent) exists necessarily.
Malcolm employs many arguments to substantiate this proposition while recognizing objections like the following:[17]

(Hume 3) "Necessity" is applicable to "relations-of-ideas" types of propositions; thus, the phrase "the Necessary Existent" is not legitimate.[18]

(Kant 2) For any x and any proposition, 'x exists,' it is possible to conceive 'x does not exist' to be true; thus the second part of Malcolm's affirmation (Malcolm 1), "necessarily exists," is not supportable.[19]

IBN SĪNĀ AND THE ONTOLOGICAL ARGUMENT

In this section we shall turn to some passages in the ibn Sīnian corpus which deal with the ontological argument—especially to those passages omitted in our earlier writing on this subject.[20]

To begin with, we note that the subject matter of the Necessary Existent *(al-Wājib al-Wujūd)* is the most prominent single concept in ibn Sīnā's metaphysical writing; in fact he places as much emphasis on it as Spinoza does on his God-one-substance in *The Ethics*. For example, in the *Dānish Nāmeh*,[21] out of fifty-seven chapters, chapters nineteen through thirty-eight and chapter fifty-five make explicit mention of the Necessary Existent in their titles. In the *Najāt*,[22] out of fifty-seven chapters, approximately nineteen take up the subject matter of the Necessary Existent, while in the *Shifā'*,[23] the sixth and the seventh sections of the first chapter, the eighth chapter, and the content of many other sections, such as the last two chapters, the ninth and the tenth, touch on the same topic. Consequently, the statements that ibn Sīnā makes about the Necessary Existent should not be viewed as standing in isolation in his system; this concept, indeed, is the most central doctrine in his metaphysics.

Let us investigate, accordingly, the logic of ibn Sīnā's argumentation and note how he would classify the truth of the conclusion about the existence of the Necessary Existent or God. We may begin with the classification of sentences in the logic of *al-Ishārāt*[24] (I, 305-310), where the discussion grows out of a context specifying the relationship between a predicate (*maḥmūl*) and its subject (*mawḍū*), which, according to ibn Sīnā, holds between both affirmative and negative propositions. The predication leads either to a contingent proposition such as "A man is a writer," or to an impossible proposition, such as "A man is a stone." Subsequently he states that the matter (*mādda*) of each proposition (as related to the predicate) results in a relation which is either necessary (*wājib*), contingent (*mumkin*), or impossible (*mumtani'*). (We note here that "*mumkin*" should be translated as "contingent," which precludes "necessary"; the usual translation of "*mumkin*" as "possible," which includes "necessary," is misleading.) Having specified the general class of necessary propositions, he subdivides them into absolute (*muṭlaq*) propositions, which are categorically necessary and are independent of any one condition (*sharṭ*), such as the realization of an essence, and those propositions that are hypothetically necessary and are based upon a condition. To illustrate the first kind, ibn Sīnā presents the proposition "God (*Allāh*)—may he be exalted—exists (*mawjūd*)" (*Ishārāt,* I, 310), whereas for the second he cites, "A man is necessarily a rational body," implying further that wherever there is a man, there is a rational body. Consequently, our knowledge of God's existence is not dependent on any condition, e.g., the existence of other entities, whereas the truth of a sentence that attributes a predicate (even an essential one) to a subject other than God assumes the existence of the subject. This interpretation corroborates also Rescher's analysis of ibn Sīnā's position on existential propositions and genuine predicates; Rescher's position, which is based upon his analysis of the logic of the *Dānish Nāmeh,* is upheld by our own reading.[25]

The next problem inviting our attention is the exploration of the meta-language status of the "Necessary Existent" in ibn Sīnā's metaphysical vocabulary. In *al-Shifā'* (pp. 5-6), ibn Sīnā notes that in each science (*'ilm*), some entities are assumed [to exist], while their modes are investigated by the science in question.[26] In metaphysics, however, the existence (*anniyya* [*Ibid.,* 5], *wujūd* [*Ibid.,* 6]) of God (*Allāh*) is not an assumption but a goal to be investigated (*maṭlūb*). Here, ibn Sīnā does not affirm our knowledge of the proposition, "The Necessary Existent exists," to be either true or false; he does establish, however, that we do not begin the science of metaphysics with the concept of the Necessary Existent as our primitive term, but develop this concept in the course of our inquiry. His statement should not be interpreted to assert that an empirical, matter-of-fact type of assumption is necessary for proving the existence of God. This problem becomes clear if we differentiate between Aquinas' concept of what constitutes a proof for God's existence and the ibn Sīnian method.

As noted, Anselm's version of the proof is based upon "the fool's" psychological awareness in his own ear that he understands what the most perfect being means.[27] Aquinas objects to the argument on the grounds that the ontological argument based upon something "psychologically evident to us" is inadequate. He might say, nonetheless, that "God exists" is syntactically self-evident. In this vein, Aquinas argues:

> I maintain then that the proposition 'God exists' is self-evident in itself, for, as we shall see later, its subject and its predicate are identical, since God is his own existence. But, because what is to be God is not evident to us, the proposition is not self-evident to us, and needs to be made evident. This is done by means of things which, though less evident in themselves, are nevertheless more evident to us by means of, namely, God's effects.[28]

Crucial to his argument is Aquinas' insistence on a proof which has to be "evident to us." At the expense of an a priori analytical proof, such an insistence leads him to offer instead an argument based upon "God's effect" in the actual world, which might be "self-evident" to the "fool" in the psalms. In this vein, Aquinas states:

> On the other hand, nobody can think (*cogitare*) the opposite of a self-evident proposition, as Aristotle's discussion of first principles makes clear. But the opposite of the proposition 'God exists' can be thought, for *the fool* in the psalms *said in his heart: There is no God.* That God exists is therefore not self-evident.[29]

It is for this reason that all five of the celebrated "ways" which Aquinas presents to prove God's existence are a posteriori cosmological arguments. Aquinas notes subsequently that "God exists" is not a proposition which is implanted in us by nature in any clear and specific way.[30] Thereafter, he quotes St. Paul to support the view that God's existence must be demonstrated by the "things he has made."[31] A close inspection of each of the five ways shows that his arguments are a posteriori in that they focus on the changes things in the world undergo, efficient causation in the observable world, the possibility and necessity of things "we come across" in the world, gradation observed in things, and order in nature.[32] Consequently, Aquinas insists that a proof for God's existence is needed in which every premise is self-evident and every concept is psychologically intuitive. Ibn Sīnā chooses a different approach. In the first place, ibn Sīnā refrains from using ordinary language to prove explicitly the God of religion to his readers. Instead, he presents a metaphysical system in which a theory about the Necessary Existent is conceptually formulated. With the exception of the last two chapters of *al-Shifā'*, a book written prior to the *Dānish Nāmeh* and the *Ishārāt*, his metaphysical writings are purely abstract, especially the *Dānish Nāmeh,* where the entire discussion of heavens and bodies is presented in an axiomatic way. The proofs refer not to "God" but to the Necessary Existent—especially the ontological proofs, which are based purely on his analytic specification of this concept, as the following analyses should clarify.

In considering the question of the self-evident nature of God's existence, ibn Sīnā does not differentiate between that, which is psychologically self-evident to us, and that, which is analytically self-evident, as he is constructing a rational schema. In this vein, he claims that it is impossible (*maḥāl*) for us to render conjectures (*faraḍ*) about the nonexistence of the Necessary Existent. He uses this doctrine to differentiate the Necessary Existent from other existents (*al-Najāt,* p. 224). The problem, as he envisages it, is to show that even though the Necessary Existent is not in Itself a primitive metaphysical concept, "That the Necessary Existent exists" is a categorically true proposition. Accordingly, we note in the *Dānish Nāmeh* an outline of such an argument, which is corroborated in his other writings.

(Ibn Sīnā 1) "Being-qua-being (*hastī*) is the most general (*'āmm*) concept recognized by the intelligence (*khirad, 'aql, nous, intelligentia*)."

(Ibn Sīnā 2) "According to intelligence, 'being-qua-being' is divided into 'impossible,' 'contingent,' and 'necessary' kinds of being."

(Ibn Sīnā 3) Consequently "The Necessary Being" is "The Necessary Existent", or "The Necessary Existent is that whose essence is existence."

Let us begin our analysis by pointing out the variations with which the argument comes to the fore in ibn Sīnā's various texts.

(1) First we notice that there are two different terms used by ibn Sīnā to discuss the subject matter of (ibn Sīnā 1), "*hastī*" and "*wujūd.*" Having discussed these terms extensively in our previous studies, we shall do no more than note those points that are significant to our present discussion.[33]

"*Huasti,*" meaning "being-qua-being," is equivalent to Aristotle's use of "τὸ ὂν ᾗ ὄν" in *Metaphysica* 1002a20 and Ockham's use of "*ens*" in *Summa Totius Logicae*[34] ("*wujūd*" is translated as "existence," "*mawjūd*" is translated as "existent," whereas "*māhiyya,*" "*dhāt*" and "*ḥaqiqa*" are translated as "essence").

(2) Ibn Sīnā has two formulations of his primary hypothesis:

(2a) In the *Dānish Nāmeh,* he asserts that "being" (*hastī*) is the most general (*'āmm*), well-known (*ma'rūf*) notion recognized by reason (*khirad* and intelligence, *'aql, nous, intelligentia*) (p. 15). In the *Najāt,* he asserts without a doubt that there is existence (*wujūd*) (p. 235). In both of these cases the following theory is proposed: there is no doubt that there is being (*Dānish Nāmeh*) and existence (*al-Nājat*), or furthermore that in its primary division existence is either necessary, contingent or impossible (*Dānish Nāmeh*). In the *Najāt,* the premise about the modalities follows immediately in the same sentence, whereas the modal doctrine follows fifteen chapters later in the *Dānish Nāmeh.* These two passages provide plausible grounds for the interpretation that ibn Sīnā regards either "being" as primary, from which it follows that "necessary being," "contingent being," and "impossible being" can be assumed to be legitimate concepts (according to the doctrine of the *Dānish Nāmeh*) or that he regards "existence" as primary, from which it follows that "necessary existence" and "contingent existence" are considered to be primary (according to the doctrine of *al-Najāt*). Obviously this variation is legitimate, since there can be impossible *beings,* e.g., the concept of a round square, but no impossible *existents.* These two perspectives could be aligned as follows: both "being" and "existence" are primary to the intelligence. When we consider being, we do so in three instances, "necessary being," "contingent being" and "impossible being." When we consider existence, that which is primary to our intelligence is "necessary existence" and "contingent existence." (By way of providing clarification, let us note that among contingent beings, those whose causes have been realized have an instance, e.g., particular man, while those whose causes have not been realized, e.g., "being a unicorn," are mere essences without existents.)

(2b) Now we shall turn to the second set of quotations to buttress the first two premises. In *al-Shifā'* (p. 29), it is asserted that the first ideas to be configured in the soul (*nafs*) are existents (*al-mawjūd*), such as being a thing (*shai'*) and being a necessity (*al-ḍarūri*) and, moreover, that there is no need to know of other configurations in order to know these (primary) ones. Similarly, in another passage in *al-Shifā'* (*al-Shifā'*, p. 37), ibn Sīnā notes that from the vantage point of the intelligence (*'aql*) any existence (*wujūd*) is either a necessary existent (*al-wājib al-wujūd*) or a contingent existent (*al-mumkin al-wujūd*). In *al-Ishārāt* (III, 19), it is stated that any existent in its own nature (*nafsahu*), is either a contingency (*mumkin*) or a necessity (*wājib*). In *'Uyūn al-Ḥikma,* ibn Sīnā reaffirms the thesis that aspect by which any thing (*shai'*) has existence is either a necessity (*wājib*) or a contingency (*mumkin*) (*'Uyūn al-Ḥikma*).[35] In these passages, ibn Sīnā seems to place ontic status on the notions of "existence" on the same level accorded to the modalities of "necessity" and "contingency." Now axiomatically for our purpose, it does not matter whether ibn Sīnā considers "being" or "existence" as the first set of notions and modalities (i.e., "necessity," "contingency," and "impossibility") a second set, or whether these two sets of notions have the same primary status. It is a fact that both sets are "nonempirical" and both provide ibn Sīnā with the basis from which to deduce that the concept of "necessary existence," i.e., one combining "existence" and "necessity," is a legitimate notion. Having made this assumption a part of what may be called his "rules of formations," he goes on to note that an understanding of the concept of Necessary Existence implies the existence of exactly one Necessary Existent.[36]

(3) Next, let us ask whether or not the positions designated as (ibn Sīnā 1) and (ibn Sīnā 2) commit him to a rationalistic ontology. Before resolving this issue, let us note first that no classical philoso-

pher doubted that there is something in the world, as the alternative would be that there is nothing, and "nothing" has been a meaningless concept in classical philosophy since Parmenides. In *al-Najāt* (p. 213), ibn Sīnā states explicitly that there is no doubt but that there is existence. This statement is not an assumption necessary to his proof but an assertion of a primary incorrigible truth. To assert that this particular passage makes ibn Sīnā's argument a cosmological argument is not legitimate for the following reasons. Descartes, in his fifth meditation, (where he states his ontological argument) and Anselm, in the *Proslogion*, (where he formulates a version of the ontological argument par excellence) assume that they themselves and their ideas do exist as actual entities. Consequently, if we make the criterion for the cosmological argument the assumption that at least something exists, then we shall not be able to call the arguments of Anselm or Descartes (fifth meditation) "ontological"—which is absurd. Typical cosmological arguments, such as the ones stated by Aquinas, refer to a feature some entity possesses in the actual world—not in mere thought or in definition. Now let us clarify further what we may mean by "rationalism" before investigating whether ibn Sīnā's claim that we are acquainted with "being" commits him to a rationalistic metaphysics. Since it is beyond the scope of this paper to discuss different schools of philosophy, we shall touch on no more than one central issue: whether or not a philosopher can claim that we can know bodies by reason and not by the senses. The most celebrated case of a "rationalistic" position on this topic is found at the end of Descartes' second meditation after his so-called "wax experiment," in which he states:

> I now know that even bodies are not really perceived by the senses or the imaginative faculty, but only by intellect; that they are perceived, not by being touched or seen, but by being understood; I thus clearly recognize that nothing is more easily or manifestly perceptible to me than my own mind.[37]

In contradistinction to such a view stands ibn Sīnā's position. In the logic of the *Ishārāt* (I, 189), he affirms that our ability to attribute "being a figure" and "being a triangle" to the same entity does not imply that "being a figure" and "being a triangle" are one and the same idea (*ḥaqiqa*); instead, the thing (*shai'*) in question which we name "a triangle" can also be named "a figure." Ibn Sīnā returns to this example in the metaphysics found in the same collection (*Ishārāt*, III, 13-14) when he asserts that the idea, essence (*ḥaqiqa*) of a triangle is dependent upon features, such as line formation, but that its existence (*wujūd*—that is, the realization of a particular triangle—is due to other causes. Moreover, in the *Dānish Nāmeh* (p. 56), ibn Sīnā makes a distinction between the meaning of a bodily substance in whose subject an essence is realized and the act of knowing that there is actually a bodily substance, on the basis that the latter belongs to the experience of an actually existing subject rather than to mere relations of ideas. Consequently, ibn Sīnā's adherence to "being" or to "existence" as an a priori concept does not commit him to a rationalistic metaphysics. He would reject Descartes' view that the validity of sensations depends on God's existence. For this reason, as well as on account of his essence-existence distinction with which we have dealt elsewhere, he could not accept the second premise of the first version of the ontological argument "(V1P2)," which specifies that existence is a perfection for any entity. The sole exception is the "Necessary Existent," as defined by ibn Sīnā.

(4) Moreover, this difference between the argument assuming "(V1P2)" and the argument merely assuming "(Malcolm 1)" and not "(V1P2)" is the means by which to differentiate between the two versions of this argument, as Malcolm points out in the following passage:

> Previously I rejected *existence* as a perfection. Anselm is maintaining in the remarks last quoted, not that existence is a perfection but *the logical impossibility of non-existence is a perfection.* In other words, *necessary existence* is a perfection. His first ontological proof uses the principle that a thing is greater if it exists than if it does not exist. His second proof employs the different principle that a thing is greater if it necessarily exists than if it does not necessarily exist.[38]

Thus, ibn Sīnā's repeated assertion that the "Necessary Existent" is a legitimate concept and that "Its essence is no other than existence" permits us to assign his and Malcolm's arguments to the second version of this argument.

Malcolm indicates that philosophers other than Anselm have called the "Necessity of existence" a perfection. For example, in his replies to objections made to his fifth meditation, Descartes asserts that existence may be a property but also that "necessary existence" is a property.

> Nay, necessary existence in the case of God is also a true property in the strictest sense of the word, because it belongs to Him and forms part of His essence alone. Hence the existence of a triangle cannot be compared with the existence of God, because existence manifestly has a different relation to essence in the case of God and in the case of a triangle.[39]

Spinoza, too, begins his treatise on *Ethics* by asserting that "By cause of itself, I understand that whose essence involves existence, or that whose nature cannot be conceived unless existing."[40] He uses his feature to clarify his notion of God by stating: "The existence of God and His essence are one and the same thing."[41] "The thesis that only in the case of God are essence and existence the same is also stated by Ockham, who asserts that God cannot not exist.[42]

This view of the ontological argument has recently found a supporter in R. Taylor, who, upon noting that the concept of the Necessary Existence has been questioned by "confused" people, attempts to clarify it in his *Metaphysics.*

> If it makes sense to speak of anything as an *impossible* being, or something which by its very nature does not exist, then it is hard to see why the idea of a necessary being, or something which in its very nature exists, should not be just as comprehensible.[43]

This argument is actually much weaker than the one presented by ibn Sīnā, for it confuses an essence with an existent. There could not be *an existent* which is an impossible being, for if it were impossible for it to have been realized, then it could not be an actual entity. Consequently, Taylor's "something which by its very nature does not exist" should be reformulated as follows: "We can conceive of various kinds of essences, e.g., being a round square, which cannot have an instance." However, from this statement it does not follow that there must be an essence which must have an instance or be equal to its own instance. The difficulty in ibn Sīnā's, Malcolm's, and Taylor's (reformulated) arguments is the assumption underlying each that the concatenation of "necessity" and "existence" is legitimate. In contradistinction to these positions stand Kant's classical remarks:

> If, in an identical proposition, I reject the predicate while retaining the subject, contradiction results; and I therefore say that the former belongs necessarily to the latter. But if we reject subject and predicate alike, there is no contradiction; for nothing is then left that can be contradicted. To posit a triangle, and yet to reject its three angles is self-contradictory but there is no contradiction in rejecting the triangle together with its three angles. The same holds true of the concept of an absolutely necessary being. If its existence is rejected, we reject the thing itself with all its predicates; and no question of contradiction can then arise.[44]

Taylor must contend with still another objection. Even if we assume that the Necessary Existent makes sense, just because we use the concept of "an impossible being," it does not follow that we are also using the concept of "the necessary being" in a comprehensible way.[45]

While we cannot disagree with "(ibn Sīnā 1)," we do not agree with his second premise "(ibn Sīnā 2)." It is obvious that there are certain propositions that are *necessarily false,* e.g., "There is the largest number," or "There is someone who is the mother of herself." There are also some *contingent* propositions, e.g., "It will rain tomorrow." And most philosophers have held that certain propositions are *analytically true* in one sense or another, such as "'2' is an even number" or "A white horse is a horse." Modalities as applied to propositions make sense, but as applied to entities violate Hume's principles as formulated in (Hume 2) and Kant's analysis as formulated in (Kant 2). This writer is baffled by ibn Sīnā's assumption that "necessity" can legitimately be concatenated with "being." We question the significance of "necessary being" (unless applied to propositions) and "necessary existence," for these concepts are used clearly only in the context of traditional ontology. Since ibn Sīnā and others do not present any argument for their position that modalities and "existence" or "being" can be combined, while Hume and Kant present explicit arguments against this position, we cannot assume that (ibn Sīnā 2) is an a priori truth or applicable to the actual world.

Another problem with the second version of the argument is the question of the legitimacy of the concept of an "essence." C. D. Broad's analysis of Leibniz's "Predicate-in-Notion" principle, to which we shall return subsequently, sheds some light on this issue by pointing out that in some cases (e.g., a circle), an essence may easily be determined, while in other cases (e.g., an ellipse), and any member of a family of some properties can constitute an essence.[46] Yet even in the case of the circle, one would need, in addition to its so-called essence, a set of other items (e.g., Euclid's axioms), from which to derive other properties.[47] In applying this objection to the concept of the Necessary Existent, we note that "being self-caused" and "having one's essence as one's existence" are interchangeable because in medieval terminology a cause is often that agent which is essential in the realization of the patient as an actual entity; consequently, "being self-caused" is identical to "existing due to oneself" which implies "existing at all times," and "having no agent for one's realization"; for otherwise, one would have to antedate one's own existence to actualize oneself. Consequently, all theorems about the Necessary Existent which use "its essence is no other than existence" may isomorphically, use the "self-caused" feature, which shows that there is no simple way of indicating the Necessary Existent.

In sum, ibn Sīnā's ontological argument is no more successful than the others we have mentioned. Having dealt with the logic of the arguments in question, let us turn to an equally important aspect of the Necessary Existent, about which ibn Sīnā's analysis will provide great insight.

THE PRAGMATICS OF THE "NECESSARY EXISTENT" FOR RELIGIOUS EXPERIENCE

What is the pragmatic significance of the ontological argument? A clue is provided by Malcolm's own argument, which tries to justify the legitimacy of the notion of the Necessary Existent by showing its use in ordinary language and by appealing to religious texts, such as the Bible, and to religious practices. Toward the end of his argument Malcolm remarks,

> Here is expressed the idea of the necessary existence and eternity of God, an idea that is essential to the Jewish and Christian religions. In those complex systems of thought, those "language games," God has the status of a necessary being. Who can doubt that? Here we must say with Wittgenstein, "This language-game is played!" I believe we may rightly take the existence of those religious systems of thought in which God figures as a necessary being to be a disproof of the dogma, affirmed by Hume and others, that no existential propositions can be necessary.[48]

We have discussed Malcolm's attempt to define God as the most independent entity and have noted the logical difficulties inherent in this method. It is nevertheless true that many agree with Malcolm that the formal version of the ontological argument finds little support in ordinary religious experience; consequently, support for the existence of God must be found elsewhere. The first alternative has been to reject this argument in particular and to substitute another formal argument which is as removed from the ordinary language as the first two versions are. Plantinga takes such a step, when he asserts:

> It is doubtful, I think, that any person was ever brought to a belief in God by this argument, and unlikely that it has played the sort of role in strengthening and confirming religious belief that, for example, the teleological argument has played. To the unsophisticated, Anselm's argument is (at first sight at least) remarkably unconvincing,

> if not downright irritating; it smacks too much of word magic.[49]

He asserts thereupon that even though many of the classical objections to the argument are invalid,[50] none of the obvious ways of stating the argument can succeed. After reviewing other types of arguments, Plantinga finally offers his own, "Hence my tentative conclusion: if my belief in other minds is rational, so is my belief in God. But obviously the former is rational; so, therefore, is the latter."[51] As this type of argumentation takes us away from the main stream of our essay, we shall not pursue it further, as numerous arguments may be offered for God's existence, each of which may be unsound.

Another alternative has been to reject the logic of any rational argument for the existence of God on the grounds that it is unsuitable for religious discourse, and to uphold instead some "ontological" feature of God, e.g., "infinity," as an essential aspect of a direct religious experience. In this vein, H. D. Lewis, a celebrated contemporary philosopher of religion, argues:

> The objections to the main arguments for the existence of God are well known. But it seems to me that what these arguments tried to express, most of all in the cases of the cosmological and the ontological ones, is the conviction of the self-subsistent supra-rational source of the world as we find it. Where the argument fails is in trying to break into a series of steps what is in fact one insight, and also in seeing to start from purely finite factors, and reason to conclusions about the infinite.[52]

Lewis clarifies his use of "the infinite" in describing the "filling" or the "content" of religious awareness:

> For it seems to me that this begins to be formed from the first onset of any properly religious life through the way the first apprehension of finite being as having a supreme and infinite source, and the emotional and other accompaniments of this awareness which we have also in mind designating it 'wonder,' impress themselves into the

> situation which prompts them by lending to that situation something of their own quality and aura of mystery.[53]

The key notion, "the first apprehension of finite being as having a supreme and infinite source," is repeated in the conclusion of Lewis's work when he attempts to emphasize the social side of religion as follows: "Moreover the moment of wondering and still appreciation of finite facts as having an infinite or transcendental source, in deepening our sense of the unity of our natural environment, will intensify in the same way our sense of affinity and kinship with other persons."[54] The notion that the concern of religious experience is not to prove God's existence but to recognize the so-called "infinite basis of our finite being" is often encountered by a historian who attempts to point out the major features of an important thinker. For instance, after pointing out the Christian background of Hegel, Copleston, in his essay on "Hegel and the Rationalization of Mysticism," asserts: "In the second place Hegel was convinced that from the philosophical point of view the finite is not intelligible except in the light of the infinite whole, which is the ultimate reality. His philosophy is therefore concerned with exhibiting the nature of the ultimate reality rather than with trying to prove its existence."[55]

Often another transcendent term is substituted for the word "infinite," while the door is kept open to possibilities of relating this feature to other terms. For example, in the conclusion of his excellent study on *The Varieties of Religious Experience* William James notes three of the broadest characteristics of the religious life. He has found:

1. The visible world is part of a more spiritual universe from which it draws its chief significance;
2. Union or harmonious relation with that higher universe is our true end;
3. Prayer or inner communion with the spirit, be that spirit "God" or "Law," therefore is a process wherein work is really done, and spiritual energy flows in and produces effects, psychological and material, within the phenomenal world.[56]

The key point in James's account is this: the dependence of every aspect of the visible universe upon a spiritual aspect attests to the possibility of an "inner communion" with the "spirit."

At this point we shall investigate the possibility of merging the basic concepts of the ontological argument with what appears to be a major theme in religious experience, according to the writers quoted, who imply that the affinity between "the finite" and "the infinite" or an immediate dependence upon the divine is the core of religious experience and may well be a source of "ordinary logic" or of belief in a God.

TOWARD A THIRD VERSION OF THE ONTOLOGICAL ARGUMENT

At the outset we wish to distinguish between two different kinds of a priori awarenesses or acquaintances. For example, prima facie, I may be aware of the truth of the mathematical proposition that "2+2=4," or that I am seeing a valley, without being at the same time immediately aware of other facts, as for instance that "2" is the only even prime number, or that the sighting of a valley implies the concurrent sighting of a hillside. These two kinds of epistemic states have already been distinguished by Descartes in the passage below, which is embedded in his fifth meditation, where he presents the ontological argument for God's existence,

> Of the things I thus perceive, some are obvious to anybody; others are discovered only by those who undertake closer inspection and more careful investigation, but, when discovered are regarded as no less certain than others.[57]

The examples he provides begin with the truths of mathematics, which are certain but not immediately apparent, and continue to his notion of God. The first kind of awareness is immediate, whereas the second kind of awareness, even though it requires no empirical datum for support, requires nevertheless further conceptual analysis to make the concept in question clear; once we are aware of the first type of proposition, we are in a sense able to deduce other propositions of which we were not aware, in the first sense of "awareness." For example, once we understand the axiomatic system, i.e., the rules and the signs of a formal system, such as Euclidean geometry, we also "know," in the sense that we can generate, all theorems which can be deduced from the axioms in question. Let us, for purposes of clarity, name the first type of epistemic state, a "phenomenal a priori" state and the second a "discursive a priori" state. Having made this distinction, let us now formulate the ontological argument in question.

(V3P1) In a "phenomenal a priori" mode, I know that I exist as an agent who is acting, since my acts presuppose some agent and they are "my" acts. It is impossible for me to be nothing and act simultaneously.

(V3P2) In a "discursive a priori" state, I know that I can only coexist as an aspect of something, or as a derivative from a source of my dependence, which is a kind of *x* (where the value of *x* differs in each context, e.g., the "One Substance of Spinoza", or the "Necessary Existent of ibn Sīnā"); one case of *x* is the Necessary Existent. A complete notion of myself, in the Leibnizian sense of a "predicate-in-notion principle" involves the description of *x*.

(V3C) *x* exists, since *x* coexists as an aspect of myself.

An example of an intuitive but inadequate representation of this argument is the following: "I think, therefore there is at least a mental aspect of me. This mental aspect can exist only through the mediacy of the Necessary Existent. The Necessary Existent must coexist with me, and I in context of it." Before clarifying this thesis, let us note a fundamental difference between this argument and the cosmological argument for God's existence. For the latter at least one of the premises must be a posteriori, such as the assumption of the existence of some contingent entity outside the subject, independent of analytical consideration. But variations of "(V3P1)" and "(V3P2)" all claim to be a priori; consequently, this argument as represented in this essay has the form of the ontological argument.

Let us cite some of the many illustrations the history of philosophy offers to shed light on the first premise. As has been stated, no serious ancient or medieval philosopher has ever doubted the existence of at least something in the world, for otherwise he would have had to uphold the meaningfulness of the statement "There is nothing." This general disclaimer holds even for the most extreme skeptics. For example, in his *Lives of Eminent Philosophers,* Diogenes Laertius mentions the doctrine of the most extreme skeptic, Pyrrho, whose followers declared, "For we admit that we see, and we recognize that we think this or that, but how we see or how we think we know not."[58] In defense of the skeptics against the criticism of the dogmatists, it is said that, "[The skeptics] do not deny that we see. 'We admit the apparent fact,' they say, without admitting that it really is what it appears to be."[59] Accordingly, the problem is not whether or not there is at least one entity in the world but with what degree of certainty we know a concrete entity of a specific kind.

The first set of passages to be considered is taken from St. Augustine, who first formulates the view corresponding to "(V3P1)." In his work *On Free Choice of the Will,* he introduces the following questions:

> Augustine: Let us take up our search in the following order, if you will. First, how is it proved [*manifestum*] that God exists? Second, are all things whatsoever, insofar as they are good, from God? Finally, is free will to be counted as a good? When we have answered these questions, it will be quite clear, I think, whether free will was rightly given. Therefore, to start at the beginning with the most obvious, I will ask you first whether you yourself exist. Are you, perhaps, afraid that you are being deceived by my questioning? But if you did not exist, it would be impossible for you to be deceived.[60]

From thinking, such as doubting, which is incorrigible, he deduces the existence of an agent and a thought. Perhaps the argument supporting this rather sketchy deduction assumes that the following premises are true: (i) I cannot doubt that I am doubting, (ii) doubting must be an event, (iii) all events presuppose a substance, and a mental event (e.g., doubting) presupposes the existence of the substance, i.e., myself. In this passage the argument is used specifically to affirm God's existence; in a celebrated quotation from *The True Religion,* he notes,

> If you do not grasp what I say and doubt whether it is true, at least make up your mind whether you have any doubts. If it is certain that you indeed have doubts, inquire whence that certainty.[61]

Augustine does not explicitly assert here that there is a person who entertains doubts; he asserts however that the experience of doubting is certain. He wishes to show here that the result is a truth which we experience, as is evident from the contiguous passage:

> Every one who knows that he has doubts knows with certainty something that is true, namely that he doubts. He is certain, therefore, about a truth.[62]

The truth, however, is the fact that he doubts, which, according to the passages concerning the freedom of the will, signifies that the agent exists. Another set of passages could be cited from the *Meditations* of Descartes, where he concludes that he exists because he doubts. In this vein, Descartes asserts, "I am. I exist; that is certain." He continues, "For the present I am admitting only what is necessarily true: so 'I am' precisely refers only to a conscious being (*cogitans*)."[63] Sufficient discussion about Descartes' position exists in the philosophical literature which shows the relevance of his philosophy for the support of "(V3P1)."[64]

Ibn Sīnā's celebrated argument of the flying man manifests the same pattern.

> Let us suppose that one of us is created in an instant, and created perfect. But his eyes are blindfolded and cannot see any external objects. He is created floating in the air, or rather in the void, so that the resistance of the air which he might feel, does not affect him. His members are separated, and therefore do not meet or touch one another. Then he reflects and asks himself if his own exis-

> tence is proved. Without any hesitation he would reply that he exists, although he could not prove the existence of his feet or his hand, of his entrails, his heart or his brains, or any exterior thing; but he would nevertheless affirm that he exists, without establishing the fact that he has length, breadth or thickness.[65]

In this passage, Ibn Sīnā observes that epistemically the knowledge of his existence as a nonphysical entity or the nonphysical aspect of himself as prior to the knowledge of other entities. Moreover, in every one of the passages we quoted about the priority of "existence" or of "being," ibn Sīnā assumes that either the soul (*nafs*) or the intelligence (*'aql, khirad*), which receives these a priori truths, exists. Consequently either ibn Sīnā assumes that the soul or the intelligence aspect of persons exists as the receiver of a priori truths or he states explicitly that we know the existence of the soul aspects of ourselves a priori. In sum we found passages in the works of Augustine, Descartes, and ibn Sīnā which shed light on the first premise. Whereas ibn Sīnā places the discussion in a context other than the argument for God's existence, Augustine and Descartes relate the argument of the self directly to God's existence. Consequently we cannot assert that ibn Sīnā uses "(V3P1)" as a direct premise of an ontological argument; however, we can assert that he knows incorrigibly his own existence in a phenomenal a priori mode.

The second premise, "(V3P2)" has been variously shaped in the writings of numerous philosophers, to whose formulation of this premise we shall attend so as to clarify our argument.

Returning to Augustine's discussion of the fact that he exists because he cannot doubt that he doubts, we observe that he buttresses his argument as follows. Conceptual analysis demonstrates that only a living agent can doubt. (The step calls obviously for an a priori mode of knowledge, because the problem concerns the meaning of the words "agent" and "being alive" as applied to an entity which can doubt.) Next, Augustine notes that of all the faculties, such as external and internal senses and the understanding, reason is the best epistemic state, as it includes other states while it is not determined by them. (Here again the analysis is a prior.) Finally, Augustine comments that the eternal truths known by reason, e.g., mathematics, are necessary, immutable, and eternal. (This step is also a prior.) From experiencing these truths, Augustine deduces that God exists. He asserts, accordingly, "You granted, moreover, that if I showed you something higher than our minds, you would admit, assuming that nothing existed which was still higher, that God exists. I accepted your condition and said that it was enough to show this. For if there is something more excellent than truth, this is God. If there is not, then truth itself is God. Whether or not truth is God, you cannot deny that God exists, and this was the question with which we agreed to deal."[66] Later in the same paragraph he notes that in addition to religious faith, the existence of God can be proved by a tenuous form of reason. The most intuitive insight Augustine reveals concerning the relationship between the self and the divine lies embedded in his celebrated assertion in his *Soliloquies*, "God and the Soul, that is what I desire to know." When asked, "Nothing more?" he answered, "Nothing whatever."[67] Augustine's inquiring mind does not fail to note a special affinity between himself and God, as is evident from *The Confessions,* especially in two chapters titled "That the God Whom We Invoke is in Us; and We in Him," and "Everywhere God Wholly Filleth All Things, but Neither Heaven nor Earth Contain Him." Augustine asks, "And how shall I call upon my God—my God and my Lord? For when I call on Him I ask Him to come into me."[68] As he ponders further, he feels himself related to God and is uplifted and filled with the Divine.

> And when Thou art poured forth on us, Thou art not cast down, but we are uplifted; nor art Thou dissipated, but we are drawn together. But, as Thou fillest all things, dost Thou fill then with Thy whole self, or, as even all things cannot altogether contain Thee, do they contain a part; and do all at once contain the same part? Or has each its own proper part—the greater more, the smaller less? Or is it that Thou art wholly everywhere whilst nothing altogether contains Thee?[69]

Evidently, Augustine's writings contain not only clarifications of the third version of the ontological argument, but indicate also the significance of the interrelationship between the knowledge of his self-soul and God, topics embedded in the first two premises of the third version of this argument.

In turning to the most celebrated case of defense of "(V3P2)," found in Descartes' third meditation, we observe that in spite of the phenomenal a priori mode by which he knows that he exists as a mental substance, he has a better knowledge of God's existence than of his own existence by means of a discursive a priori mode, as is evinced in the passage below:

> I must not think that my conception of the infinite has come about, not through a proper idea, but by a denial of the finite—as I conceive of rest and darkness by way of the denial of motion and light; on the contrary I clearly understand that therefore in a way my primary concept (*perceptionem*) is rather of the infinite than of the finite—rather of God, than of myself. How could I understand my doubting and desiring—that is, my lacking something and not being altogether perfect—if I had no idea of a more perfect being as a standard by which to recognize my own defect?[70]

We should recall that Descartes does not use the term "infinite" loosely, for in principle XXVI of his *Principles of Philosophy*, he repeats Aristotle's objection to the notion of the actual infinite.[71] Nevertheless, in principle XXVII, he consciously departs from such strictures by permitting the application of "infinity" to God:

> We shall use the term *indefinitely great* (*indefinita*) rather than *infinite* in order to confine the term *infinite* to God; only as regards to God is it a matter of our not merely failing to apprehend any limit in any respect, but positively knowing there are none. We have no such positive knowledge that other things are in some respect unlimited; we merely make the negative admission that, if they have limits, at any rate they are not discoverable by us.[72]

Consequently, Descartes distinguishes between our epistemic state of knowing God as an infinite entity, of knowing Him absolutely, and the difficulties attendant upon the application of the term "infinite" to others. The most important distinction between God and others, however, is a metaphysical distinction, states in principle LI (fifty-one):

> We can mean by *substance* nothing other than a thing existing in such a manner that it has no need of no other thing in order to exist. There can indeed be only one substance conceived as needing absolutely no other thing in order to exist; namely, God. We can see that all other substances are able to exist only by means of God's cooperation.[73]

As Descartes' ontological argument as stated in the fifth meditation is well known, it is omitted here. Passages in this meditation coming after the formulation of the ontological argument specifically illustrate Descartes' sense of knowing God as a source of the world's dependence, e.g., "But now . . . I have discerned that God exists, and have understood at the same time that everything depends on him, and that he is not deceitful."[74] Descartes notes that the essence of God is no other than existence. That he considers this theme to be a primary discursive idea is evident from the following passage:

> For what is intrinsically more obvious than that the Supreme Being is; that God, to whose essence alone existence belongs, exists? And though it took careful consideration for me to see this, yet I am as certain of it as I am of anything else that appears most certain; not only that, but I can further see that certainty of anything else depends on this, so that apart from this no perfect knowledge is ever possible.[75]

According to Descartes, first one knows "(V3P1)," then "(V3P2)," and finally a stronger version, "(V3C)," specifying that God exists as that infinite entity through which one's own finite aspects can be understood.

The Cartesian view of God as the only infinite entity has been taken up in various senses and from various vantage points. Leibniz, for example, comments on the idea of the absolute infinite in his critique of Locke's doctrines on "Innate Ideas," in *New Essays Concerning Human Understanding*. As vehicle he has chosen the dialogue whose first participant, "Philalethes," proceeds to discard the idea of absolute infinite, whereas the second, "Theophilus," concludes by asserting that there is an (innate) idea of an infinite which is a true idea, an idea which can be applied ". . . as an absolute or attribute without limits which exists reference to *eternity*, in the necessity of the existence of God, without depending upon parts and without the notion of being formed by addition in time."[76]

Another set of passages is found in the works of Spinoza, who introduces the notion of God into his *Ethics*, defining God as an infinite entity, noting that "finiteness is in truth partly negation, and infinitude absolute affirmation of existence of some kind. . . ."[77] He proves, moreover, the existence of God in several ways; after giving an a priori proof based upon the notion that God's essence is existence, he proceeds to explain the matter only with an a posteriori proof, not without adding, however, that an a priori proof can be established on the same grounds, and concluding, ". . . of no existence can we be more sure than of the existence of the Being absolutely infinite or perfect, that is to say God."[78]

Before focusing on the thematic contours of terms that ibn Sīnā utilizes in "(V3P2)," we shall approach the genesis of the argument by turning to the contemporary remarks of two scholars who have discussed ibn Sīnā's corpus in the context of mysticism.

In his classic work, *Mysticism, Sacred and Profane,* R. C. Zaehner differentiates between two kinds of mysticism, "monism" and "theism." Whereas one of the essential features of "monism" is its method of "integration," the essential feature of "theism" is its method of "isolation." By way of clarifying "monism," Zaehner remarks, "The nature mystic identifies himself with the whole of Nature, and in his exalted moments sees himself as being one with Nature and as having passed beyond good and evil."[79] Of a version of isolation, Zaehner states: "It [isolation] holds that man's spirit is an immortal, immutable and passionless monad, and that neither the body nor the reason, nor what Aristotle and the Muslim philosophers call the lower soul, really belong to him. He is essentially other than they, and his eternal destiny is to rid himself forever of the whole psycho-physical apparatus. This is the reverse of integration. There is no vision of the unity of man with Nature, nor is it a case of this vision being utilized to build up the whole man."[80] In commenting on ibn Sīnā, Zaehner points out, "Avicenna, and following him most of the Muslim writers in psychology, distinguished two distinct parts in the human soul—the higher or rational soul which naturally strives upward and whose goal is the acquisition of knowledge of God, and the lower soul usually called the *nafs* or 'self' which is tripartite, being composed of the imagination, anger, and lust. These three are indissolubly attached to the rational soul, and no escape from them is possible or even desirable during this life."[81] Subsequently Zaehner's statement is actually corroborated by *Ishārāt* (IV, 125). Zaehner quotes relevant passages from ibn Sīnā's *Ḥayy ibn Yaqẓān,* which disclose that ibn Sīnā recommends accepting the lower faculties in recognition of the disaster that may result if one attempts to suppress them altogether. Zaehner reaches the conclusion, "Thus, for Avicenna as for Jung, integration of the personality was man's first aim on earth, and his lower soul does not seem to differ greatly from Jung's collective unconscious."[82] In several representative cases of Islamic mysticism Zaehner examines, there is no question but that a person is not only essentially related to God as implied by "(V3P2)," but that the statements uttered suggest an identity of persons with God. In describing these cases, Zaehner (an adherent of religious theism), follows a roundabout interpretation of the passage in question until he finally labels the entire tradition as confusing and derivative. Nevertheless, a strong support for the presence of "(V3P2)" in the Islamic tradition, to which ibn Sīnā belongs, is offered by the quotations Zaehner selects, such as the following:

> This is probably what Junayd, the founder of the 'middle' school of Muslim mysticism, meant when he spoke of his ecstatic (one is tempted to say 'maniac') predecessor, Abū Yazid of Bistām, as having reached the first stage only on the mystic's path when he made such astonishing statements as 'I am He', and 'Glory be to me,

> how great is my glory,' implying thereby that he was actually identical with the Deity.[83]

Zaehner sides, of course, with Junayd, who asserts that Abū Yazid's utterances are only a way of talking about a union permissible according to religious laws, rather than the problem of identity, or about Ghazālī's designation of such states as mystical intoxications. Nevertheless, even Ghazālī acknowledges this to be a very interesting description of mysticism, which corresponds closely to "(V3P2)." Ghazālī notes accordingly,

> The mystics, after their ascent to the heavens of Reality (Truth), agree that they saw nothing in existence except God. Some of them attained this state through discursive reasoning, others reached it by savouring it and experiencing it.[84]

He continues as follows,

> Nothing was left to them [the mystics] but God. They became intoxicated with an intoxication in which their reason collapsed. One of them [Ḥallāj] said, 'I am God (the Truth.)' Another [Abū Yazid] said, 'Glory be to me! How great is my glory,' while another said, 'Within my robe is naught but God.'[85]

Ghazālī goes on to show how "identity" actually refers to a union in this context, disclosing at the same time that there are truths in these sayings which he was not at liberty to reveal.[86]

Evidently, according to Zaehner's scheme, ibn Sīnā's position supports "(V3P2)" in the following manner: (i) ibn Sīnā's normative psychology is the foundation of an ethical system which is remarkably similar to that of nature mystics who consider man's essential task to be the recognition of his unity with nature—God, a unity that is to be achieved by integration; and (ii) ibn Sīnā does not stand in isolation but is part of a Muslim tradition embracing many mystics who have claimed an identity with God (Zaehner would prefer "nature" to "God") and affirmed that knowledge of one's self-soul leads to knowledge of God.

J. Houben is another scholar to claim that there is a difference between what he designates as true "religious" mysticism and the naturalistic mysticism of ibn Sīnā.[87] He points out that inherent in ibn Sīnā's depiction of the chain of being connecting God and man is a nonreligious monism.[88] In relating the (mystical) knowledge of God (*ma'rifat Allāh*) to ibn Sīnā, Houben notes,

> The fact which glares into our eyes is that the highest knowledge and beatitude of man is of the same nature as the usual human knowledge, though pitched to a higher degree. The highest degree, this *ma'rifat Allāh* consists therein that the mystic firstly sees in his own soul as in a mirror the intelligibles which are traces of the Divine Truth, and further in the higher stage it perceives as reflected object, God's Truth Itself.[89]

Houben mentions that this knowledge of God, received from one's own soul, is for ibn Sīnā another case of intellectual contemplation, as the soul has no (will) for God but to be reflected like a polished mirror.[90]

It appears then that Houben's account corroborates our proposal that there is some evidence that ibn Sīnā supports "(V3P2)." Having established the nature of the support of our position, let us now discuss a few important passages in ibn Sīnā's texts which specifically disclose his adherence to "(V3P2)."

At the outset we wish to establish that in no single passage does ibn Sīnā present one concise proof with "(V3P1)," "(V3P2)," and "(V3C)" following each other in sequence. The first premise, "(V3P1)," occurs only in his psychology, but as we have shown, nowhere does ibn Sīnā entertain doubts about the existence of at least one actual entity, for time and again he refers to the fact that existence (*wujūd*) is an obvious primary datum for the soul (*nafs*) and for the intelligence (*'aql*). The problem of doubting the existence of entities is not the problem of ibn Sīnā, the medieval philosopher. The second premise emerges out of the fundamental metaphysical doctrines designated as (ibn Sīnā 4) and (ibn Sīnā 5) which we shall illustrate as follows:

(Ibn Sīnā 4): The Necessary Existent is not a sustance (*jawhar*).

If the knowledge of one's own existence is to be essentially related to the knowledge of the existence of the Necessary Existent, certain conditions must be absent. For instance, if the individual existent and the Necessary Existent are substances of such difference that no total description of the individual in the Leibnizian sense will involve a reference to the Necessary Existent, then the individual will need something in addition to himself to obtain knowledge of the Necessary Existent. Consequently, both the Necessary Existent and the individual could not be two substances totally independent of each other. But in his metaphysical writings, as has been shown in our previous studies, ibn Sīnā (i) asserts explicitly that the necessary Existent is not a substance (*Dānish Nāmeh,* pp. 56-57); (ii) affirms that certain features, e.g., "genus," "differentia," "having no subject," which apply to ordinary substances, do not apply to the Necessary Existent (e.g., *al-Shifā',* p. 347; *al-Ishārāt,* III, 53; *al-Najāt,* pp. 226-27); (iii) explicitly rejects the notion that the Necessary Existent is a substance proper, to which one can apply "substantiality" and merely mean thereby that it is not in a subject (*al-Shifā',* p. 348, p. 367; *al-Najāt,* p. 231); and (iv) lists substances but never includes among such a list the Necessary Existent (*al-Najāt,* p. 208; *Dānish Nāmeh,* p. 16; *al-Shifā',* p. 60). In contradistinction to this view stands that of Aristotle, who regards God (θεῖὸς) as an *ousia,* a term usually translated as substance, which ibn Sīnā identifies with *jawhar.*[91]

(Ibn Sīnā 5): The concept of the world is essentially contained in the concept of the Necessary Existent.

Going beyond our attempt to ascertain how knowledge of ourselves implies knowledge of this particular nonsubstance type of entity, we note that ibn Sīnā's metaphysical system contains principles which make the specification of the concept of all actual entities dependent upon certain features of the Necessary Existent, such that our knowledge of actual entities implies concurrent knowledge of the Necessary Existent.

The essential features of reality (*ḥaqq*), particularity (*khuṣūṣiyya*), necessity (w*ājibi*), and even the demonstrable reason (*burhān*) for all things are found in the notion of the Necessary Existent as it is portrayed by ibn Sīnā. For example, at the beginning of a chapter titled "that the Necessary Existent is a reality in all the meanings of reality," ibn Sīnā asserts that in its essence *(dhāt)* the Necessary Existent is absolute reality and truth (*ḥaqq*), for the essence of each thing (*shai'*) is the instantiation (particularization—*khuṣūṣiyya*) of its existence by the agent of its actualization (*yathbat*). There is no reality (*ḥaqq*) that is more real than the Necessary Existent, and a belief in its existence (w*ujūd*) is truthful according to ibn Sīnā *(al-Shifā'*, p. 356; *al-Najāt*, p. 229).

In *al-Shifā'* (p. 356), ibn Sīnā repeats verbatim the assertion made in *al-Najāt* that the Necessary Existent is reality (*ḥaqq*) and that the reality of everything is the particularization (*khuṣūṣiyya*) which instantiates *(yathbata)* that entity; he affirms again that this is the most true belief one can hold. Prior to this assertion he lists terms related to the Necessary Existent by privation and proceeds to acknowledge that there is no demonstration (*burhān*) for the Necessary Existent, while the latter is necessary to the demonstration of other entities (*al-Shifā'*, p. 354). In ensuing passages he identifies the Necessary Existent with absolute perfection *(fawq al-tamām)*, for all entities flow (*fāḍil*) and emanate (*fa'iḍ*) from it. It is further identified with existence (*huw al-wujūd*) or the perfection of existence (*al-kamāl al-wujūd*). Existence is a good (*khair*) and the Necessary Existent, as the perfection of existence, is the Good of all existence (*al-Shifā'*, p. 356). The notion that the Necessary existent is the absolutely perfect entity is mentioned also in tile *Dānish Nāmeh* (pp. 79-80) following the account of the emanation of first entities. Entities are either imperfect (*nāqiṣ*, perfect (*tamām*), or absolutely perfect (*fawq al-tamām*). While the imperfect entity cannot exist by itself, and while the perfect entity can and does exist by itself, the absolutely perfect entity alone can exist by itself and be at the same time the source of the realization of all other entities. In this sense, ibn Sīnā's argument implies that as an absolutely perfect entity, the Necessary Existent is without will, since will is analyzed by knowledge and acts as the source from which the world emanates. However, as imperfect entities (e.g., in Descartes' sense of knowing himself as a finite entity), our understanding of our own realization must be due to knowledge of the existence of an absolutely perfect entity.

This essential dependence relation is corroborated in the context of many other themes fundamental to ibn Sīnā's philosophy. Two such themes are two aspects of causality which are often overlooked when the medieval thinkers emphasize a new dimension of the notion of the final cause in their description of the relationship between persons and the ultimate being:

(a) As the first sense of a cause ibn Sīnā establishes the beholder, operative for instance in the case of the house and the laws governing the element's physics as well as in the case of elements which compose the entity in question (*Dānish Nāmeh,* p. 50). The cause, ibn Sīnā repeats, is that which necessitates (*wājib*) the persistence (*istādan*) of the entity in question, namely, the house. Now the Necessary Existent appears repeatedly in ibn Sīnā's texts (*Dānish Nāmeh*, p. 81; *al-Shifā',* p. 363; *al-Najāt*, p. 249) as the knower of the Good Universal Order (*al-Niẓām al-khair kulli*) in existents, whose will for the realization of the actual world is identical with its knowledge. In the ibn Sīnian system, as a result of its knowledge of the laws, the Necessary Existent is the beholder and the cause of the persistence of actual entities. Consequently, a discursive a priori knowledge of ourselves, if it includes the knowledge of the cause of our persistence, includes also a knowledge of the existence of the Necessary Existent. This doctrine, moreover, is embedded in the Spinozistic axiom, "The knowledge (*cognitio*) of an effect depends upon and involves the knowledge of the cause."[92]

(b) A cause can also be a cause of perfection (*kamāl*), depicted for instance in the *Risāla fī al-'ishq*,[93] where all entities are specified in terms of love, which leads them to complete their own perfection; here the ultimate perfection is identified with The Good (*al-Khair*) [*'ishq*, 21 (*khair maḥḍ*)], an absolute entity, which many passages identify with the Necessary Existent [*Dānish Nāmeh*, p. 80 (*khair*); *al-Najāt*, p. 229 (*khair maḥḍ*); *al-Shifā'*, p. 355 (*khair*)]. Accordingly, in the normative sense, our own concept of the perfect self implies the notion of the absolutely perfect entity as the cause of our completion—namely, the Necessary Existent.

Among the positions held on this issue is one that would make the conception of the Necessary Existent dependent on the conception of what emanates from it. Since features of the Necessary Existent include absolute perfection and being the cause of the realization of others (i.e., of the actual contingent world), a complete conception of the Necessary Existent will include the conception of entities in the actual world. Perhaps it is for this reason that Spinoza specifically begins with the following definition of substance. "By substance I understand that which is in itself and is conceived through itself; in other words, that, the conception of which does not need the conception of another being from which it must be formed."[94] Measured by this concept of substance, the ibn Sīnian version of the human soul-person is not a substance because the Necessary Existent ultimately defines its formulation, and is its ultimate cause. On the other hand, the Necessary Existent and the entire actual realm form one substance because of their interdependence through the various features of the Necessary Existent (e.g., "Absolute perfection," "being the beholder of the world," and "being the ultimate cause of the completion or the perfection of each entity"). This position is actually upheld by Spinoza when the One substance, namely God, is identified with Nature; he asserts that a substance is necessarily infinite (Proposition VIII), and that apart from God, no substance can be conceived (Proposition XIV). As we already pointed out for Descartes, in the strictest sense of the concept of substance, there is actually one substance which Spinoza identifies with God when he asserts, "There can indeed be only one substance conceived as needing absolutely no other thing in order to exist; namely, God. We can see that all other substances are able to exist only by means of God's co-operation."[95]

Moreover, we have already had occasion to point out in another study that the Self is to be united with the Necessary Existent—a concept which appears confusing in a substance-event language interpretation of the ibn Sīnian system but becomes workable in a process-language interpretation of his system.[96] That a reference to the Necessary Existent is essentially embedded as an essential constituent of a person becomes manifest when one considers the Neoplatonic delineation of the mystical return, which is the undergirding of the ibn Sīnian system. In the *Dānish Nāmeh*, "*paivand*" (union) describes how the ultimate happiness of a person lies in a union (*paivand*) with the Necessary Existent (pp. 71-76). The term union (*ittiḥād, muttaḥid)* is used both in *al-Najāt* and in the *Risāla fī al-'ishq*. In the former, it designates the aim of the rational soul to be united (*muttaḥid*) with the beloved (*al-Najāt,* p. 293); in the latter, *ittiḥād* is used by mystics to refer to a means of attaining perfection by approximating that of the absolute Good (The Necessary Existent) (*'Ishq*, p. 22).

(c) In *al-Ishārāt* (III, 53), there is another striking passage in which an equally affirmative feature of the Necessary Existent emerges. Here ibn Sīnā asserts that the only way in which one can indicate or point to (*ishāra*) the Necessary Existent is by way of mystical intelligence (*al-'irfān al-'aqlī*).

But a close reading of his text fails to reveal any one passage in which he explicitly asserts that the soul does in fact preserve its individuality. In an interesting passage in *al-Ishārāt*, he states that the rational soul (*al-'aql al-nāṭiqa*) does not become the soul of the active intelligence (*al-'aql al-fa'āl*), and notes specifically that it becomes connected (*ittiṣāl*) with the active intelligence (*al-Ishārāt,* p. 293).

In sum, it appears that monistic system emerges in which the concept of the Necessary Existent is implied in the concept of every actual entity, that is, in the individual whose self-knowledge is phenomenal a priori, whereas the knowledge of the Necessary Existent is discursive a priori; Necessary Existence here is part of the complete description of the subject in the Leibnizian form.

CONCLUDING REMARKS

Evidently, several key passages in ibn Sīnā's metaphysical texts, when carefully considered in the light of his fundamental philosophical doctrines, do in fact support the second version of the ontological argument. It is remarkable that no philosophical system which supports the ontological argument (e.g., those of Augustine, ibn Sīnā, Anselm, Descartes, Spinoza, Malcolm, and Taylor) can adequately respond to the devastating criticism by Hume and Kant of all ontological arguments. We deem these arguments logically unsatisfactory—valuable only for the pedagogical study of metaphysical concepts used in the argument itself.

Its logical inadequacy notwithstanding, a more important aspect of God's existence has yet to be "proven." We note with Augustine, and perhaps with many others, that the search for knowledge of God is closely tied to the quest for self-knowledge; both are considered to be primary objects of inquiry. Moreover, many religiously inclined philosophers, e.g., H. D. Lewis, envision the so-called "infinite" basis of the "finite" self as the core of religious experience and reject the experiential significance of the ontological argument. In this vein Lewis notes that in religious experience ". . . wondering and stilled appreciation of finite facts . . . [have] an infinite or transcendent source. . . ."[97] Following such a train of thought, we explored the possibility of constructing an argument which takes account of the phenomena felt to be significant by those taking a religious perspective, but can be aligned, at the same time, with a systematic philosophical perspective. Accordingly, we depicted a third version of the ontological argument and clarified its premises by drawing on the works of well-known philosophers who have addressed themselves to the issues in question. We demonstrated, moreover, that ibn Sīnā's metaphysical system contains doctrines of great consequence to the depiction of the premises of the argument under consideration. In spite of its "mystical monism," which is in agreement with the views of many Muslim mystics, as pointed out by Zaehner, Houben, and our own previous inquiry, ibn Sīnā's monism is unacceptable to the devout on account of its naturalistic presentation of the world, which conflicts with "religion" in the sense we have specified.[98] Moreover, we have rejected the notion of essence, the assumption about the predictability of existence, and the significance attached to the application of "necessity" to "things" on the grounds that they are philosophically inadequate.

In conclusion, we turn once more to Augustine's quest, a quest he limited to obtaining knowledge of "God" and "his own self-soul" and to the answer given in an old Arabic proverb saying, "He who knows himself, knows his God," as well as to the answer given by the mystic Ḥallāj, "I am God-Reality." Obviously, neither Augustine nor contemporary religious philosophers such as Zaehner and Lewis would find these answers acceptable.

Notwithstanding the clarification of ibn Sīnā's texts and the philosophical analysis of a few concepts proffered in this essay, we have little to offer except to note that all three forms of the ontological argument fail—the first two being at least logically inadequate, and the third being unacceptable to religious systems, its mystical insights notwithstanding. But such a failure should not be viewed as a shortcoming—for a legitimate application of philosophy to theology is not to justify the dogmas of the latter, but to analyze its significant problems openly and to disclose by such probing whether a rational reconstruction of a phenomenon which is important for religious experience is found to be in conflict with traditionally approved religious maxims.

NOTES

* Originally published in *Islamic Philosophical Theology*, Parviz Morewedge, (Albany: State University of New York Press, 1979).

1 *The Many-Faced-Argument,* ed. John H. Hick and Arthur C. McGill, (New York: Macmillan), 1967, p. vii.
2 *The Ontological Argument,* ed. Alvin Plantinga, (New York: Doubleday, 1965); hereinafter all references to this text will be cited as *OA* and will be preceded by the name of the individual contributor. R. Taylor, *OA,* vii.
3 *Philosophy of Religion,* ed. George L. Abernethy and Thomas A. Lanford, (New York: Macmillan, 1969), p. 170.
4 *St. Anselm: Basic Writings,* trans. S. N. Deane and intro. C. Hartshorne, (La Salle: Open Court, 1963), p. 1; (hereinafter cited as *St. Anselm*).
5 Originally appeared in *The Philosophical Review*, LXIX, no. 1 (January, 1960), pp. 41-62. We shall make reference to its printed version in *OA*.
6 Malcolm, *OA*, 136.
7 For the rejection of the first version, see Malcolm, *OA*, 140; for his defense of the second version, see *OA,* 141-157. In a counterattack on Kant's criticism of "existence as a predicate" doctrine, Malcolm states, "To these remarks [Kant's] the reply is that when the concept of God is correctly understood one sees that one cannot 'reject the subject.' 'There is no God' is seen to be a necessary false statement" (*Ibid.*, p. 148).
8 P. Morewedge, "Ibn Sīnā (Avicenna) and Malcolm and the Ontological Argument," *The Monist* 54, no. 2 (April 1970): 234-49.
9 For example, Anselm states, "And, indeed, we believe that Thou art a being than which nothing greater can be conceived," and proceeds to argue against the objection of the fool who said in his heart that there is no God, concluding, "Hence, even the fool is convinced that something exists in understanding, at least, than which nothing greater can be conceived. For, when he hears of this, he understands it." *St. Anselm,* 7-8. Another classical occurrence of this theme is in the fifth meditation of Descartes, where he states, "I assuredly find in myself the idea of a God—of a supremely perfect being—no less than the idea of a figure or a number" (*Descartes, Philosophical Writings,* trans. and ed. E. Anscombe and P. T. Geach with intro. A. Koyre, London, 1963, p.103; hereinafter cited as *Descartes, A. and G.*, followed by the page

number from this text.) There are at least two forms of this first premise: a syntactical one which defines the notion of God as that which is the most perfect being and an epistemic one which states that there is an idea of God in our minds than which nothing greater can be conceived. The syntactical version assumes that the concept is not logically contradictory; the epistemic version is rather vague, for the ability to conceive an idea is a psychological matter, which varies from person to person and cannot serve as a universal a priori truth.

10 Anselm argues, "And assuredly that, than which nothing greater can be conceived, cannot exist in the understanding alone. For suppose it exists in the understanding alone: then it can be conceived to exist in reality; which is greater." *St. Anselm*, p. 8.

11 *New Essays Concerning Human Understanding by Gottfried Wilhelm Leibniz*, trans. A. Gideon Langley, (La Salle: Open Court, 1949), includes one version of Leibniz' objection. He notes, "It [the ontological argument] is not a paralogism, but it is an imperfect demonstration, which assumes something that must still be proved in order to render it mathematically evident; that is, it is tacitly assumed that this idea of all-great or all-perfect being is possible, and implies no contradiction. And it is already something that by this remark it is proved that, *assuming that God is possible, he exists*, which is the privilege of the divinity alone. . . . The other argument of Descartes, which undertakes to prove the existence of God because of the idea of him in our soul, and must have come from the same origin, is still less conclusive. For in the first place this argument has this defect, in common with the preceding, that it assumes that there is in us such an idea, i.e. that God is possible" (p. 504; hereinafter we shall cite this text as "Leibniz, *New Essays*," followed by the appropriate page number).

12 Kant states that "'being' is obviously not a real predicate; that is, it is not a concept of something which could be added to the concept of a thing. It is merely the positing of a thing, or of certain determinations, as existing in themselves. Logically, it is merely the copula of a judgment. The proposition, 'God is omnipotent' contains two concepts, each of which is its object—God and omnipotence. The small word 'is' adds no new predicate, but only serves to posit the predicate *in its relation* to the subject. If, now, we take the subject (God) with all its predicates (among which is omnipotence), and say 'God is,' or 'There is a God,' we attach no new predicate to the concept of God, but only posit the subject in itself with all its predicates, and indeed posit it as being an object that stands in relation to my concept" (Immanuel

Kant's *Critique of Pure Reason*, trans. N. Kemp Smith, London: Macmillan, 1953, pp. 504-505).

13 Hume's basic premise is that "all the perceptions of the mind are of two kinds, *viz.*, impressions and ideas, which differ from each other only in their different degrees of force and vivacity. Our ideas are copied from our impressions, and represent them in all their parts" (*A Treatise of Human Nature*, ed. L. A. Selby-Bigge, London, 1964, p. 96). A similar passage is found in *Enquiry Concerning Human Understanding* and *Enquiry Concerning the Principles of Morals*, ed. L. A. Selby-Bigge, (London, 1955), p. 18. In the *Enquiry* he divides "all objects of human reason" into relations of ideas and matters of fact (p. 25). Subsequently he states that ". . . nor can our reason, unassisted by experience, ever draw any inference concerning real existence and matters of fact" (p. 27). Since existence types-of-statements are matters and a priori types-of-statements, e.g., "(VIPI)" and "(VIP2)" are claimed by "reason alone," then the entire argumentation is not legitimate, according to Hume.

14 Hume states, "Our ideas reach no further than our experience: We have no experience of divine attributes and operations: I need not conclude my syllogism: You can draw the inference yourself" (*Dialogues Concerning Natural Religion,* ed. N. Kemp Smith, New York, 1947, pp. 142-43). Consequently, Hume questions the claim that we have an idea of a most perfect being. In this vein Hume argues against Descartes' claim of calling an "innate idea" of a deity the source of power, "For if every idea be derived from an impression, the idea of a deity proceeds from the same origin; and if no impression, either of sensation or reflection, implies any force or efficacy, 'tis equally impossible to discover or even imagine any such active principle in the deity" (*Treatise,* p. 160). Here Hume hints that the idea of a deity must be also derived from impressions and cannot be postulated as the source of power. The previous quotations question whether there is an impression of a divine attribute. In another passage in the *Treatise,* Hume attends to "existence" as applied to a deity, saying that, "Thus when we affirm, that God is existent, we simply form the idea of such a being, as he is represented to us; nor is the existence, which we attribute to him, conceived by a particular idea, which we join to the idea of his other qualities, and can again separate and distinguish from them. But I go farther; and not content with asserting, that the conception of the existence of any object is no addition to the simple conception of it, I likewise maintain, that the belief of the existence joins no new ideas to

those, which compose the idea of the object. When I think of God, when I think of him as existent, and when I believe him to be existent, my idea of him neither increases nor diminishes" (*Treatise*, p. 94). Consequently for Hume, God cannot be defined in terms of a source of power or as any entity of which we have no impression; merely postulating that "God exists" does not add any reality to God; and, moreover, at least according to one of the three figures in *The Dialogues Concerning Natural Religion,* we have no impression of an attribute of God.

15 *Malcolm, OA,* 140.

16 *Ibid.,* 147.

17 See P. Morewedge, "Ibn Sīnā (Avicenna), Malcolm, and the Ontological Argument."

18 Hume asserts, "The contrary of every matter of fact is still possible; because it can never imply a contradiction, and is conceived by the mind with the same facility and distinctness, as if ever so conformable to reality" (*Enquiry*, p. 25).

19 Kant states, "But if, on the other hand, we admit that all existential propositions are synthetic, how can we profess to maintain that the predicate of existence cannot be rejected without contradiction? This is a feature which is found only in analytic propositions, and is indeed precisely what constitutes their analytic character" (*Critique of Pure Reason*, p. 504).

20 See P. Morewedge, "Philosophical Analysis and ibn Sīnā's 'Essence-Existence' Distinction," *Journal of the American Oriental Society* 92:3 (July-September 1973), 425-435.

21 The *Dānish Nāmeh 'ali (Ilāhiyyāt)*, ed. M. Mo'in, Tehran, 1952. Page references to this text are taken from my own translation of this work in P. Morewedge, *The Metaphysica of Avicenna* (*ibn* Sīnā), (London: Routledge and Kegan Paul; New York: Columbia University Press, 1973; hereinafter all references to this text will be cited as *Dānish Nāmeh*, followed by the page number taken from my text.

22 *Al-Najāt*, (Cairo: Muḥyi al-Din al-Kurdi Press, 1938).

23 *Al-Shifā': Al-Ilāhiyyāt* (*La Metaphysique*), ed. G. Anwati, M. Y. Mussa, S. Dunya, and S. Zayed, 2 vols., (Cairo, 1960); hereinafter all references to this text will be cited as *Al-Shifā'*.

24 *Al-Ishārāt wa-l-Tanbihāt*, ed. S. Dunya, 4 vols., (Cairo, 1960).

25 N. Rescher, *Studies in Arabic Philosophy*, (Pittsburgh: University of Pittsburgh Press, 1966), p. 73. An adequate symbolization of the ibn Sīnian system is difficult if not impossible to obtain. If we let "a" be any in-

dividual first substance and "Φ" a genuine predicate, then if "Φa" is true, then "E!a"—meaning that affirming a genuine predicate of a subject—implies existence of the subject. Consequently no affirmative predication can be made of nonactualized entities like unicorns or "the king of France." There is no difficulty in this part of the theory. However, then we note that no adequate symbolism for the Necessary Existent can be found, for if it is not an individual substance we must conclude that the same sign cannot be applied to individuals, such as Zayd, and The Necessary Existent. See also Aristotle, *Analytica Posteriora,* 71a 20-23. All references to Aristotle will be cited from *The Works of Aristotle,* ed. W. D. Ross, 12 vols., (London, 1908-52), unless differently indicated in the notes.

26 Aristotle mentions in *Analytica Posteriora* 71a 10-13, "The preexistent knowledge required is of two kinds. In some cases admission of the fact must be assumed, in others comprehension of the meaning of the terms used, and sometimes both assumptions are essential." The passage cited indicates that in each science one begins with a set of assumptions concerning the existence of a subject matter for the inquiry in question. In metaphysics, it is not immediately assumed that "The Necessary Existent" is apprehended prior to any other notion, but since we comprehend "existence" (*wujūd*) and "necessity" (*wājibi*) as primary terms, metaphysical analysis teaches us that "the Necessary Existent" is a meaningful notion which has certain features—the most important of which is that the Necessary Existent exists. In modern axiomatical methods a similar procedure is adopted. For example, Carnap notes that the axioms and theorems of an axiomatic system, AS, assume certain constants (names) as "axiomatic constants." Then he continues. "Some of them [the axiomatic constants of the AS] are given without definitions; they are called *the axiomatic primitive constants of the AS.* All other axiomatic constants are introduced by definitions on the basis of the primitives" (*Introduction to Symbolic Language and Its Application,* tr. W. H. Meyer and J. Wilkinson, New York: Dover, 1958, p. 171). In the Carnapian sense, "being" or "existence" and modalities such as "necessity" are *axiomatic primitive constants.* Thereafter a rule of formation specifies that "being" and "existence" can legitimately be concatenated. Finally, theorems about "the Necessary Existent" are deduced. In this context the ontological argument in an a priori sense is deduced without the use of any nonprimitive and observable datum.

27 Gaunilon's objections to Anselm capitalize on the factual aspects of the argument (*St. Anselm,* p. 146). Accordingly on behalf of "the fool,"

Gaunilon makes a difference between the temporal state of "the having of an object in the understanding—and what is subsequent in time—namely, the understanding that an object exists; . . ." But an analytical formulation of the problem moves the argument into an atemporal aspect which is nonempirical, cf. the difference between an atemporal "category" and a temporal "schema" in Kant.

28 St. Thomas Aquinas, *Summa Theologiae,* vol. 2, (New York: McGraw-Hill, 1964), p. 7.

29 *Ibid.,* pp. 5-6.

30 *Ibid.*

31 *Ibid.,* p. 9.

32 *Ibid.,* pp. 13-17.

33 P. Morewedge, "Ibn Sīnā's Concept of the Self," *Philosophical Forum,* IV, no. I (Fall 1972), pp. 49-73.

34 *Ockham, Philosophical Writings,* ed. and trans. P. Boehner, London: Nelson, 1967, p. 90. Here Ockham points out that in one sense (uno modo), being (ens) is associated with a concept that is common to all things. Moody clarifies Ockham's position by pointing out that, "'being' (ens), and the transcendental terms convertible with it, cannot, as Aristotle proves, be a genus or in a genus." Moody continues by noting that for Ockham, ". . . the subject matter of metaphysics is "being," and there is no term or concept prior to or more universal than 'being'" (Ernest A. Moody, *The Logic of William of Ockham,* New York: Russell and Russell, 1965, p. 118).

35 *'Uyūn al-Ḥikma,* ed. A. Badawi, (Cairo, 1952), p. 55.

36 The classical argument for the uniqueness of the Necessary Existent assumes that the Necessary Existent is a simple entity, for if it were a complex one, then its parts would be its causes. But it is the cause of itself; thus, it has no parts. Accordingly, if there were two different cases of the Necessary Existent, then each case would have an essential differentiating feature that would have to be accounted for in its essence. Now either each of these two differentiating features would come under the same essence, which would not make them two different features; or, each of these differentiating features would be unique and a necessary condition for the specification of each Necessary Existent—thereby the unique differentiating feature would be more necessary than the Necessary Existent as its necessary condition. Since these are the only two logical possibilities and both lead to absurdity, there cannot be two Necessary Existents. See *Dānish Nāmeh,* 54-55.

37 *Descartes, A. and G.*, p. 75.

38 Malcolm, *OA*, 142.

39 *The Philosophical Works of Descartes,* trans. E. S. Haldane and G. R. T. Ross, (London: Cambridge University Press, 1968), vol. II, p. 228.

40 *Ethics: preceded by On the Improvement of Understanding,* ed. J. Gutmann, (New York: Hafner, 1967), p. 41.

41 *Ibid.*, p. 60.

42 Ockham states, "The reason why the saints and others say that God is His very existence is this. God exists in such a manner that He cannot not exist; in fact, He exists necessarily; and He is not from something else." Ockham proceeds to show that there is a difference between God and all other entities since only He *necessarily* exists. *Ockham*, pp. 94-95.

43 R. Taylor, *Metaphysics*, (Englewood Cliffs: Prentice-Hall, 1963), p. 93.

44 Kant, *Critique of Pure Reason*, trans. N. Kemp Smith, New York: St. Martin's Press, 1965, p. 502.

45 A symbolization of Taylor's argument is as follows: Let "M" be "modalities," "N" be "is necessary," "C" be "is contingent," and "I" be "is impossible." Then, using ordinary logical signs, we translate his argument as follows:

$$(x)\ (Nx \vee Cx \vee Ix)$$
$$\exists x Cx$$
$$\underline{\sim\exists x Ix}$$
$$\therefore \exists x Nx$$

The scheme of this argument is obviously invalid. (Of course a more adequate symbolization of Taylor's argument would be in intentional logic, with modal signs that we shall not pursue here.) From the fact that "M" is divided into three classes and the second premise, it does not follow that the class corresponding to "(x) Nx" is not empty. In addition, the first premise assumes that "Necessity" can be applied to individuals—but in ibn Sīnā's system, at least, the Necessary Existent is not an individual.

46 C. D. Broad, "Leibniz' *Predicate-in-Notion Principle* and Some of its Alleged Consequences," *Theoria*, XV (1949), reprinted in H. G. Frankfurt, ed.; *Leibniz: A Collection of Critical Essays,* Modern Studies in Philosophy, (Garden City, 1972), pp. 4-5.

47 *Ibid.*

48 Malcolm, *OA*, 153.

49 A. Plantinga, *God and Other Minds,* (Ithaca: Cornell University Press, 1967), p. 26.

50 *Ibid.*, p. 64.
51 *Ibid.*, p. 271.
52 H. D. Lewis, *Our Experience of God*, (London: George Allen and Unwin, 1959), p. 41.
53 *Ibid.*, p. 112.
54 *Ibid.*, p. 289.
55 *Royal Institute of Philosophy Lectures*, vol. 2, 1967/8, ed. G. N. A. Vesey et al., (New York: St. Martin, 1969), p. 120.
56 *The Varieties of Religious Experience*, (New York: Collier Books, 1971), p. 377.
57 *Descartes, A. and G.*, pp. 105-106.
58 *Diogenes Laertius. Lives of Great Philosophers*, ed. and trans. R. D. Hicks, vol. 2, The Loeb Classical Library, (Cambridge: Harvard University Press, 1958), p. 515.
59 *Ibid.*
60 *On Free Choice of the Will*, trans. A. S. Benjamin and L. H. Hackstaff, (Indianapolis, 1964), p. 40.
61 John A. Mourant, *An Introduction to the Philosophy of Saint Augustine*, (University Park: Pennsylvania State University Press), 1964, p. 76.
62 *Ibid.*
63 *Descartes, A. and G.*, p. 69.
64 For example, we note a list of 3612 works on Descartes in G. Sebba, *Bibliographica Cartesiana*, (Hague: Martinus Nijhoff, 1964), where only the literature from 1800 to 1960 is considered. The most illuminating modern work on the subject in question is by J. Hintikka, "*Cogito*, Ergo Sum: Inference or Performance," *The Philosophical Review*, LXXI, I (January 1962), 3-32.
65 See A. M. Goichon, "The Philosopher of Being," in *Avicenna Commemoration Volume*, ed. V. Courtois, (Calcutta, 1956), pp. 109-110.
66 Augustine, *Free Will*, p. 71.
67 *Soliloquies*, II, 7, i, in *Basic Writings of Saint Augustine*, ed. W. J. Jones, vol. 1, (New York: Random House, 1948), p. 262.
68 *Ibid.*
69 *Ibid.*
70 *Descartes, A. and G.*, p. 85.
71 *Ibid.*, p. 186. Aristotle, *Physica*, Book III, B.
72 *Descartes, A. and G.*, pp. 186-87.
73 *Ibid.*, p. 192.
74 *Ibid.*, p. 107.
75 *Ibid.*, p. 106.

76 G. Leibniz, *New Essays Concerning Human Understanding*, p. 164.
77 *Ethics*, p. 45.
78 *Ibid.*, p. 50.
79 R. C. Zaehner, *Mysticism, Sacred and Profane*, (London: Oxford University Press, 1967), p. 109.
80 *Ibid.*, p. 125.
81 *Ibid.*, p. 106.
82 *Ibid.*
83 *Ibid.*, p. 114.
84 *Ibid.*, p. 157.
85 *Ibid.*, pp. 157-158.
86 *Ibid.*, p. 158.
87 J. J. Houben, "Avicenna and Mysticism," in *Avicenna Commemoration Volume*, p. 207.
88 *Ibid.*, p. 217. See also George F. Hourani, "Ibn Sīnā's Essay on the Secret of Destiny,"" *Bulletin of the School of Oriental and African Studies* XXIX, Part 1 (1966), pp. 25-48. In this important essay, as Hourani's penetrating analysis shows, ibn Sīnā holds adamantly to the complete determination of the world by God as due to the necessity of His nature.
89 *Ibid.*, p. 219.
90 *Ibid.*, p. 220.
91 See P. Morewedge, "Ibn Sīnā's Concept of the Self." Ibn Sīnā equates the Arabic "*jawhar*" with the Greek "ousia" when he lists the categories in the *Kitāb fi al-Ḥudūd* in *Tis Rasā'il*, (Cairo, 1908), defs. 3. 4 and in *Ishārāt* (II, 343-450) and *Dānish Nāmeh* chaps. 3, 47, and 55.
92 Spinoza, *Ethics*, p. 41.
93 "*Risāla fī al-'ishq*," ed. M. A. von Mehren in *Traités mystiques d'Aboū Ali al-Hosain b. Abdallāh b. Sīnā ou d'Avicenne; text arabe avec l'explication en français*, 3 vols., (Leiden, 1849).
94 Spinoza, *Ethics*, p. 41.
95 *Descartes, A. and G.*, p. 192.
96 See P. Morewedge, "Ibn Sīnā's Concept of the Self." The argument in question points out that whereas substances can never be united with each other in an ethics of process of self-realization, one process may merge into another process, e.g., a state-station (*ḥāl-maqām*) leads to another state-station (*ḥāl-maqām*) until the final unity (*tawḥid*) *is* achieved, which implies both the destruction of the personal ego (fanā') and the eternal persistence of what remains (*baqā'*).
97 H. D. Lewis, *Our Experience of God*, p. 289.

98 See P. Morewedge, "The Logic of Emanationism and Ṣūfism in ibn Sīnā," *Journal of the American Oriental Society,* 91, no. 4 (1972): 467-76 and 92, no. 1 (1972): 1-18. In this essay the conflict between ibn Sīnā's philosophy, and religion is discussed.

THE ANALYSIS OF "SUBSTANCE" IN ṬŪSĪ'S *LOGIC* AND IN THE IBN SĪNIAN TRADITION*

INTRODUCTION

ṬŪSĪ'S TEXT AND THE METHODOLOGY OF OUR INQUIRY

The aim of this paper is to clarify the salient features of a method by which Nāṣir al-Dīn Ṭūsī, a thirteenth century Iranian Muslim philosopher-scientist, presented an analytical exposition of the concept of "substance" (*jawhar*) in his fundamental text on logic.[1] Before we turn to the detailed analysis of this concept, let us note some of the striking features of this work.

The text bears the title *Asās al-Iqtibās,* hereafter cited as *Asās,* which can be translated as "Principles of Inference" or "Foundations of Learning (Deduction)." Examination discloses the work to be a Persian version of Aristotle's logical works as well as of Porphyry's *Isagoge* [εἰσαγωγή] (Introduction). In agreement with Rescher we note that as yet no major study has appeared on this important Persian version of Aristotle's logic, although it is well known among western scholars that Aristotle's logical works with their Porphyrian introduction have been extensively translated and commented upon in Syriac and Arabic.[2]

The reader should be warned at the outset not to expect from this text any attempt on Ṭūsī's part to "Persianize" the logical vocabulary already present in both Greek and Arabic; Ṭūsī follows the Arabic terminology closely. Even in the titles for his nine books, he uses both the transliteration of the Greek term and the Arabic term. Accordingly, the first book carries the double title *Isāghūjī*...a transliteration of the Greek εἰσαγωγή, and its Arabic version, *Madkhal,* both meaning "introduction." The other eight books in the collection follow the order for logical texts adopted by medievalists (the standard name for each text is given here, followed by Ṭūsī's Arabic usage): "Categories" (*Maqūlāt*), "Hermeneutics" (*'Ibārāt*), "Prior Analytics" (*Qiyās*), "Posterior Analytics" (*Burhān*), "Topics" (*Fadal*), "Sophistics" (*Mughāliṭah*), "Rhetoric" (*Khiṭābah*), and "Poetics" (*Shi'r*). Ṭūsī presents a detailed treatment of these topics in a text of approximately 600 pages, which, because of its size, the editor called a major work on logic in Islamic philosophy, second only to the *Manṭiq* of ibn Sīnā's *Shifā'*.[3] In comparing its size with ibn Sīnā's texts on logic (*manṭiq*) found in the two other encyclopedic texts, the *Dānish Nāmeh 'Ala'ī* and *al-Ishārāt wa al-Tanbīhāt*, we observe that it exceeds both in length.[4]

Extrinsic considerations alone point to the significance and the eminent position of this text in the corpus of logic in the peripatetic tradition of Islamic philosophy. But its deeper significance lies in the methodology to which Ṭūsī resorts in explaining "substance" and in its unusual display of his analytical ability, which enabled him to avoid difficulties inherent in some metaphysical approaches to this concept.

As the present inquiry concerns itself with the topic of substance, traditionally a part of metaphysics, but presented by Ṭūsī in a text on logic, we shall begin by examining some of the problems inherent in the Aristotelian notion of metaphysics. We shall then proceed to some parallel topics in tile works of other Islamic philosophers who preceded Ṭūsī in order to indicate that his work does not stand in isolation or show a break in the continuity of philosophical development in the Muslim tradition. The major part of this paper will consist of a systematic reconstruction of a philosophical scheme in which the notion of "substance," and the set of conceptual terms associated with it, can be formulated without the confusions that will be enumerated in the following sections of our introduction. We shall also turn to a few topics that appear in other works of Ṭūsī, in which he presents a view of substance that differs radically from the standard Aristotelian analysis of substance. Finally, we shall offer a few tentative conclusions about Ṭūsī's philosophy and voice a note of caution against the common practice of classifying philosophers by categories that, though pedagogically convenient, are not entirely accurate. Thus the usual estimates of Ṭūsī do not take account of his non-peripatetic works.

METAPHYSICS AND ITS SUBJECT MATTER

Since metaphysics is a branch of theoretical inquiry, we shall note here Aristotle's list of the principal types inquiry and point out some of the difficulties which have a bearing upon our discussion. Aristotle divides inquiries into three general kinds: theoretical (θεωρητική), practical (πρακτική), and productive (ποιητική).[5] The differences among them are attributed to differences in their aims. Whereas it is the aim of theoretical inquiries to arrive at true statements regardless of any pragmatic utility they have, it is the aim of practical inquiries to attain to those truths which correspond with proper desires.[6] Productive inquiries are concerned with the production of useful objects.[7] In order to determine the distinction between metaphysics and natural science (or physics), it is necessary to subdivide the theoretical sciences into three groups: natural science or physics (φυσική), mathematics (μαθηματική), and metaphysics, to which he refers by various terms.[8] Aristotle explains at some length the difference between natural science and mathematics. Whereas natural science investigates movable bodies in the actual world,[9] mathematics studies quantities, e.g., volume, surface, point and line, the relationships among quantities, and methodology.[10] For this reason the conceptual analysis of substance lies outside the domain of these disciplines.

Aristotle's renowned analysis of the scope of metaphysics is not without difficulties. The first problem, that he gives three different explanations of metaphysics without making their relationship clear, has been noted by scholars such as Ross, Owens, Merlan, and Jaeger and we shall not belabor it here.[11] Aristotle interprets metaphysics in three ways: first as "first philosophy" (η πρώτη φιλοσοφία) which studies "being qua being" (τὸ ὂν ᾗ ὄν), next as an inquiry into principles and causes (αρχάς καὶ αἰτιάς), and finally as theology (θελογική) which investigates God (θεῖος) as a motionless (ακί νητος), everlasting (εἰδος) entity.[12] The difficulty particularly relevant to our discussion is as follows. If we assert that metaphysics studies substances, it is not clear which substance is meant, e.g., a conceptual specification of "being qua being," a cause for the composition of entities, or an elementary part of the universe derived from the divine being. For this reason Owens agrees with Jaeger's observation that there are at least two contradictory notions concerning the subject matter of primary philosophy; the first concerns a notion about a supersensible or immobile being, while the second describes a notion about a general concept of being which applies to particulars.[13] The former relates to the notion of metaphysics as theology, whereas the latter belongs to metaphysics as ontology.

A second difficulty with Aristotle's theory of metaphysics resides in the question of the emptiness of metaphysics. Obviously, no sense impression can be used to prove that the objects of metaphysics exist. Even if we grant that natural science is a legitimate study because it deals with physical bodies, which we take to exist, and concede further that mathematics is legitimate because its concepts are abstracted by definition from these sensible movables, there is still no guarantee that metaphysics is not empty, for its objects are not related to sensible movables either conceptually or by definition. Consequently, metaphysics cannot be introduced as the science which investigates purely abstract concepts, because it may be meaningless to speak about entities which are in no way related to sense experience. If one takes such an empiricist position, the assertion that metaphysics is based upon abstractions from physics and mathematics will be beset by difficulty. One cannot claim, without presenting further arguments, to have an experience of entities such as "causality" and "God," as the well-known controversies over such topics would seem to prove. In sum, it is not entirely evident that metaphysics contains subject matter such as substances. Perhaps, instead of assuming the existence of substance, we should employ logic and analysis to clarify the proper uses of the terms that designate substance in a philosophical system.

In addition to the difficulty with metaphysics, questions related to the subject matter of physics pose another serious problem in Aristotle's philosophy. Ross, for instance, points out, "It cannot be said that in practice the distinction between physics and metaphysics is maintained by Aristotle, and it may be noted that the bulk of the *Physica* is what we should call metaphysics. It is not an inductive inquiry into natural law, but an a priori analysis of material things and events that befall them."[14]

Further difficulty may be encountered in the attempt to interpret the Aristotelian theory of natural science in the light of contemporary views on philosophy of science, as is illustrated by some of the doctrines of Hempel, Carnap, and other contemporary philosophers. If we accept their view that empirical sciences are concerned with observational statements, then we are at a loss to find a basis for such statements in Aristotle's theory of scientific inquiry.[15] Although the philosopher clearly recognizes the distinction between what may be called "observational-epistemic" terms, such as "perception-sensation" (ἄισησις), "experience" (ἐμπειρία), and "memory" (μνήμη), he does not extensively employ these terms in his discussions of science,[16] but relies heavily on two terms, 'ἐπιστημή' and 'νοῦς' for the description and the premises of "scientific knowledge." Neither one of these terms is a satisfactory component upon which to base an observational statement. ἐπιστημή is the ability to deduce true statements or to generate valid arguments, a task that a computer can perform for simple languages.[17] Aristotle states that of the two, the more important term for scientific knowledge is νοῦς, supposedly an infallible ability which is able to grasp the first principles.[18]

If we read Aristotle in the light of contemporary views on conditions that characterize "observational statements," we are faced with the following specific problems. Requirements for observational statements, such as confirmation and testability, rule out incorrigible and at the same time infallible first person statements, such as "I am in pain;" instead, these requirements apply to corrigible statements voiced by many persons, such as statements concerning the length of a rod based on the approximated measurements of several observers. According to Carnap's view, the idea of "observable" in an empirical science includes fallible cases of epistemic experiences, such as data received from measurements which have been approximated.[19] Measured by Carnapian criteria, Aristotle's notion of intuition cannot serve as an adequate basis for an empirical theory of science. It is beyond the scope of this paper to elaborate upon this point; we terminate this argument by pointing to the often-overlooked passage in which Aristotle states that "intuition" enters as an outside element and calls it a "divine" element.[20]

Most problematical, for our purposes, is not the logical difficulty mentioned, but the obscurity spelled out below, which is probably not unrelated to the other problems embedded in his concept of metaphysics and natural science. Aristotle fails to make a sharp distinction between "being" and "substance." This obscurity poses such acute difficulties, particularly the problem of substance, that several scholars like Owens and Hope do not employ the term "substance" in their translations of Aristotle's works, preferring neutral terms, such as "primary being" and "entity."[21] As we shall have occasion to note subsequently, this complication does not exist in Ṭūsī's work or in the works of other Muslim philosophers, who define their terms sharply. Perhaps one might argue that such thinkers did not reject Aristotle's framework as much as they clarified and specified the ambiguity found in the Aristotelian texts.

Consequently, the nature of metaphysics, which is supposed to investigate substance as well as the meaning of the term "substance," is not clarified by Aristotle's inquiry into metaphysics. Inasmuch as his definition of natural science labors under difficulty, and his anti-Platonic views preclude any contribution from mathematics to the study of "substance," we must look to his logic for an answer. When we turn to Aristotle's logical works, we note that his concept of the categories discussed in *Categoriae* is absent from his metaphysical treatise. Consequently, we are not in a position to make a definite connection between what may be called his logical and his metaphysical uses of the concept of substance as "οὐσία." Having acquainted ourselves with the major recognized problems and ambiguities related to the problem under consideration, let us leave the Aristotelian domain and investigate how some of these doctrines were received and modified by some of the significant predecessors of Ṭūsī in the Islamic cultural tradition.

NON-ARISTOTELIAN FEATURES OF METAPHYSICS IN ISLAMIC PHILOSOPHY

Ṭūsī's analytical treatment discussed in the next section should be seen against the background of some Aristotelian concepts and their modifications in Islamic philosophy. As has been observed by several writers, Islamic philosophers distinguished clearly between the meaning of the science of nature (*al-'ilm al-ṭabī'ī*), corresponding to the Greek φυσική, and metaphysics.[22] Like the Greeks, they embedded this distinction in the broader classification of a speculative or theoretical type of inquiry (*naẓarī*) and a practical kind of inquiry (*'amalī*).[23] However, more specific distinctions between the subclasses of inquiries are to be found in the texts of various philosophers. By mentioning this distinction and attributing it to Aristotle, Fārābī definitely demonstrates his awareness of it.[24] Calling physics "the science of nature," he contrasts it with the science which comes after (*mā ba'd*) nature, i.e., metaphysics.[25] Among Fārābī's well-known works, one finds a fourfold division of speculative inquiry into mathematics, the science of nature, metaphysics, and politics-civics.[26] In his most celebrated text on the subject, natural science is divided into eight parts and metaphysics into three parts. According to Fārābī, metaphysics investigates (1) the nature and characteristics of bodily existents, (2) the principles of demonstrations in particular sciences or metasciences, and (3) the nature of non-bodily existents.[27]

A more penetrating look at a newly edited text of Fārābī, a work on metaphysics of great significance, contains some points which are of particular import to this discussion.[28] In this work Fārābī explicitly distinguishes between "substance" (*jawhar*) and "being" (*mawjūd*).[29] He identifies substance with the Greek οὐσία and mentions that Aristotle, in his *Categoriae,* differentiates between "first substance" and "second substance."[30] His concept of substance, however, is obviously presented in a more detailed manner than Aristotle's. For example, he gives an analysis of one of the ordinary Arabic meanings of the term, "a precious entity," which does not appear in the Greek extended meaning of the term,[31] and states that the philosopher's applications of "substance" are derived from common usage—a theory for which we should look in vain in the works of Aristotle.[32] The care he takes in his analysis is notable, for instance, in the case of "being" (*wujūd*), when he admits the lack of an Arabic term corresponding to the Persian, Greek, and Sogdian equivalents of this concept and mentions, moreover, that philosophers writing in Arabic eventually resort to *wujūd* as a substitute.[33] Accordingly, his distinction between words taken from common usage by philosophers to enrich the philosophical vocabulary and the difficult concepts for which philosophers have invented words or have postulated novel usages is quite clear.

Another example of the modification the Aristotelian doctrines related to metaphysics underwent is found in the works of ibn Sīnā. Even the medieval writer ibn Khaldūn regards ibn Sīnā's treatment of the science of nature as an original doctrine in which the philosopher departs from the Aristotelian philosophy.[34] Before turning to an examination of ibn Sīnā's analysis of "inquiry," we should take notice of an ambiguity in the translation of "science," for which two common meanings exist: (1) "science" as a general area of inquiry which includes the productive and practical disciplines as well as physics, mathematics, and metaphysics, and (2) "science" as natural science in terms of physics (*'ṭabī'yyāt*). To designate the first set of inquiries, which resembles Aristotle's general doctrine of intellectual virtue, ibn Sīnā uses three terms: *'ilm, ḥikma,* and *dānish.* The last term is reserved for his Persian texts; as might be expected, either *'ṭabī'yyāt* or *al-'ilm al-ṭabī'ī* is employed in referring to the second category.[35]

Ibn Sīnā follows Aristotle's general division of theoretical sciences and distinguishes among three kinds of speculative inquiries: physics (*'ṭabī'yyāt*), mathematics or syntax (*riyāḍiyāt, farhang*), and metaphysics, variously designated, to which we shall attend next.[36]

The term *ilāhiyyāt* is regularly employed for metaphysics in most of ibn Sīnā's works.[37] However, in two texts, the Persian *Dānish Nāmeh 'Alāī* (*Ilāhiyyāt*) and the Arabic *'Uyūn al-Ḥikma,* a more specific formulation of metaphysics is presented. In the *Dānish Nāmeh* he uses *'ilm-i barīn* for metaphysics, which is translated into Persian as first science or inquiry; it is distinct from natural science and mathematics. He states further that *ilāhiyyāt,* also termed *'ilm-i rubūbiyya,* is a part (*para*) of yet another inquiry which he names *'ilm-i barīn,* the latter being a higher and more general inquiry than the former.[38] Similarly, in the *'Uyūn al-Ḥikma,* he mentions *al-falsafa alawwaliyya* (first philosophy) and its part (*juz'*) *al-falsafa al-ilāhiyya,* also known as *al-rubūbiyya,* which is identical with the term used in his Persian text.[39] These data, as well as the arguments found in the *Dānish Nāmeh* and the metaphysical texts of *al-Shifā', al-Najāt, al-Ishārāt wa al-Tanbīhāt* lend support to the following lemmata. It is legitimate to say that in some of his writings, ibn Sīnā postulates that metaphysics proper investigates "being" (*wujūd, hastī*) and topics that are abstract entities, depending neither in their conception (*tawahhum*) nor in their definition (*hadd*) upon material bodies. A branch of this discipline is theology, which examines the Necessary Existent (*wājib al-wujūd*).[40] This study follows logically the more abstract study of first philosophy proper, which includes the concept of substance. However, the more specific study is not a study of a substantial entity, for the Necessary Existent is not a substance. We may note then that some of the confusion observed in the Aristotelian system among the different senses of metaphysics has been avoided by ibn Sīnā.

In addition to this novel feature in the ibn Sīnian formulation, there is the suggestion of another new conception, which, however, is not supported by much evidence. In specifying mathematics, ibn Sīnā often refers to it as *riyāḍī,* as well as "an instructive science" (*ta 'līmī*), "an intermediate inquiry" (*miyānagī*), and as "syntax" (*farhang*).[41] The last designation is rather significant, for it implies that mathematics is a structural and axiomatic inquiry rather than a science dealing with mere quantities. Although Aristotle's works include investigations into music, astronomy, geometry, and arithmetic, ibn Sīnā's formulation of mathematical systems, as, for instance, in the *Shifā',* is far more elaborate than any one of these studies.

With respect to the natural sciences, a division of speculative inquiry, we find ibn Sīnā's treatment to be as extensive and elaborate as its Aristotelian counterpart.[42] Undoubtedly, ibn Sīnā's formulation is more original and substantial than Aristotle's, because of his familiarity with post-Aristotelian science, a topic which we shall omit from this essay. It is evident that in physics, as well as in metaphysics, Islamic philosophers like ibn Sīnā developed a more systematic view of inquiry. Consequently, we may claim that an Islamic philosopher, such as Ṭūsī, could have held an analytically more precise doctrine of substance than Aristotle, especially if the modifications that his predecessors adopted on the Aristotelian system were relevant to his analysis of the subject.

Before turning to Ṭūsī's own work, we should note that we have omitted ibn Sīnā's analysis of being and its relationship to substance from this discussion because we have dealt with these points in terms of his celebrated "essence-existence" distinction in another paper.[43] One of the conclusions reached in that essay is relevant to the present discussion, namely that the essence-existence distinction is to be applied to a distinction between a method of analysis of concepts and an inquiry into the nature of actual existents. The logical analysis of substance, as will be pointed out subsequently, belongs to the former type of inquiry. As we claimed in the aforementioned essay that ibn Sīnā's distinction is significant from the point of view of methodology, we affirm in this study that the present subject of inquiry falls into the continuous tradition indicated in the previous arguments as well as in the aforementioned study.

A RECONSTRUCTION OF ṬŪSĪ'S ANALYSIS OF SUBSTANCE

While Ṭūsī follows the traditional Peripatetics in the general format of his division of sciences, he demonstrates at the same time his originality in his detailed analysis of concepts related to substance. Let us take cognizance of the special features of his division of inquiries.

ṬŪSĪ'S REMARKS ON METAPHYSICS AND RELATED DISCIPLINES

The two terms Ṭūsī uses in *Asās* in referring to metaphysics in the peripatetic sense are *ilāhī* and *falsafa-i awwalī,* terms commonly used by Muslim philosophers (*Asās,* pp. 404-405, *et passim*). In his well known work on *The Naṣirean Ethics,* he refers to metaphysics as *ilāhī,* but—following Fārābī's usage as well—notes that it is a science which is also called "that which studies *mā ba'd al-ṭabī'iyya* (an Arabic transliteration of "metaphysics").[44]

Ṭūsī's debt to the Aristotelian doctrine as it was transmitted by the Arabic tradition also becomes apparent from a study of his vocabulary. For example, for every term he adopts for a branch of logic, he lists the Arabic word and a transliteration of the Greek term in the Arabic rather than the Persian version, although the text is written in Persian (*Asās,* pp. 34, 61, 186, 340, 515, 529, and 586). For instance, τοπικα is transliterated as *taubiqā*, in spite of the fact that its Persian transliteration, *tupikā* phonetically resembles the Greek term more closely.

Ṭūsī's recognition of Aristotle's importance is evident from his attempt to draw an important distinction between metaphysics and natural science. Of the many arguments he presents in this endeavor, he correctly attributes one to Aristotle, the doctrine that any science which is demonstrative, e.g., natural science, makes use of a middle term (το μέσον) assumed by it but analyzed by another demonstrative science of a higher level.[45] Ṭūsī notes, moreover, that if two sciences investigate objects at different levels, then they must be different. Upon observing that there are many divers entities, he cites "body" and "eternal movement" as examples of entities whose existence is presupposed by natural science, but whose nature is analyzed by metaphysics. Thereupon he concludes that metaphysics must be different from natural science since the former studies entities that are presupposed by the latter.[46]

Ṭūsī takes great care in his delineation of the sciences. He explains in great detail, in a section corresponding to Aristotle's *Analytica Posteriora,* that each science has a subject matter, a set of presuppositions, and certain problems in need of solution (*Asās,* p. 393). He also cites some special cases, such as the notion of a body (*jism*), drawing a distinction between a "natural body" (*jism-i tabīʿī*) and "an instructional [representation of a] body" (*jism-i ta ʿlīmī*) (*Asās,* p. 401). The former is the subject matter of natural science (*ʿilm-i ṭabī ʿī*), whereas the latter is the subject matter of the science of solids (*mujassamāt*).

Ṭūsī affirms that logic (*manṭiq*) is definitely a science (*ʿilm*) with a specific subject matter proper to it and that it investigates concepts of second intention, such as the universal, the particular, the essential (*dhātī*) and the accidental.[47] Concepts derived from first intentions are substance, accident (*ʿaraḍ*) unity, plurality, and related concepts (*Asās,* p. 399). It follows that logic uses "substance," but does not itself define "substance" specifically. This distinction is of utmost importance to philosophical analysis, for Ṭūsī's various uses of the concept of substance in different contexts illuminate the meaning of this concept more adequately than do attempts that limit themselves to defining this term. In his logical text, however, Ṭūsī commits an apparent contradiction when he specifies substance. Nevertheless, a closer investigation of the relevant passages establishes clearly that in the aforementioned contexts he does not employ logic in the narrow sense in which logic is used to construct proofs about universal predictions and similar topics, but rather, makes use of analysis in dealing with metalogical problems, as for instance, when he employs the concept of substance in order to distinguish between particulars and universals, these latter being mental concepts of the second intention. Interestingly enough, because Ṭūsī is forced to introduce new refinements into the use of the concept, he gives us a family of features that characterize concepts (such as substance) as no categorical style of definition had done previously. The various philosophical theories of meaning and the numerous definitions which explain the reasons for the success of this method are well known and need not be reiterated in a paper which intends to do no more than to investigate Ṭūsī's theory.[48]

NOTES ON THE USE OF *JAWHAR* (SUBSTANCE)

As has been pointed out, Fārābī uses *jawhar* for Aristotle's οὐσία, which is ordinarily translated as "substance." Parallels for such usage can be found in the works of many Muslim philosophers. For example, in his *Book of Definitions* ibn Sīnā names the first ten categories, attributes them to Aristotle, and equates the first category with substance (*jawhar*).[49] It appears that the term *jawhar* has been used uniformly as distinguished from *wujūd* in the Arabic texts; in Persian texts *gauhar* is distinct from *hastī*, having been introduced by ibn Sīnā chiefly through the usage he establishes in the *Dānish Nāmeh 'Alāī*.[50] Throughout the *Asās*—as well as in his other texts—Ṭūsī resorts to the Arabic-Persian term *jawhar*, even though the text is written in Persian and *gauhar* is directly derived from Middle Persian. Yet Ṭūsī's usage is not unconventional, for inspection of the works of the philosophers following ibn-Sīna will reveal that ibn Sīnā's Persian vocabulary, in this respect, did not find acceptance with philosophers such as Suhrawardī and Kāshānī.[51]

Jawhar, as one might expect, was regarded as the first substance belonging to the ten categories (*maqūlāt*). Since "being qua being" in Islamic peripatetic philosophy is held to be a general idea that includes even the concept of the categories, we shall focus our attention next on its analysis and proceed thereafter to more determinate theories, examining for each one the special uses of *jawhar*.

BEING QUA BEING

For Ṭūsī, the most common, general, and determinable term is "being" in the Aristotelian sense of "τὸ ὂν ᾗ ὄν." To this concept, in the ibn Sīnian sense of "*hash*," we shall turn next. Ibn Sīnā uses two words to designate "being qua being," *hastī* and *wujūd*. The former, *hastī*, is a Persian term to which he refers in *Dānish Nāmeh: Ilāhiyyāt* as the most determinable concept in the language.[52] Reason (*khirad*) recognizes that it is without definition (since it has neither a genus nor differentia) and description (since it is the most common notion).[53] Moreover, in this work ibn Sīnā identifies *anniyya* with *wujūd*. He clearly distinguishes *hastī* (being qua being), from *anniyya* and *wujūd* (existence).[54]

In his Arabic writings, however, ibn Sīnā uses the term *wujūd* to signify "being," as is illustrated in the celebrated passage in the first chapter of the *Ilāhiyyāt* of *a-Shifā'*, where he indicates that the primary ideas ("*ma'nā*," which can be translated as "εἶδος") are *mawjūd* ("existent"), *shāi'* ("thing"), and *ḍarūrī* ("necessary").[55] In this passage *mawjūd* does not appear as *the* most primary concept, but as one of the three most primary concepts.

Ṭūsī seems to follow the ibn Sīnian doctrine, which is expressed in *al-Shifā'* in more detail than in the *Dānish Nāmeh*. Ṭūsī asserts that most philosophers agree that there are intelligibles that are more common (*'āmm*) than the ten categories. Among such intelligibles he mentions two classes: (1) the class of "existence" (*wujūd*), "necessity" (*wujūb*), and "contingency" (*imkān*), and (2) that of entities which are related to the specification of some species, such as "unity" (*waḥdat*), and "point" (*naughṭa*).[56] In another passage, Ṭūsī observes a distinction among the ideas which are receptive to intelligences and minds. Those assigned to the first class are either absolutely intelligible (*ma 'qul-i maḥḍ*) or they are sensible and receptive to the external and internal senses. Among the absolute intelligibles he lists "existence" (*wujūd*), "necessity" (*wujūb*), "contingency" (*imkān*), and "impossibility" (*imtinā'*). As examples of entities to which the external senses are receptive, he mentions heat and cold, color, light and darkness. Corresponding to the internal senses, he cites several feelings, such as happiness, sadness, satiety, and hunger. The criteria by which they are distinguished are these: whereas the first is of a universal nature, the second and third kinds possess particular natures [*Asās*, 412].

Let us note two different ways in which Ṭūsī's doctrine can be stated and name them for purposes of clarification: "epistemic-phenomenological" and "syntactical" explanations. From the first point of view, in the familiar Kantian language, "that there is a being" is a transcendental condition of experience. Since it is implicitly assumed that "nothing" does not denote anything, and that whatever we experience is a "something," we know necessarily that there is a being. The specific nature of this being, of course, depends on the peculiarity of sensations and other factors that are a posteriori to experience. In the syntactical way, the concept of "being" is handled quite simply, without the traditional metaphysical importance attached to it.[57] Syntactically, the meaning of "being" can also be considered in the following way. Some words in the language can be arranged on different levels on the basis of the degree of determination they possess, which in turn depend partially upon whether or not a sign can be predicated on another sign and result in a well-formed expression. For example, "man" is more determinable than "Socrates;" consequently, "Socrates" is more determinate than "man" because "the man Socrates" (which reads "Socrates is a man") is a significant expression in the language. "Animality" is more determinable than "humanity." (The cases of predicates with different numbers of places can easily be taken into account, as is illustrated in type-theoretical languages). Accordingly, the concept of *being* is explained as the designatum of a sign of the highest level in the language, which is predicated on a sign of any other level in the manner of a transcendental term, e.g., a number which is predicated on properties of different levels.[58]

It is legitimate to inquire whether we are reading modern themes into the philosophies of Ṭūsī and ibn Sīnā or whether these philosophers actually subscribed to a syntactical philosophy of being. The answer to this question is obviously in need of certain qualifications and clarifications, as these philosophers were not acquainted with the tools of contemporary symbolic logic, such as the theory of types. Nevertheless, from examples that both Ṭūsī and ibn Sīnā provide, it appears that each upholds a syntactical rather than epistemological sense of priority of "being" in the sense indicated. For instance, both make use of syntactical paradoxes to show that "substance" is not identical with "being;" e.g., if we substitute "substance" for "is" (*hast*) in the sentence "A substance is," we get "A substance substance," which is nonsensical.[59]

In sum, both Ṭūsī and ibn Sīnā attempt to present what might be termed a syntactical way of discussing "being." The so-called "necessity of being" would not be a difficult ontological problem for them. If a finite number of levels of predication alone explains our experience adequately, then there must be an upper boundary to the levels of predication. "Being" is that concept which is of the highest level. Ibn Sīnā considers it legitimate to combine "being" with modalities. Accordingly, he uses "being" with "actuality" in the following ways: "a Necessary Being is actual," "an impossible being is never actual," and "if the cause of a contingent being is actual, then the contingent being itself is actual." Employing such reasoning and certain premises about the nature of "goodness" of the "Necessary Being," he sets out to derive a proof for the existence of actual entities in this world.[60]

CATEGORIES

Apart from carrying many significant implications of a philosophical as well as an historical nature, the concept of "categories" is a useful tool in the exegesis of complex passages concerned with key terms, such as "substance."

Within a philosophical context, there are two questions that may legitimately be asked of a philosopher who uses the apparatus of categories. We could inquire whether he makes a distinction between logic and metaphysics and, if so, to which of these disciplines the theory of categories belongs, and, if to both, how the transformation is carried out from one to the other. A related question concerns a more acute problem since it touches on the very nature of the categorical investigation. The problem arises when the apparently simple, legitimate question is asked: what are the categories about? In the attempt to answer this question, what might prima facie be taken as two distinct possibilities present themselves: first, linguistic expressions, and second, the ultimate nature of entities in the nonlinguistic aspect of the world. In our present exposition we should note these problems but should also observe that these problems are of concern to us—not to the Islamic philosophers, who, not having been faced with them, cannot justly be accused of having evaded them. It is not surprising, therefore, that there is no clear-cut discussion of these points in Aristotelian works; ibn Sīnā assumes a position, and although Ṭūsī is aware of the problem, he merely follows ibn Sīnā's views on these controversial points after having offered minor arguments for the justification of his views.

Almost without exception, Islamic philosophers followed a

set of fixed Arabic equivalents for the original Greek terms. In the *Dānish Nāmeh*, ibn Sīnā introduces Persian names for the categories, which are not adopted by Kāshānī and other Persian writers after ibn Sīnā. In this text as well as elsewhere, Ṭūsī follows the Arabic version of ibn Sīnā's list given in his texts other than the *Dānish Nāmeh*. The list is presented below:[61]

English	*Greek*	*Arabic*	*Persian*	*Latin*
1. substance	οὐσία	Jauhar	gauhar	substantia
2. quantity	πόσον	kammiyya	chandī	quantum
3. quality	ποιόν	Kaifiyya	chigūnagī	quale
4. relation	πρός τι	iḍāfa	nisbat	ad aliquid
5. place	ποῦ	'ayn	Kujā ī	ubi
6. time	ποτέ	Matā	kaī ī	quando
7. posture	κεῖσθαι	Waḍ '	Nahād	quando
8. possession	ἔχειν	Mulk	dāsht	habere
9. action	ποιεῖν	An yaf'al	kinish	facere
10. passion	πάσχειν	An yanfa'il	bakunīdan	pati

Having discussed the terminology of individual categories, let us now turn to certain difficulties that arise in Ṭūsī's reformulation of Aristotle's original formulation. Even though Aristotle's philosophy, in which "substance" is the prime category, uses the notion of categories indirectly throughout its explanations, only in the *Categoriae* itself and in *Topica* 103b 21-25 do we find an explicit reference to a list. Moreover, the *Metaphysica* does not mention that the general notion of categories is an essential part of metaphysical analysis, even though some of its significant sections, notably Book Zeta, are devoted to the clarification of one of the most important categories, "substance." It should be noted that this difficulty may not be inherent in Aristotle's views but may be due to the incomplete or faulty transmission of his works. The attempt to find a connection between his metaphysical and his logical works is especially complicated because the entire order of what we take to be his *Metaphysica* is based upon nothing but tentative premises and fragmentary evidence, as indicated by attempts such as those of Jaeger to emend the text according to some reasonable order.[62]

In view of differences in terminology and emphasis in his *Categoriae* and *Metaphysica*, it is not surprising that several commentators express disagreement about the intention and the use of the doctrine of the categories and its place in Aristotle's philosophy.[63] For example, Moody, in his able exposition of Ockham's views on this topic, presents a comprehensive interpretation of Aristotle's *Categoriae* as part of his *Organon,* an idea implicitly supported by Bocheński.[64] Kneale and Kneale, on the other hand, consider the *Categoriae* as a metaphysical work.[65]

The doctrine of categories, as Aristotle asserted it, could not have been accepted by Neoplatonists (especially since it reduced genera and species to secondary substances), as has been noted by A. C. Lloyd and substantiated by the famous attack on this doctrine by Plotinus in *Enneads,* VI.[66] One of Plotinus' main objections was that the categories could not be interpreted in his own dualistic realms, viz., the realm of the sensible and the realm of the intelligible. Porphyry, in his specification of the nature of the categories, took Plotinus' objections into account by making the categories directly applicable to the sensible realm and applicable to the intelligible realm only by analogy.[67] The confusion about the meaning of the categories, however, remains in the Neoplatonic philosophies and has continued in contemporary discussions of Aristotle's philosophy.[68] In making historical notes on the topic of the categories, one should attempt to avoid the tendency of some modern philosophers like Anscombe and Ryle to interpret Aristotle's categories purely on the linguistic level and to criticize his linguistic shortcomings, as well as those of other ancient and medieval philosophers.[69] But the results of the efforts of those who attempt to establish what can be said of the text of the *Categoriae* without reading into Aristotle's work any specific intention are often in disaccord. For example, Ackrill observes that Aristotle's categorical analysis is about things and suggests that in order to carry out his investigation, Aristotle has to pay attention to linguistic usage. Accordingly, the categories can be arrived at by means of two aspects: (1) the different kinds of questions that can be asked about substance, and (2) the various kinds of answers to a particular question which can be asked about any entity.[70]

In view of these diversities, we conclude that Aristotle's analysis of categories is by no means clear in its aims or in its actual results. When we turn to ibn Sīnā and Ṭūsī, the doctrine becomes more specific.[71] Ibn Sīnā asserts three times that the study of the categories belongs to logic—first in his momentous work on the *Cate-*

goriae in the "Logic" of *al-Shifā'*, second in the "Metaphysica" of *al-Shifā'*, and finally in *al-Najāt*.[72] He adopts the Aristotelian category divisions, by passing, therefore, both Plotinus' rejection and the system of the four categories adopted by the Stoics. For the Stoics, Bocheński argues the theory that the categories belong to physics rather than logic.[73] The difference between the views of Aristotle and ibn Sīnā on this topic amounts to more than the mere specification of categories by the former as a part of philosophy and by the latter as a part of logic. One important distinction is that ibn Sīnā's metaphysical systems expressed in *al-Shifā'* and the *Dānish Nāmeh* are based explicitly on the doctrine of the categories, whereas Aristotle offers no explicit discussion of the categories in his *Metaphysica* or of lists as we know them from the Islamic philosophers.[74]

Ṭūsī, in *Asās* (pp. 34-35), demonstrates his awareness of the controversy about the nature of categories among his contemporaries. According to him they hold the view that the study of the categories does not belong to logic because neither the specification of the nature of universals nor the description of what exists, i.e., substances and accidents, belongs to logic. But he notes that definition, description, and deduction of the premises of deductions cannot be undertaken without consideration of the logical distinction among individual categories. He affirms the value of categorical analyses in stating that they can assist us in our discussion of cases in the actual world; moreover, such cases are employed only for pedagogical purposes to elucidate the logical relationship between individual categories.

Ṭūsī's discussion points to a significant problem concerning the use of syntactical categorical schemes in science. Even though categorical analyses may be logically independent of actual objects, nevertheless, the logical distinctions among the conceptual relationships of categorical terms illuminate our understanding of the domain with which science is concerned. Let us consider, for example, the problem of choosing a language for a physical theory. The problem lies essentially in choosing some primitive terms, a language, and a set of axioms, in the context of a Carnapian type of syntax.[75] Some considerations with which a scientist must deal are factors about the meaning of the categories of "space" and "time," e.g., the reversibility of the spatial realm and the irreversibility of temporal units, and the kinds of languages in which it is possible to express physical properties of the world, such as metric and topological languages.

Such languages entail a study in the logic of quantities, such as comparisons of cases of coordinate systems with a logic of relations expressing topological relations suited to the physical theory in question.

When a philosopher considers these factors, his analysis, to the extent that it is expressed in terms of the categories, does not go beyond concepts, for it does not take into account empirical facts, e.g., what the Muslims called properties and relations of sensible movables. Nevertheless, such an analysis results in alternative languages among which the scientist has to make a choice. In this sense then, a logical independence of categorical analysis from science does not imply that categories are irrelevant to science; it implies instead that the analysis of the categories is part of the theoretical aspect of a scientific inquiry.[76] In his syntactical analysis of the categories, Ṭūsī does not employ them as part of "science proper" but as a tool which is concerned with those languages science can use. He insists that the primary aim of logic is to clarify intelligible ideas, "*ma 'anā-yi 'aqlī*;" it is not a mere concern with linguistic expression for its own sake (*Asās*, p. 187). Ṭūsī notes that logic is a science of sciences, for its subject matter consists of the second intelligibles, which are abstracted from the first intelligibles, such as substance, but are nonetheless useful for the derived sciences (*Asās*, p. 399). It follows then that philosophy concerns itself with concepts from which those general instances can be abstracted which serve as the theoretical framework of sciences. In this sense, logic becomes an intermediate tool between philosophy and science. However, since Ṭūsī does not discuss this point clearly, it is unwarranted to present him in the garb of a twentieth century constructionalist in philosophy of science. From his discussion of the categories, it has become evident that there is a difference between science and philosophy; even though their subject matters are logically independent, in the practical sense philosophical analysis can serve science through the medium of logic.

ṬŪSĪ'S CONCEPT OF "SUBSTANCE"

The notion of "substance" is generally associated with several problems of both an historical and a philosophical nature. Of course, "substance," derived from the Latin "*substantia*" was not used by Aristotle, who, it is thought, was the first philosopher to specify this concept by using "οὐσία" in *Categoriae* and "τί ἐστι" in *Topica* 103b 20-5 as the first of the categories. He discusses the meaning of "οὐσία" extensively in *Metaphysica,* especially in Book Zeta. Since the task of specifying the Aristotelian notion of substance is beyond the scope of this study, we offer the following notes upon which the subsequent discussion will be based.

1. From the philosophical point of view, Aristotle's text on "substance" is prima facie confusing, as the following examples will demonstrate. (a) In *Categoriae*, he presents the primary substance as consisting of individuals, and the secondary substance of species and genera; (b) he emphasizes in the *Metaphysica* the notion of concrete individuals as the primary case of being; (c) in the last chapter of *Metaphysica:* Zeta, he attributes substantiality to what can be called a definition and a cause; and (d) in *Metaphysica*: Lambda, he takes a non-sensible eternal God to be a "substance."[77]
2. As far as terminology is concerned, it is questionable whether "ουσία" can adequately be translated as "substance." In all probability, a clear presentation of Aristotle's views, as Owens has indicated, must "reconstruct" this notion under a "neutral" label, such as "entity."[78] To state, therefore, that "*jawhar*" means "ουσία" does not contribute to an understanding of details of ibn Sīnā's or Ṭūsī's use of "*jawhar.*"
3. In taking the historical perspective, we note that the term "ουσία" underwent numerous diverse renderings in the Latin philosophical texts, and that we may not, therefore, take the liberty of regarding "ουσία" as the equivalent of "substantia" merely on the basis of Boethius' use of these terms as equivalents in his commentary.[79]

These difficulties notwithstanding, we shall assume hypothetically the following theses: (a) Aristotle formulated two concepts of substance in the first of his categories—the first naming concrete individuals and the second species and genera; (b) although the primary existing entities were individual substances, we refer to their essences in defining them; and, finally (c) Aristotle was not explicit in the presentation of his views on substance concerning what he called "ουσία."

Let us now turn to ibn Sīnā's analysis of "substance." Here we notice a very clear separation of "substance" from "being," "essence," and "existence," a separation that we have discussed elsewhere.[80] Ibn Sīnā distinguishes explicitly between the concept of "the first substance" designating it as "*al-jawhar al-shakhṣī*,"[81] "*al-jawhar al-awwalī*,"[82] and that of "the second substance," which he designates as "*al-jawhar al-thānī*."[83] In his works this distinction becomes almost the cornerstone of an empiricistic view in the realm of his ontology.[84] For example, in the *Dānish Nāmeh* he relates the differences between the two substances to the difference between the conceptual analysis of an object and the empirical acquaintance with it. In discussing the nature of "substance," he draws a distinction between the "essence" (*ḥaqīqa*) of a substance (*jawhar*) and its existence (*wujūd*). Asserting that there is a priori knowledge that an entity, such as an independent body, is a substance, he affirms that such knowledge is necessary and independent of observation. On the other hand, the question whether or not an instance of a secondary substance has been realized (*ḥāṣil*) cannot be answered a priori, since such knowledge depends on observation of a subject (*mawḍū'*, ὑποκεί μενον).[85] For reasons like these, the distinction he makes between essence and existence is connected to the distinction between substances. The domain of the analysis of the secondary substances falls under syntactical inquiries, while propositions concerning existential facts about first substances can be justified only by an acquaintance with the material substratum, the subject matter of the first substance. Thus the difference between the two substances corresponds to the difference between an empirical inquiry, which illustrates a scientific kind of activity, and a conceptual inquiry, which is a philosophical activity.

Another point of interest in ibn Sīnā's analysis of substance is the fact that he makes distinction between the first substance (*al-jawhar al-awwalī*), a particular (*al-shakhṣ*), the second substance (*al-jawhar al-thānī*), a species (*naw'*), and the third substance (*al-jawhar al-thālith*), a genus.[86]

Ṭūsī continues the ibn Sīnian doctrine, emphasizing, however, the syntactical aspect of the concept of the substance. For instance, in his first division of substance he establishes three categories: (a) individual particulars, which are first substances, (b) species, which are second substances, and (c) genera, which are third substances (*Asās*, p. 38). He accentuates also the differences between primary and other kinds of substances on the grounds of having previously drawn distinctions between a particular (*juz'ī*) and a universal (*kullī*). Some of these salient points stressed by him in his presentation of the subject are enumerated below:

1. In his attempt to provide a precise syntactical interpretation of the terms "universal" (*kullī*) and "particular" (*juz'ī*), Ṭūsī points out that in any consideration of terms the range of what they can designate should be established. A particular term can designate exactly one entity in the actual domain, whereas a universal term designates, or can designate, more than one. His discussion of various kinds of proper names (*Asās,* p. 17) shows an awareness of the possibility of reducing definite descriptions of terms to a combination of properties needed to specify the term in question.
2. Of significance is his notion that "universality" and "particularity" can be considered in the context of the predication of a sentence, rather than as semantic determinants of the interpretation of the sentence in question. For example, "humanity" is a universal with respect to its predication of individual but is a particular with respect to its relation to "animality."
   In this context Ṭūsī's attempts to explicate universals and particulars can be clarified by pointing to their formulation in the contemporary language of determinables and determinates. Accordingly, if "an expression θ of a level n is predicated of an expression Ψ of a level $n\text{-}1$ in a well-formed sentence," then "ψ is a particular relative to θ," and "θ is a universal relative to ψ."
3. A further distinction is drawn by him between the intensional aspect of universality (*kullī*) and the extensional feature of the sum of a class. This distinction is carefully couched in a language in which the accent falls on the explication of concepts rather than on references to existents. The only extension recognized by him is a sum (*majmū'*) of distinct parts (*juz'iyyāt*), and the only intension to which he refers is related to individuals by definition (*ḥadd*). The existence of the extension (or the sum) depends upon the existence of the individuals, whereas the nonexistence of the case would not destroy the meaning of the intension (the concept).
4. Whereas for some cases the extension (the sum) can be con-

ceived, the totality of an intension may not be conceivable. For example, if there were only two human beings in the world, we could conceive the total extension of "humanity," although we might have some difficulty in conceptualizing the meaning of the concept of humanity, which is the intension of the term "humanity."

5. While instances of an extended class are limited, the applicability of the intension (concept) is unlimited. Even though the class as a whole cannot be a part of particular elements in the class, an intension is attributed to its members.
6. The extension (the sum) does not exist in the particular individuals, which comprise the extended sum, whereas the intension is attributed to every individual in the extended sum. For example, the set of all numbers is not a number, whereas "numerosity" is a feature of every particular number.

   Another way of making this point is to assert that the conception of the extension is not presupposed in the conception of a particular, whereas the conception of the intension (the concept) is presupposed in the conception of the essence of a particular.

Ṭūsī follows ibn Sīnā and Fārābī in specifying the meaning of substance in the Aristotelian manner, as (a) not existing in a subject; (b) not having an opposite; (c) not admitting of degree; and (d) being the subject of contrary qualities in respect to its substratum [*Asās*, p. 37].[87] Nevertheless, in the actual exposition of the idea of substance, we observe its syntactical presentation in terms of the exposition of the concepts of "universality" and "particularity." That Ṭūsī is less involved in an "ontological inquiry" than in a syntactical conceptual inquiry is indicated by the manner in which he relativizes such concepts as "being a substance" and "being a genus." In the sense that they are universals, universals exist only in the intelligence and in the understanding, but when they are instantiated in a particular (*Asās*, p. 29), they exist as actual entities. An entity "*x*" is a "genus" in relation to another entity "*y*," if "*y*" is a "species" with respect to "*x*." If "*x*" is a "species" with respect to some "*y*," then it is possible to consider "*x*" as a "genus" with respect to some "*z*," if "*z*" is of a lower level than "*x*." A "real" (*ḥaqīqī*) species is an entity that contains only particular existents under which nothing can be subsumed. That Ṭūsī's concept of this hierarchy of being is conceptual rather than ontological is apparent from the following example: Any given concept which is regarded as a genus may be transcended by another concept which is also considered a genus; however, we cannot conceive (*taṣawwar*) an idea (*ma'nā*) of infinite levels. It follows, then, that there is such a concept as the highest genus, called "*jins al-ajnās*" (literally, the genus of genera), and that the same entity can actually be termed a species with respect to a higher level of predication, while it can be considered as a genus with respect to a lower level of predication. If we grouped entities in terms of species (*naw'*), then the highest level conceivable would be the highest species (*naw'-i 'ālī*) [*Asās*, pp. 29-30].

Ṭūsī is well aware of the difference between talking about kinds of entities, such as "a body," and actual entities, which may include a set of specific bodies. For example, from the names he assigns to them, calling the former "*jism-i ta' īmī* " and the latter "*jism-i tabī' ī*," we learn that a syntactical exposition of a bodily substance is distinguished from its naturalistic exposition, a task which belongs to science.

In sum, we note that Ṭūsī's analysis of substance is closely related to the distinction he upholds between science and metaphysics. It is possible to reconstruct his theory in two forms: either (1) by taking his distinction as the set of his premises for his proposition about substances, or (2) by considering his theory about substances as a premise from which to justify a distinction between science and philosophy. The arguments are sufficiently interrelated to permit either construction.

PROBLEMS IN EXTENDING OUR ANALYSIS TO SELECTED WORKS OF ISLAMIC PHILOSOPHY

So far our analysis has shown how an analytical and syntactical construction of the concept of substance both supports and illustrates the attempts of Muslims, like Ṭūsī and ibn Sīnā, to distinguish between philosophy and science. As has been illustrated, many texts corroborate our interpretation of the views of Ṭūsī and ibn Sīnā on this issue. In the light of the data cited, there might be a temptation to consider our exposition of "substance" as typical and representative of nearly all Islamic philosophical works on this subject. Among the works of virtually every Islamic philosopher, including ibn Sīnā and Ṭūsī, we find several texts with the following special features: the use of "substance" in the context of metaphysics, which Rescher calls "evaluative metaphysics," rather than in a context which places emphasis on the peripatetic traditional discussions of the categories.[88]

In such writings substances such as "the self" (*nafs*, ψυχή, *anima*, *jān*) and "intelligences" (*'aql*, νοῦς) are usually cited in support of doctrines, which resemble what Rescher calls "the value of personhood." Even a cursory inspection of these texts leaves one with the impression that the concept of substance is used in a way which differs from our presentation.

Since an extensive illustration of this point is beyond the scope of this paper, we refer the reader to other studies in which he will find such an illustration as well as a discussion of several other issues associated with this topic.[89] But we shall offer some evidence in support of our thesis that the syntactical interpretation of substance should be restricted to the kinds of texts we have mentioned.

For instance, ibn Sīnā speaks of the "union" (*paivand*) of persons with the Necessary Existent. It is obvious that such a relation cannot be applicable to substances, for the reason that the only kind of changes substances can undergo are generation and destruction, and for the additional reason that the Necessary Existent, according to ibn Sīnā's explicit assertion, is not a substance.[90]

Ibn Sīnā confronts us, then, (i) with a doctrine which is definitely non-Aristotelian, i.e., any "mystical union" of *psyche* with the "prime mover" would be nonsensical in Aristotle's system, while mystical union with the Necessary Existent is a cornerstone of ibn Sīnā's thesis, and (ii) with a complicated process of "union" (*paivand*), which no simple syntactical apparatus, such as the "particular-universal" distinction we have outlined, can express or explain adequately.[91]

The material we have quoted here stands by no means isolated in ibn Sīnā's works. For example, in *Ma'rifat al-Nafs* we find a reference in which the soul is first described as belonging to the category of relation (*iḍāfa*) but is also viewed as a substance, *jawhar*, after the death of the body[92] and, upon reaching its ultimate state, is connected with the Divine Light.[93]

Similarly, in *al-Ishārāt wa al-Tanbīhāt*, he points to the mystical intelligence as the only means by which we can relate to the Necessary Existent.[94] Consequently, it is highly questionable whether the syntactical view of substance described previously explains adequately the view of substance presented in ibn Sīnā's mystical writings.

When we consider the mystical works of Ṭūsī, we discover a similar situation. For example, in his *Awṣāf al-Ashrāf* and the *Aghāz wa Anjām,* Ṭūsī follows the point of view outlined by ibn Sīnā. In his analysis of *tauḥīd* (a mystical state denoting "unity"), he claims that there is essentially no existent but the highest being, "God," and that which has emanated from God.[95]

The point here is that for the mystic there should be no differentiation between the phenomenon of the self and the world. Thus, "the value of personhood" is explained in terms of the self's non-alienating union with the ultimate being—the world, which is essentially similar to ibn Sīnā's *paivand* with the Necessary Existent. Ṭūsī points out that the aim of *ittiḥād* (unification) with God is to become one (*yagānagī*) with God.[96]

Higher than *ittiḥād* is the stage of *waḥdat* (unity), in which all differentiation between persons and the world is to disappear.[97] A similar doctrine of the "unity of being" (*waḥdat al-wujūd*), in which the traditional substantial differentiations among entities are repudiated, is also advocated in another work of Ṭūsī. In *Aghāz wa Anjām,* Ṭūsī notes, for instance, that only through the annihilation (of the ego) of persons can we be led to an eternal mode of existence in God.[98]

Numerous discussions in this text deal with and support similar themes. For example, he considers the perfection of the mystic to be that stage in which there will be no essential (*dhātī*) difference between him and God. Such a depiction permits the union of the soul (*nafs*) with God in a process of self-realization, where God would be the last stage in the process of the soul's self-realization.[99]

It is not necessary to stress that this doctrine of *waḥdat al-wujūd* and the related themes to which we have pointed in the texts of Ṭūsī and ibn Sīnā are by no means as clear as we wish them to be. But a part of the noticeable confusion and complexity is specifically due to the fact that these doctrines deal with a process that cannot be explained by our traditional Aristotelian notion of substance. And this mystical tradition, it should be noted, cannot be overlooked or dismissed as theosophy or magic, if only for the reason that any objective inspection of the Islamic philosophy, not limited to what was available to the Latin and Hebraic translators, reveals a vast amount of material written about the themes of *waḥdat al-wujūd* and similar doctrines. So far we have pointed out a few examples in philosophy, but it is actually in the later medieval Persian poetry that such philosophical themes find their major expression, as the following few lines will illustrate:

Rūmī:

> Let me be emancipated from this soul (*nafs*) and this bodily element [lit. air]
> Neither alive nor dead do I have a source of Grace (*faḍl*) but God.[100]

Ḥāfiẓ:

> I shall not cease to seek until my perfection is reached
> When my life reaches the life [source] of life—when this life leaves the body.[101]

Jāmī:

> The entire world is but an image
> It is but a ray of that Beauty.[102]

Aṭṭār:

> Let your self be annihilated, so that all the birds [mediums] of the way
> Make way for you in the everlasting state in [His] Court.[103]

These are but a few of thousands of lines which one familiar with Persian literature might cite on the theme of "the unity of being" (*waḥdat al-wujūd*). It is well known that one does not find in such poems a systematic exposition, that is, an attempt to produce a valid argument from well-established premises about the truth of this doctrine, for treatments of such a nature belong to philosophy rather than to the realm of poetry. Nonetheless, the existence of such poems suggests that themes such as *waḥdat al-wujūd*, which are related to a non-Aristotelian view of nature, do not stand in isolation in the Islamic tradition; instead, they are essential aspects of the Islamic *Weltanschauung*, and, taken in such a context, help to clarify the philosophical doctrines which are part of the same tradition, e.g., the nature of the soul. One cannot dismiss the mystical texts of ibn Sīnā and Ṭūsī as "incidental" but should consider them as integral parts of their philosophy. The first consequence of such an acceptance would be greater caution in applying the definition of "substance" found in texts such as *Asās* to the "self" described in Ṭūsī's mystical works, in spite of the fact that Ṭūsī asserts in the *Asās* that the self is a substance. Having discussed this particular issue, let us note some of the possible results of our inquiry.

We close our paper with remarks of a philosophical as well as a methodological nature. Methodological distinctions, such as "analytic," "synthetic," and "essence-existence," should be judged not only in isolation by themselves or by their ontological meaning, but rather, by their use. Such distinctions may frequently be useful to the philosopher because they allow him to undertake a legitimate study in conceptual analysis without demanding that his work ultimately relate to the existents.

It appears that both Ṭūsī and ibn Sīnā made use of the twofold meaning of "substance" in their works for the purposes we have indicated. To the methodological remarks already put forward, we should append that the analysis of "substance," like the analysis of other concepts, with which for lack of space we have not dealt here, should not be restricted to the works of Near Eastern philosophers written in the analytical, classical style of Greek philosophy. This is particularly true with regard to philosophers in the eastern part of the Islamic world, since almost every one of them wrote mystical texts containing ideas which were harmonious with the rich Ṣūfī tradition, especially in poetry, and were received at least in part by an audience familiar with their analytic writings. One problem upon which scholarly attention should focus is whether the analytical and mystical works are consistent in content. To complete an adequate inquiry on this topic, we should specify what we mean by these respective traditions and on what particular problem we have focused our attention, as has been illustrated elsewhere.[104] We should note that if the philosophers regarded their analyses not as descriptions of existents, but as analyses of concepts, then they would not be restricted to the construction of only one philosophical model.

A philosopher endowed with such freedom could develop an analytic of essences in the language of the mathematician, a set of physical substances in the scientific terminology, and a nonalienating doctrine of the unity of being for the mystic. But regardless of whether or not such a tentative hypothesis is correct, at least one recommendation should be made at this point. If we study the primary sources of Near Eastern philosophy, as we have attempted to do in the case of "substance," we may expose new trends and doctrines. These new insights may question, if not disprove, the old cliché that Near Eastern philosophy is a derivation of Greek philosophy and Islamic theology. For in addition to being part of the heritage of the world, Islamic philosophy and secular sciences may have messages and insights to offer which make them worthy of a study on their own terms.

It is our hope to have added to such insight through the data presented in this paper in support of the thesis that in Islamic philosophical texts, as for instance, in Ṭūsī's *Asās*, a distinction is drawn between "philosophy" and "science," a distinction that is corroborated by syntactical treatments of the important concept of "substance."

NOTES

* Originally published in *Essays in Islamic Philosophy and Science*, ed. G. Hourani (Albany, New York: SUNY Press, 1975), pp. 158-188. This article was translated into Persian and published in *Shiite Theology and Philosophy*, ed. M. Mohaghegh (Tehran: University Press, 1985).

1 Ṭūsī, *Asās al-Iqtibās*, ed. M. Muddras-Raḍawī (Tehran, 1948) (hereafter cited as *Asās*). This text is mentioncd in N. Rescher's *The Development of Arabic Logic* (Pittsburgh, 1964), p. 198, and in Carl Brockelmann, *Geschichte der arabischen Literatur*, 2 vols., 2nd ed. (Leiden, 1943-49); 3 suppl. vols. (Leiden, 1937-43). See 1, bk. 2, p. 673. Brockelmann mentions 59 texts of Ṭūsī, whereas Raḍawī lists 113 items, including minor letters, in addition to 21 works of doubtful authorship, Brockelmann, *Ibid.*, pp. 670-76; Raḍawī, pp. YJ-YH. *Khāwja Naṣīr* al-Dīn Ṭūsī Abū ja'far Muḥammad ibn al-Ḥasan Abī Bakr (b. 18 Feb. 1201; d. 26 June 1274) is best known for his works on astronomy and ethics and a commentary on ibn Sīnā's *al-Ishārāt wa al-Tanbīhāt.* The last work mentioned ed. S. Dunya in 4 vols. (Cairo, 1960). The most popular text of Ṭūsī, his *Akhlāq-i Nāṣīrī*, has been translated into English as *The Nasirean Ethics*, by G. M. Wickens (London, 1964). See *Encyclopaedia of Islam*, 1st ed., vol. 4 (Leiden, 1913-42): 980-82; B. H. Siddīqī, "Naṣīr al-Dīn Ṭūsī" in *A History of Muslim Philosophy* ed. M. M. Sharif, vol. 1

(Wiesbaden, 1963): 560-80; M. Madrisī, *Sarguzasht wa' aqā' id-i Falsafiyya Khāwja Naṣīr al-Dīn Ṭūsī* (Tehran, 1954); S. H. Nasr, *Science and Civilization in Islam* (Cambridge, Mass., 1968), pp. 321-28.

2 On the *Isagoge*, including Boethius' translation, see *Commentaria in Aristotelem Graeca*, ed. A. Busse 1, vol. 4, pt. 1, (Berlin, 1887). For a discussion of Porphyry's *Isagoge* in Islam, see I. Madkour, *L' Organon d' Aristote dans le monde arabe* (Paris, 1934), pp. 70-75; A. Badawi, *La Transmission de la Philosophie au monde arabe* (Paris, 1968), pp. 105-106; M. Steinschneider, *Die Arabischen Ubersetzungen aus dem Griechischen* (Graz, 1960), pp. 75-78, 136-37; F. E. Peters, *Aristoteles Arabus* (Leiden, 1969), pp. 8-9; F. E. Peters, *Aristotle and the Arabs* (New York, 1968), pp. 79-87. On the controversy between ibn Sīnā's and Porphyry's views, see J. Finnegan, "Avicenna's Refutation of Porphyrius" in *Avicenna Commemoration Volume*, ed. V. Courtois, (Calcutta, 1956), pp. 179-186. For two criticisms of Porphyry's views, see (1) E. A. Moody, *The Logic of William of Ockham* (1935; repr. New York, 1966), pp. 65-117 and (2) R. I. Aaron, *The Theory of Universals*, 2nd ed. (London, 1967), pp. 1-17. The remarks on the lack of studies on this text appear in Rescher's *The Development of Arabic Logic*, p. 198, in which he translates the title as "The Bases of Learning in Logic."

3 *Asās*, p. yb. Of the nine books of *al-Manṭiq of al-Shifā'*, the following have been edited: (i) vol. 1, *The Isagoge*, ed. A. F. Ahwani (Cairo, 1959); (ii) vol. 2, *Categories* (*al-Maqūlāt*), ed. M. Khodeiri, A. F. Ahwani, G. Anawati, and S. Zayed (Cairo, 1959); (iii) vol. 4, *Syllogism* (*al-Qīyās*), ed. S. Zayed (Cairo, 1964); (iv) vol. 5, *Demonstration* (*al-Burhām*), ed. A. Afifi (Cairo, 1956); (v) vol. 6, *Dialectic* (*al-Fadal*), ed. A. F. Ahwani (Cairo, 1965); (vi) vol. 7, *Sophistic* (*al-Safsata*), ed. A. F. Ahwani, rev. ed. (Cairo, 1958); (vii) vol. 8, *Rhetoric* (*al-Khiṭāba*), ed. M. Salem, rev. ed. (Cairo, 1954); and (viii) *Poetics*, (*al-Shi'r*), ed. A. Badawi (Cairo, 1966).

4 For Raḍawī's remark see *Asās*, p. yb. The notion of the categories is not developed in the *Manṭiq* of the other encyclopedic works of ibn Sīnā, such as *al-Najāt* (Cairo, 1938), *al-Ishārāt wa al-Tanbīhāt*, and *Dānish Nāmeh 'Alā'ī: Manṭiq*, ed. M. Mo'in and S. M. Mashkut (Tehran, 1951).

5 Aristotle uses different terms for the heading of this general division that might confuse his simple triadic division. For example, in *Metaphysica*, 993b 19-20, he mentions that "philosophy [τήν φιλοσοφί χν] is a knowledge (science) [έπιστήμην]" that seeks truths, and proceeds to divide these into the theoretical and the practical. Cf. 1026b 4-6. In *Metaphysica*, 1025b 25, Aristotle mentions that "all thoughts [πάσα δί ανοια]" are productive, practical, or theoretical, and then proceeds to

say in *Metaphysica*, 1026a 18-20, that "theoretical philosophies" [φιλοσοφί αι θεωρητιχαί] are divided into mathematics, physics, and theology. A few lines later he names the third subdivision "first philosophy" [πρώτη φιλοσοφία]. In *Ethica Nicomachea*, 1139a 25-31, he refers to thinking [διάνοια] as being either practical theoretical or productive, and proceeds to classify "scientific knowledge" [ἐπιστήμην] as a "virtue" [ἀρετή]. Our choice of the neutral word "inquiry" is based on the wish to avoid apparent confusion; it follows the method of using a neutral word for an Aristotelian term that has multiple meanings, as initiated by J. Owens in his *The Doctrine of Being in Aristotelian Metaphysics* (Toronto, 1963), see pp. 315-65.

6 *Ethica Nicomachea*, 1139a 25-31. Later in the same text, Aristotle notes that "practical wisdom [φρό ησις]" is "a truth-attaining quality, concerned with action in relation to things that are good and bad for human beings." *Ibid.*, 1140b 3-6.

7 *Ethica Nicomachea*, 1140a 26. For Aristotle, a mark of practical inquiry and of art [τέχνη], the paradigm of productive inquiry, is their concern with variable states; theoretical inquiry deals with constant states.

8 *Metaphysica*, 1026a 18-22. See above, no. 5.

9 *Metaphysica*, 1061b 28-30, 1064a 15-18, and *Physica*, 193b 23-25.

10 *Physica*, 193b 22-194b 15.

11 See, for instance, "The subject matter of metaphysics is stated differently by Aristotle in different places." W. D. Ross, *Aristotle's Metaphysics*, 2nd. ed. rev. (London, 1958), I: lxxix, and "Aristotle himself appears conscious of no inconsistency or contradiction in these various designations. Even when raising a question of what today seems to bring an antinomy to the fore, he writes as though unaware of any real difficulty. He does not seem in the least perturbed by what the modern commentators find embarrassing if not impossible." J. Owens, *The Doctrine of Being;* see p. Merlan, "Greek Philosophy from Plato to Plotinus," in *The Cambridge History of Later Greek and Early Medieval Philosophy* (London, 1967) pp. 51-52; W. Jaeger, *Aristotle: Fundamentals of the History of His Development*, trans. R. Robinson, 2nd ed. (London, 1960), pp. 217-219.

12 See *Metaphysica*, 1026a 24 for "metaphysics" as equated with "first philosophy"; 1003a 20-21, 1060b 31 for the study of "being qua being"; 982a 1-3, 982b 9-10 for the study of "principles and causes"; 1026a18-22 for "theology" as a branch of "theoretical inquiry," and for several references to God, see 983a 8, 1026a 19-23, 1064b 1-6, 1069a 30. His "motionless" features are mentioned in 1071b 1-5,

1073b 3-5; "everlasting" in 1071b 1-5, 1073b 3-5; and finally "separated from sensible entities" in 1073b 3-5.

13 Owens, *The Doctrine of Being*, p. 36; Jaeger, Aristotle, pp. 222-28.

14 Ross, *Aristotle's Metaphysics*, I: lxxix.

15 R. Carnap, for instance, states, "In the discussion on the methodology of science, it is customary and useful to divide the language of science into two parts, the observational language and the theoretical language. The observational language uses terms designating properties and relations for the description of observable things or events." "The Methodological Character of Theoretical Concepts," in *Minnesota Studies in the Philosophy of Science*, ed. H. Feigel and M. Scriven (Minneapolis, 1965,) p. 38; see C. G. Hempel, *Aspects of Scientific Explanation* (New York, 1965), p. 177.

16 In *Analytica Posteriora*, 100a 3-5, he mentions that perception-sensation leads to memory from which experience is derived, *cf. Metaphysica*. 980a 28.

17 *Ethica Nicomachea*, 1139b 15.

18 *Analytica Posteriora*, 100b 5-16

19 R. Carnap, *Philosophical Foundations of Physics* (London, 1966), p. 225.

20 *De Generatione Animalium*, 736b 25-30.

21 See Owens, *The Doctrine of Being*, pp. 316-28 (especially p. 317). Here Owens uniformly replaces what is traditionally translated as "substance" by the term "entity." As far as substance is concerned, he asserts that "substance" and "essence" seem to be the only translations of φύσις. Neither is satisfactory for a detailed study of Aristotle's "Being," (pp. 148- 49). In the same passage, Owens objects to Cherniss' use of "reality" to explain this term. The reference is to the latter's *Aristotle's Criticism of Plato and the Academy* (New York, 1962), p. 364. Hope systematically uses "primary being" for the usual translations of "substance," *Aristotle's Metaphysics*, trans. R. Hope (Ann Arbor, 1960).

22 See N. Rescher, *The Development of Arabic Logic*, p. 47; G. E. von Grunebaum, *Islam*, 2nd ed. (London, 1964), p. 117; S. H. Nasr, *Science and Civilization in Islam*, p. 126. Nasr points to the proximity between the Islamic view of "physics" and the teaching of Aristotle in its basic outlines. In the case of natural science, the concept is common in Islamic philosophy, e.g., Ghazālī, *al-Monqidh min aḍ-Ḍalāl*. ed. and trans. F. Jabre (Beirut, 1959), p. 23; *Maqāṣid al-Falāsifa*, ed. S. Dunya (Cairo, 1961), p. 136. Apparently there is a clear relationship between "nature" in Arabic (*tabī'a*) and φύσις: see L. Massignon, "Nature in Islamic

Thought," in *The Mystic Vision,* ed. J. Campbell (Princeton, 1968), pp. 315-18.

23 See *Dānish Nāmeh 'Alā'ī, Ilāhiyyāt,* ed. M. Mo'in (Tehran, 1952), chap. 1; *al-Shifā', al-Ilāhiyyāt,* ed. G. C. Anawati, Mohammed Yousef Moussa, Solayman Dunya, and Sa'id Zayed (Cairo, 1960), 1:3, *et passim; 'Uyūn al-Ḥikma,* ed. A. Badawi (Cairo, 1952), p. 16. A similar division also appears in the later philosophers. For example, Suhrawardī divides sciences into practical (*'amalī*) and theoretical (*naẓarī*) sciences, subdividing the latter into metaphysics (*ilāhī*), mathematics (*rīyāḍī*), and physics (*ṭabī'ī*); see Shihābaddīn Yahyā Al-Suhrawardī, *Opera Metaphysica,* ed. Henry Corbin, vol. 1 (Istanbul, 1945), p. 196.

24 D. M. Dunlop's translation of an unpublished manuscript, "The Existence and Definition of Philosophy, from an Arabic Text Ascribed to al-Fārābī," *Iraq* 13 (1951): 76-94, in which Fārābī acknowledges Aristotle's division of theoretical philosophy into natural, mathematical, and divine philosophy; see Fārābī *Falsafat Arisṭūṭālīs,* Arabic text, ed. Muhsin Mahdi (Beirut, 1961), where Fārābī contrasts Aristotle's notion of natural science with what he calls "the voluntary science" (p. 72) and comments on the nature of metaphysics, to which he refers as *ilāhī* and *ḥikma* (wisdom), as well as other designations, such as "the wisdom" (see p. 77).

25 Fārābī, *Fuṣūl al-Madanī,* Arabic text ed. and trans. D. M. Dunlop (London, 1961), p. 166.

26 D. M. Dunlop, "al-Fārābī's Introductory Risālah on Logic," *Islamic Quarterly,* 3 (1957), p. 227.

27 Fārābī, *Iḥṣā' al-'Ulūm,* ed. O. Amine (Cairo, 1968), pp. 111-123.

28 *Al Fārābī's Book of Letters (Kitāb al-Ḥurūf) Commentary on Aristotle's Metaphysics,* ed. M. Mahdi (Beirut, 1969). The text is divided into three parts: Particles and Categories; The Origin of words, Philosophy, and Religion; and Interrogative Particles. For our purposes, the most important section of this work is the first part, which is divided into eighteen chapters. Each chapter is devoted to a verbal as well as a philosophical concept important in metaphysics; it may extend beyond discussions found in the Greek version of any one text because of its precise references to the Arabic usage of the terms analyzed.

29 *Ibid.*, pp. 97-105 discusses *jawhar* and its main use in Arabic as well as in philosophy. See pp. 110-28 for a discussion of *mawjūd* as a word constructed to convey the concept expressed in Greek, Persian, and Sogdian. The distinctions between the two concepts are very clear.

30 *Ibid.*, p. 102. He mentions that Aristotle's use of "first substance" con-

cerns that which is not in a subject, while his use of "second substance" refers to universals.

31 *Ibid.*, pp. 97-98. Here Fārābī uses examples of sentences from ordinary Arabic to clarify the sense of *Jawhar.*

32 *Ibid.*, p. 102. In this passage, he is referring to the notion of "absolute substances" as well as the use of "substance" as an auxiliary to the thing in question.

33 *Ibid.*, p. 111 *et passim.*

34 See ibn Khaldūn, *The Maqaddimah,* trans. Franz Rosenthal, 2nd ed., vol. 3 (Princeton, 1967): 147-48, in which he mentions that in the "Physics" of *al-Shifā',* ibn Sīnā disagrees with Aristotle over many issues. Ibn Khaldūn himself describes four distinct steps in the study of metaphysics so as to distinguish the study from physics, the subject of which is bodies and their motions, p. 152. See M. Mahdi, *Ibn Khaldūn's Philosophy of History* (Chicago, 1967), p. 76 for the fourfold division of theoretical sciences into logic, mathematics, physics, and metaphysics.

35 *'Ilm* is used uniformly throughout most of his writings—even concurrently with other terms; e.g., *al-Shifā', al-Ilāiyyāt* (*La Métaphysique*), ed. G. C. Anawati, Mohammad Yousef Moussa, Solayman Dunya, and Sa'id Zayed, vol. 1 (Cairo, 1960): 4, 5 *et passim. Ḥikma* usually means "wisdom" (σοφία), resembling the Persian term *khirād;* it is used extensively in ibn Sīnā's *'Uyūn al-Ḥikma,* ed. A. Badawi (Cairo, 1952), p. 17, *et passim,* and in the *Dānish Nāmeh 'Alā'ā, Ilāhiyyāt,* where *'ilm* and *ḥikma* appear together, pp. 1, 99, 100 *et passim. Dānish* is used only in Persian texts and is equivalent to the Arabic-Persian *'ilm* in ordinary usage and in poetry.

36 See *'Uyūn al-Ḥikma,* p. 17; *Al-Shifā', Ilāhiyyāt,* p. 4; *Dānish Nāmeh, Ilāhiyyāt,* pp. 1-3; *Najāt,* ed. M.S. Kurdi (Cairo, 1938), pp. 98, 198; *Fī Aqsām al- 'Ulūn al-'Aqlīyya* in *Tis' Rasā'il* (Cairo, 1908), p. 105; *Dānish Nāmeh Alā'ī, Ṭabī'iyyāt,* ed. S. M. Mishkāt (Tehran, 1952), p. 2.

37 *al-Shifā',* p. 3 *et passim.*

38 *Dānish Nāmeh Ilāhiyyāt,* pp. 5, 8.

39 *'Uyūn al-Ḥikma,* p. 17.

40 Ibn Sīnā, *al-Ishārāt wa al-Tanbīhāt,* ed. S. Dunya. We express this generalization not without some reservation; for example, in *al-Ishārāt wa al-Tanbīhāt,* mystical experience rather than the "Necessary Existent" is emphasized and the political philosophy found in the *Shifā'* (chap. 10) is absent from ibn Sīnā's other metaphysical texts.

41 For *ṭa'līmī,* see *al-Shifā',* p. 4, *Dānish Nāmeh, Ilāhiyyāt,* p. 3; for *farhang*

see *Dānish Nāmeh,* p.1, 3, *et passim.*

42 Ibn Sīnā's "physics" explicitly includes various sciences as subdisciplines, e.g., in his largest text, *al-Shifā',* "physics" comprises: (i) "physics proper" in four sections dealing with topics such as the nature of motion, the four elements, space and time; (ii) "The Heavens and the World" in ten chapters dealing with topics such as simple and composite bodies, the nature of the moon and the stars, and the problem of "infinity": (iii) "On Generation and Corruption," addressing itself to changes in the sublunary realm of bodies; (iv) "Action and Passion" in two sections, dealing with further changes in the class of elements, qualities such as coldness and heat, and the nature of sensible qualities; (v) "Metals and Meteorology" in two sections, discussing subjects such as mountains, water, temperature, metals, rainbows, and winds; (vi) the celebrated work on "The Soul" in five sections, including topics such as the definition of the soul, various faculties and kinds of souls, internal senses and the agent intellect; (vii) "the plants" in seven chapters, comprising the generation of plants, the principles of nutrition, distinctions among various kinds of plants, and the effect of temperature on plants; and (viii) "the animals" in nineteen chapters, observing distinctions among animals with respect to organs and internal elements, the various faculties of the animal genera, disease among animals, and differences of character among them.

For discussions of the various manuscripts of *al-Shifā',* see G. C. Anawati, *Mu'allafāt Ibn Sīnā: Essai de bibliographie avicennienne* (Cairo, 1950), pp. 29-79; Y. Mahdavi, *Bibliographie d'ibn Sīnā* (Tehran, 1954), pp. 125-74.

For editions of the "Physics," see the various publications directed by I. Madkour, particularly: (1) *Al-Shifā':* "Physics," 2. *The Heavens and the World,* 3. *Generation and Corruption,* 4. *Action and Passion,* rev. ed. text established Maḥmoud Qāssem (Cairo, 1969); (2) *al-Shifā':* "Physics," 5. *Mineralogy and Meteorology*; text established and ed. 'Abd el-Ḥalim Montasir, Sa'id Zayed, 'Abdallah Isma'il (Cairo, 1964), and, by the same authors, (3) *al-Shifā'* "Physics," 7. *Plants* (*al-Nabāt*) (Cairo, 1965). Book 6 of the "Physics," its *De Anima* has been edited as *Avicenna's De Anima,* ed. F. Rahman (London, 1959), and Ibn Sīnā (*Avicenna*): *Psychologie d'après son* oeuvret *Aš-Šifā,* ed. and trans. Jan Bakoš, 2 vols. (Prague, 1956); *Fan-i Samā'-i Ṭabī'ī Az Kitāb-i Shifā',* trans. M. 'Ali Fūrūqī (Tehran, 1938), being a translation of the first Book of the "Physics" of *al-Shifā'* into Persian; ibn Sīnā, *Kitāb al-Shifā',* incomplete, 2 vols. (Tehran, 1886).

43 P. Morewedge, "Philosophical Analysis and Ibn Sīnā's 'Essence-Existence' Distinction," *Journal of the American Oriental Society*, 92 (1972), pp. 425-35.

44 N. Ṭūsī, *Akhlāq-i Nāṣirī*, ed. A. Tehrani (Tehran, 1967), pp. 14, 45.

45 The use of the expression "higher level" here implies that the objects of philosophy are more determinable than the objects of the science of an "inferior" level; thus, a study which investigates particular bodies on earth is considered as being on a "lower" level than the study which investigates the logical relationship between various aspects of the concept of a body, e.g., "dimension," "extension."

46 For a more elaborate discussion of the distinction between "metaphysics" and "natural science" based on the general features of the former, see E. A. Moody, *The Logic of William of Ockham*, p. 118 *et passim*. E. A. Moody's discussion is based upon Ockham's view that metaphysics is not a discursive science. Aristotle makes some interesting remarks on this topic in *Analytica Posteriora*, 76b 36 *et passim*.

47 For a detailed theory of logic in medieval times as a theory of second intentions, see I. M. Bocheński, *A History of Formal Logic* (Notre Dame, 1966), pp. 154-56. Basically, the distinction is between entities of the first intention, which are outside of the soul, and entities of the second intention (*intentiones, ma'qūlāt*), which are thought or conceptual entities. The latter constitute the subject matter of logic.

48 Problems related to attempts of the ancient and medieval philosophers to use the concept of "real definitions" for analysis have been well criticized by contemporary philosophers. For example, see R. Robinson, *Definitions* (London, 1962), pp. 149-92. Presumably now no one would hold the view that the purpose of philosophizing is to define a concept such as "substance." An example of the application of the contemporary tools of analysis to classical philosophy is found in M. Lazerowitz, "Substratum," in M. Black, *Philosophical Analysis* (New Jersey, 1963), pp. 166-82. Contemporary discussions of this general problem in defining a concept by a single term are often expressed in reference to the presupposition of a picture theory of meaning in the doctrine of logical atomism. For a brief history of this issue, see J. O. Urmson, *Philosophical Analysis* (Oxford, 1963), especially pp. 130-62.

49 Ibn Sīnā, *Livre des Définitions*, ed. and trans. A. M. Goichon (Cairo: Institut Français d'Archéologie Orientale du Caire, 1963), p. 23-25.

50 Afnan claims that *gauhar* comes from the Middle Persian *gav*, which means "to grow," *Philosophical Terminology in Arabic and Persian* (Leiden, 1964), p. 93. Ibn Sīnā makes extensive reference to "*gauhar*" and uses

it interchangeably with "*jawhar*" in the Dānish Nāmeh, e.g., p. 11. The translation of "*gauhar*" as "*jawhar*" could not have started with ibn Sīnā because many philosophers prior to him made extensive use of "*jawhar*." For example, Kindī resorts to "*jawhar*" in his works, *Rasā'il al- Kindī al-Falsafīya*, ed. M. Abū Rīdah, 2 vols. (Cairo, 1950, 1953), pp. 10, 12, 14 *et passim*. Afnan points out that Ikhwān al-Ṣafā and Rāzī reportedly resorted to "*jawhar*" in their works. In Persian poetry, however, the use of "gauhar" is extensive, as illustrated by poems of Jāmī and Ḥāfiẓ, *Divān-i Ḥāfiẓ*, ed. S. A. Anjūwi (Tehran, 1968), p. 87; *Divān-i Kāmil-i Jāmī*, ed. S. S. Gauharin (Tehran, 1964), pp. 5, 6, 17, 18, 23, 31, 851, 853, *et passim*.

51 Persian philosophers reverted apparently to the Arabic "*jawhar*" and ignored ibn Sīnā's altempt to popularize "*gauhar*." See S. Y. Suhrawardī, *Oeuvres Philosophiques et Mystiques*: vol. 2, *Oeuvres en Persan; Opera Metaphysica et Mystica*, vol. 3, ed. S. H. Nasr, (Tehran, 1970), pp. 6, 14, 31, 66 *et passim*. Afḍal al-Dīn al-Kāshānī, *Muṣannafāt* vol. 2 (Tehran, 1954), p. 591; in this text Kāshānī discusses the ten categories using the Arabic terms, omitting ibn Sīnā's Persian vocabulary presented in the *Dānish Nāmeh*.

52 It corresponds to the first sense of *ens*, as Ockham states in *Summa Totius Logicae*, I. cxxxviii, clarifying it as "a concept which is common to all things and can be predicated of all things in the manner of quiddity, in the way that a transcendental term can be predicated in the manner of quiddity." *Ockham's Philosophical Writings*, ed. P. Boehner (New York, 1962), p. 90.

53 *Dānish Nāmeh*, chap. 3.

54 *Ibid.*, pp. 8-9.

55 For a detailed analysis of this point, see P. Morewedge, "Philosophical Analysis and ibn Sīnā's 'Essence-Existence' Distinction," *Journal of the American Oriental Society*, 92 (1972): 425-35.

56 The notion of "common" (*'āmm*) is very confusing here. Obviously, Ṭūsī cannot mean that the concept of a "point" is presupposed in every experience in the sense that "being" (*hastī*) might be considered to be presupposed in every experience. His use of the concept of a "point" may give us a clue that he is using *'āmm* as meaning simple, i.e., having no part, without being a logical construction out of other ideas (such as "uncle" can be explained in terms of "parent" and "brother"). In what may be called the "mystical cosmology" of a peculiar text attributed to ibn Sīnā, a point "*naughṭa*" has a special meaning. Here the

author of the text states, "Know that the primary entity in the material universe is a point," elaborating on the theme that, due to its simplicity, a point is the primary intelligible physical entity, presumably depicting the atom of fire. *Risāla dar ḥaqīqat wa kafīyat-i silsila-i mawjūdāt wa tasalsul-i asbāb wa musabbabāt,* ed. M. ʿAmid (Tehran, 1952), p. 17. However, there is no reason for us to assume that Ṭūsī refers to this peculiar doctrine in the *Asās*. The doctrine that "point" is primary is not new in Islamic philosophy. For an interesting discussion of the doctrine of the Pythagoreans on *point* as the beginning of dimensions, see W. K. C. Guthrie, *A History of Greek Philosophy,* 3 vols to date. (London, 1962), 1: 261.

57 For examples of the metaphysical import attached to the concept of "being," note Heidegger's *Being and Time,* trans. J. Macquarrie and E. Robinson (New York, 1962). Here Heidegger cites the traditional features of "being" which resemble Ṭūsī's views, e.g., "indefinability" and "self-awareness" (p. 23). But Heidegger goes further in "investigating" being in terms of "*Dasein* (being-in-the-world)" and features such as "temporality" and "care." For Ṭūsī, as well as for ibn Sīnā, "being" does not pose any "philosophical problem;" it is merely the most determinable, the most indefinite concept, due mainly to the meaning of the term.

58 For examples of type-theoretical languages, see P. Andrews, *A Transfinite Type of Theory With Type Variations* (Amsterdam, 1965); A. A. Frankel and Y. Bar-Hillel, *Foundations of Set Theory* (Amsterdam, 1958), pp. 168-74; A. Church, "A Formation of the Simple Theory of Types," *Journal of Symbolic Logic,* 5 (1940) pp. 56-68. In the context of "types" and "levels" of languages, "being" would be a sign of the highest level. For an interesting philosophical description of "determinables and determinates," see W. E. Johnson, *Logic* vol. 1 (reprinted New York, 1964), pp. 173-75. According to this terminology, "being" is a supreme determinable. On the notion of "transcendental terms," note Moody's succinct explanation in *The Logic of William of Ockham,* pp. 45-46. Ṭūsī uses the term "being" in such a sense that it applies to both categorematic and syncategorematic terms.

59 Several instances can be cited where both philosophers show an awareness of the differences between verbal and semantic relations. See *Dānish Nāmeh,* p. 37. Ṭūsī states that the intelligence (*ʿaql*) does not consider or necessarily presuppose a cause for "blackness" as a case of "color," or for "a triangle" as a case of "figure." Here a relationship exists between concepts as cases of "being." Ṭūsī observes, further,

that when we note the existence (presence) of an actual patch of color or a triangular entity, we do seek its cause (or realization).

60 See P. Morewedge, "Ibn Sīnā's Analysis of Metaphysical Concepts," *Philosophical Forum* (forthcoming).

61 See N. Rescher, *Studies in Arabic Philosophy* (Pittsburgh, 1966), p. 50. Rescher's list includes *ayyu* for "quality," whereas the standard Arabic term is *kayfa;* Rescher also lists *kayfa* as "accident," whereas this term is usually rendered as *'araḍ*. Rescher's list is especially instructive, for it covers predicables (χατηγορούμενα) and special questions. See also A. Afnan, *Philosophical Terminology in Arabic and Persian* (Leiden, 1964). Afnan mentions an earlier Arabic list by ibn al-Muqaffa' which differs from that of ibn Sīnā. Ibn Sīnā's list recurs throughout his works, e.g., *al-Najāt* (Cairo, 1938), p. 80. *al-Shifā': al-Manṭiq: al-Maqūlāt,* ed. M. Khodeiri, G. Anawati, A. F. Ahwani, S. Zayed (Cairo, 1960), p. 93; *Dānish Nāmeh, Ilāhiyyāt,* pp. 29-31. *Kāshānī, Muṣannafāt,* 2: 591. In his Persian text, Kashānī uses the Arabic terminology; Ṭūsī does likewise in his *Asās* (pp. 34-59).

62 Jaeger, *Aristotle,* pp. 167-227.

63 D. J. Allan, *Aristotle,* rev. ed. (London, 1963), p. 111.

64 Moody, p. 68, *et passim.* I. M. Bocheński, *A History of Formal Logic,* ed. and trans. I. Thomas (Notre Dame, 1961), p. 53. For Bocheński's discussion of different lists of the categories, see I. M. Bocheński, *Ancient Formal Logic* (Amsterdam, 1968), pp. 33-35; see C. Prantl, *Geschichte der Logik im Abendlande* vol. 1 (Leipzig, 1927): 207, n. 356.

65 W. Kneale and M. Kneale, *The Development of Logic,* rev. ed. (London, 1962), p. 25.

66 A. C. Lloyd, "Neoplatonic Logic and Aristotelian Logic," *Phronesis,* 1 (1955-56), pp. 58-72; 2 (1957), pp. 146-60. Plotinus, *The Enneads,* trans. S. MacKenna, 2nd ed. rev. (London, 1956), p. 443.

67 Lloyd, pp. 65, 151; see *Enneads* VI. 1.

68 *The Cambridge History of Later Greek and Early Medieval Philosophy,* ed. A. M. Armstrong (London, 1967), p. 79. W. D. Ross, *Aristotle* (New York, 1967), p. 27.

69 G. E. M. Anscombe and P. T. Geach, *Three Philosophers* (London, 1961); Anscombe states for example, "Aristotle's intention was to find a complete list of fairly simple kinds of things, with significant logical differences between them, that might be said about a subject," p. 15. G. Ryle, "Categories," in *Logic and Language,* ed. A. Flew (New York, 1953), pp. 281-98. Ryle states, "In the main, Aristotle seems to content himself with taking ordinary language as his clue to the list of predi-

cates, and so of types of predicates," p. 283.

70 J. L. Ackrill, *Aristotle's Categories and De Interpretatione* (London, 1963), pp. 78-81.

71 For translations into Arabic and various texts of the *Categoriae*, see F. E. Peters, *Aristoteles Arabus*, pp. 7-12; K. Georr, *Les Catégories d'Aristote dans leur Versions Syro-Arabes* (Beyrouth, 1948).

72 *al-Shifā' al-Manṭiq: al-Maqūlāt*, pp. 4-5; *al-Shifā': al-Ilāhiyyāt*, I, 93; *al-Najāt*, p. 208.

73 The Stoics adopted four divisions of the categories and the concept of an "indefinite something" (τὸ τὶ). The four categories were (1) το ὑποχεί μενον (substratum-subject), (2) το ποί ον (quality), (3) το πως ἔχον (state), and (4) το πρὸς τὶ πως ἔχον (relation); το τι represented the highest notion. See B. Mates, *Stoic Logic* (Berkeley, 1953), pp. 18-19; C. I. Khan, "Stoic Logic and Stoic Logos," *Archiv für Geschichte der Philosophie*, 51(1969), pp. 158-72; Bocheński, *Ancient Formal Logic*, p. 87.

74 Ibn Sīnā lists the categories in the *Metaphysica of al-Shifā'* p. 93, and in the *Metaphysica of Dānish Nāmeh*, pp. 28-31. For a discussion of the ibn Sīnian "categories," see I. Madkour's introduction to *al-Shifā': al-Manṭiq: al-Maqūlāt*, pp. vii-xxvii.

75 We are using "syntax" here in Carnap's sense of the term. See R. Carnap, *Symbolic Logic and Its Application*, p. 197-212.

76 For an example of the constituents of "theoretical aspects," see R. Carnap, "The Methodological Character of Theoretical Concepts." in *Minnesota Studies in the Philosophy of Science*, ed. H. Feigel and M. Scriven, vol. 1 (Minneappolis, 1956): 38-78.

77 See Jaeger, *Aristotle*, p. 46 for a nominalistic interpretation of Aristotle's doctrine of substance in the *Categoriae*. Jaeger questions seriously the composition of what we regard as Book Zeta. For a comprehensive defense of Aristotle's views expressed in this section, see M. I. Woods, "Problems in Metaphysics Z." in *Aristotle*, ed. M. E. Moravcsik, pp. 215- 38, and Allen, *Aristotle*, pp. 111-12.

78 J. Owens, *The Doctrine of Being*, pp. 137-54: Owens states, "'Substance' and 'essence' seem the only two current translations of οὐσία. Neither is satisfactory for an express study of Aristotelian being." *Ibid.*, pp. 148-49.

79 *Ibid.*, p. 143. In the attempt to present a consistent reconstruction of Aristotelian views, even a sympathetic interpreter like Moody notes a discrepancy in Aristotle's own usage and confusion regarding substance, *Logic of William of Ockham*, p. 137.

80 P. Morewedge, "Philosophical Analysis and ibn Sīnā's 'Essence-Existence' Distinction," *Journal of the American Oriental Society*, 92 (1972), pp. 425-35.

81 Ibn Sīnā, *al-Shifā': al-Manṭiq: al-Maqūlāt*, p. 96.
82 *Ibid.*, pp. 91, 95.
83 *Ibid.*
84 P. Morewedge, "Ibn Sīnā's Analysis of Metaphysical Concepts," *Philosophical Forum* (forthcoming).
85 *Dānish Nāmeh*. p. 77.
86 Ibn Sīnā, *al-Shifā': al-Manṭiq: al-Maqūlāt*, pp. 95-111
87 These features, noted by Aristotle in the *Categoriae*, 4a5 *et passim*, were reiterated by Muslim philosophers, such as al-Fārābī. (e.g., *Kitāb al-Ḥurūf*, pp. 102-103), and ibn Sīnā: *Dānish Nāmeh: Ilāhiyyāt*, pp. 9-10; *Kitāb al-Ḥudūd*, p. 24; *al-Shifā': al-Manṭiq: al-Maqūlāt*, p. 91 *et passim; al-Shifā': Ilāhiyyāt*, I, 57 *et passim.*
88 N. Rescher, "Evaluative Metaphysics," in *Metaphysics and Explanation* (Pittsburgh, 1964), p. 62.
89 See, P. Morewedge, "Ibn Sīnā (Avicenna), Malcolm and the Ontological Argument," *The Monist*, 54, no. 2 (1970), pp. 7234-49, where a nonsubstantial view of "the Necessary Existent" is described; "Ibn Sīnā's Concept of the Self," *The Philosophical Forum*, 2, no. 2 (Winter, 1969), for a discussion of logical problems encountered in any attempt to give a "substance" interpretation of ibn Sīnā's concept of "the self." See also "The Logic of Emanationism and Ṣūfism in ibn Sīnā," *JAOS* 91:4 (1971), pp. 467-76 and 92:1 (1972), pp. 1-18, in which a distinction is made between a philosophical, a mystical, and religious interpretation of the relation between the "self" and "the ultimate being" with regard to ibn Sīnā's system.
90 See P. Morewedge, "Ibn Sīnā's Concept of the Self," *Dānish Nāmeh*, p. 102, for the view of "union;" *Ibid.*, p. 77, on the nonsubstantiality of the "Necessary Existent;" cf. *al-Shifā': Ilāhiyyātt*, II, 354, for a privation of several properties from the Necessary Existent.
91 *Dānish Nāmeh: Ilāhiyyāt*, p. 11; *al-Shifā': al-Ṭab'īyyāt: Kitāb al-Nafs*, p. 10.
92 *Risāla fī Ma'rifat al-Nafs wa Aḥwālihā*, in *Aḥwāl al-Nafs*, ed. A. F. Ahwani (Cairo, 1952), p. 186.
93 *Ibid.*, p. 183.
94 *Al-Ishārāt wa al-Tanbīhāt*, III, 53.
95 *Awṣāf al-Ashrāf*, ed. H. Taqwā (Tehran, 1928), p. 65.
96 *Ibid.*, p. 66.
97 *Ibid.*, p. 67.
98 Ṭūsī, *Aghāz wa-Anjām*, ed. I. Afshār (Tehran. 1957), p. 7.
99 *Ibid.*, p. 33.

100 *Rūmī, Kulliyyāt-i Shams*, ed. B. Furauzānfar (Tehran, 1966), I, 31, poem 485.

101 *Dīvān-i Ḥīfiẓ*, ed. S. A. Anjuwī (Tehran, 1968), p. 71.

102 *Dīvān-i Kāmil-i Jāmī*, ed. H. Radi (Tehran, 1963), p. 100, poem 2026.

103 *Aṭṭār's Manṭiq al-Ṭair*, ed. S. S. Gauharin (Tehran, 1964), p. 251, poem 4543.

104 For a comparison of "the process" and "substance" theories of the self, see P. Morewedge, "Ibn Sīnā's Concept of the Self;" for a comparison of a "mystical," a "religious," and a "typically philosophical (Aristotelian)" depiction of the relationship between "man" and "God," see *Id.*, "The Logic of Emanationism and Ṣūfism in ibn Sīnā."

TWO SENSES OF MYSTICISM IN THE NEOPLATONIC AND SUFIC TRADITION

I
PLATONIC AND NEOPLATONIC SOURCES OF MYSTICISM

While many contemporary scholars observe an essential link between Neoplatonism and mysticism (both monistic and theistic types), they disagree on compatibility between monism and theism. This study proffers a new refinement of monistic mysticism, attempting to clarify the mystical dimensions of Neoplatonism as a specific category of nontheistic monism.[1]

The search for the begetter of mysticism is brief. Most investigators point to Platonism—of all forms, especially its Neoplatonic variations—as begetter(s) of mysticism in the West and the Near East. Take a typical notion, that of the "mystics' way," the very core of the so-called "self-realization ethics." R. Otto, who expresses the views of many, does not take mysticism as a metaphysics but as a doctrine of salvation characterized by "the inward way," and "the way of unity."[2] Otto's claim is corroborated by the concept of the way (*ṭarīqa*) in Islamic mystical (sufic) literature; the mystic is referred to as the traveler (*sālik*) of the mystical path; mysticism is a series of phenomenological transformations through the stations (*maqāmāt*) due to external efforts and the intentional state (*aḥwāl*), due to degrees of authentic encounters. In Ṣufism, gnosis (*ma'rifa*) is explained not in terms of knowledge (*'ilm*) of concepts nor sense data, but a series of revealments (*kashfhā*) where the mystic's entire world-perspective is sequentially modified until mystical union is achieved. What is the source of this doctrine? Without postulating causal connections, one observes two prototypes of this sense of knowledge in the Platonic corpus: "the allegory of the cave," in the *Republic* (514 A-521 B) and, as D. E. Anderson has observed, the ladder of ascent in the *Symposium* (209 E-212 C).[3] Note the generic use of 'mysticism' in our discussion, which includes but extends beyond "theistic" types of mysticism. Classical scholars of Plato agree. In this tenor, F. M. Cornford takes Plato's demiurge not as the object of worship, the God of the Bible, or as a religious figure. Cornford sees "no justification for the suggestion, conveyed by 'God,' with the capital letter, that Plato was a monotheist."[4] J. Burnet agrees, "We must not assume . . . that Plato meant by God what a modern theist would mean . . . he is a Mind (νοῦς) . . . but not the supreme being," as God cannot be identified with the Good which is a form and not a soul. Plato as a major source of mysticism is upheld by a large number of "the friends of the forms," and they come in every nationality, from al-Suhrawardī (d. 1191), who refers to the Divine Plato, to A. N. Whitehead (d. 1947), who saw all subsequent philosophy as a series of footnotes to Plato's texts. The consensus is that the prototype of the framework for meta-mysticism is based on Plato's works. While Plotinus is taken as *the* major philosopher of mysticism, Plato is the seed, and Plotinus is the flower. Plato's corpus is pregnant with many mystical notions, but it is in the *Enneads* where Plotinus gives birth to many of them and raises them as sturdy offspring. Let me point to another central doctrine of mysticism, that of the Absolute (*ḥaqq-i muṭlaq*). Plato's ultimate beings are the normative Form of the Good (τό ἀγαθόν) (cf. *Republic* 508 C-509 B), who begets other forms, and the demiurge (δημιουργός) (cf. *Timaeus* 30 C-31 B), the maker of the universe as a living thing, the craftsman-artist in the cosmogony. Instead of these two, the Plotinian system has a single Absolute One (τὸ ὄν), which is both the Good as well as the major figure in cosmogony. But we need to look further, as the Neoplatonic One is beyond "being" or "supra-being."[5] In fact we do have a different system or even an original system. As stated by R. A. Gilbert, "he [Plotinus] was the first to set out clearly the idea of the Absolute (the One or the Good)."[6] It is Plotinus' Absolute (which is also the Good), and not the demiurge of Plato, that is the most important model for mysticism. For many, the mark of experiential mysticism is the urge to encounter some sense of union or connection with the Absolute; this is true especially in the "rational mysticism" of W. Kingsland and "interpretative mysticism" of W. T. Stace.[7] With respect to several other topics, Plotinus is his own person; consider Plotinus' cognitive aesthetics, the distinction between the beautiful and the Good, and the dearth of political philosophy and physics in Plotinus in contrast to the extensive treatment of these topics by Plato. In my opinion, even though these reasons are sufficient for the primacy of Plotinus in mysticism, the most important cause deals with people's unexamined personal convictions—namely their religions. This is the reason for the primacy of Plotinus' direct and undeniable influence on the mystical dimensions of monotheistic traditions, especially Christianity. I believe that religiously inclined scholars are attracted to Neoplatonism, partially because of its affinity with the mystical dimensions of monotheism. Recall that Findlay's wonderful article, "Why Christians Should be Platonists" was not titled "Why Platonists should be Christians"![8] In sum, I agree with many, like R.H. Jones, who consider Plotinus' philosophy an original system in spite of its Platonic background.[9]

II
NEOPLATONISM AND THEISM

W. R. (Dean) Inge, expressing a consensus on Plotinus' influence on Christianity, remarks, "Plotinian mysticism . . . closely resembles the records of the Christian mystics, and indeed all mystics, whatever their creed, date, or nationality."[10] He calls Plato the father of European mysticism, and points out that "Justin Martyr claims Plato (with Heraclitus and Socrates) as a Christian before Christ; Athenagoras calls him the best of the forerunners of Christianity, and Clement of Alexandria regards the Gospels as perfected Neoplatonism."[11] F. C. Hoopold first identifies Neoplatonism as the synthesis of Greek and Oriental philosophy. Pointing to philosophical systems such as that in *The Mystical Theology* of Dionysius the Areopagite, he notes "As a result of fusion of Christian and Neoplatonist ideas in the early centuries of the Christian era, a system of so-called mystical theology came into existence which was one of the main foundations of Christian mysticism."[12] Steven Katz holds that the "unitive Christian mystics are invariably those such as Eckhart, Tauler, and Suso, who follow Plotinus, Dionysius the Areopagite, i.e. the strong Neoplatonic current in Christian intellectual history."[13] Another major investigator in Christian mysticism, R. C. Zaehner, who in his *Zen, Drugs and Mysticism*, states, "The main-stream of Christian mysticism, for instance is probably more influenced by Neoplatonism and Pseudo-Dionysius . . . than it is by the *New Testament*."[14] Jewish mysticism displays the same influence. For example, G. G. Scholem states that Maimonides' "mystical inclination turns him in the direction of Neoplatonism. There can be no doubt that he read . . . [the Neoplatonic text which was known as] . . . 'The Theology of Aristotle.'"[15] G. G. Scholem traces Jewish mysticism's debt to Neoplatonism in later thinkers such as Abraham Cohen Herrera of Florence (d. 1635-39)."[16] M. Idel states that "Another source of motifs, concepts, and terms . . . to Jewish medieval mysticism was Neoplatonism . . . the deep religious significance of this form of philosophy has already been recognized in the cases of Islamic and Christian mysticism, and Kabbalah fully shares with these mystical systems a deep interest in Neoplatonism."[17] I. Husik notes that, "The only source of Maimonides' ideas is to be sought in Neoplatonism."[18] T. M. Rudavsky, in her analysis of the Jewish philosopher, Maimonides, notes, "echoing Plotinus, Maimonides characterizes matter as 'a nonexistent,' 'nothing which is not nothingness.'"[19] In the case of Islamic philosophy, I concur with M. Fakhry in his claim that Neoplatonism found in the so-called *Theologia Aristotelis* influenced Muslim thinkers more than the works of Aristotle.[20] With regards to Islam, I have pointed out a number of links between Neoplatonic and Islamic mysticism in several writings; for example, most Muslim philosopher-mystics abandoned the creation theory of orthodoxy for a Neoplatonic type of emanation, because mystical union can be formulated in process metaphysics, but not in a substance-event metaphysics.[21] Is there a limit to Neoplatonic influence? No limit, or only a few, according to some contemporary scholars. In this same vein, R. T. Wallis notes,

> . . . post Cartesian Continental thought has retained a substantial Neoplatonic component. Thus in the seventeenth century Spinoza's monism and Leibniz's monadism represent different developments of a common Neoplatonic substratum, while in the Nineteenth century Schelling's Plotinian-influenced thought counterpoints Hegel's more

> Procline system. [moreover] Bergson's [creative evolution]. . . restates Plotinus' philosophy of the soul. . .[22]

We need to probe further three refinements of this relationship, namely (a) "salient features of mysticism relevant to Neoplatonism," (b) "the sense in which Neoplatonism is mystical," and (c) "further clarification of Neoplatonism by examples of monisms which are mystical but not Neoplatonic."

III
BASIC TYPOLOGIES IN CONTEMPORARY SCHOLARSHIP OF MYSTICISM

Clarifying the basics of contemporary typologies, I construe distinctions between theistic, nature and the monistic dimensions of some mystical systems.

SOME CONTEMPORARY IMPRESSIONS OF ZAEHNER'S TYPOLOGY

As the most significant contemporary typology, Zaehner's theories have elicited reactions. On the one extreme, John M. Rist writes, "We shall take as guide R. C. Zaehner's *Mysticism: Sacred and Profane,* a book whose importance for the study of mysticism is so great as to make much of what has previously been written look like pointless maundering."[23] On the other extreme, F. Staal accuses Zaehner of both religious bias and emotionalism, as Staal writes, "Zaehner's approach contributes little to the serious study of mysticism. It does not establish a position from which one can do more than scratch the surface of Hindu and Muslim forms of mysticism."[24] W. T. Stace proffers a distinction between "the experience of mysticism" and "the interpretation of that experience," and claims "in my opinion, he [Zaehner was] gravely misled by his failure to hold the distinction in mind."[25] Many contemporary thinkers, such as R. T. Wallis, agree with Stace that Zaehner confuses categories of interpretation and experience.[26] A critical analysis of Zaehner's views with respect to mysticism and Neoplatonism has been stated in a previous essay.[27] Here we focus on those elements of Zaehner's typology relevant to this essay.

FUNDAMENTALS OF ZAEHNER'S TYPOLOGY

Proffering a theistic model for mysticism, Zaehner criticizes "nature mystics," who, like Spinoza, equate "nature" with "God;" Zaehner claims " . . . it is an observable fact that in Nature there is neither morality no charity nor even common decency. God, then, is reduced to the sum-total of all natural impulses in which the terms 'good' and 'evil' have no meaning. Such a God is subhuman, a god fit for animals, not for Rational Creatures."[28] The nature mystic, for Zaehner, construes a single unity out of distinct constituents of nature and in exalted moments sees himself/herself as being one with Nature and beyond good and evil.[29] The projection of a unity is understandable, as all mystics seek a unity to combat alienation. A Nature mystic reaches this feeling of unity by his/her monistic integration of the self with the rest of nature and not with a supranatural religious entity. For Zaehner, such a unity is mistaken for two reasons. First, nature contains morally negative elements; second, monism misconstrues the true nature of persons and alienates them from their divine element. The true path for him is the "theistic and dualistic" type of mysticism by those who are "abhorred" by the doctrine of nature mystic. Theistic mystics attempt to surrender worthy dimensions of themselves to a transcendent God; this is not achieved by integration, but by "isolation" of the self-soul from ephemeral nature. In defense of theistic mysticism, he warns of the cardinal mistake of the nature mystic, who is "deceived by the mere sensation of union or of unity into the belief that the object of such a union must be the same."[30] By knowing his/her limit, a theist is a dualist who recognizes God as an entity transcending creatures; on the other hand, an absolute Monist denies existence of the real God, because the proper monotheistic God is a transcendent being. "Monism in practice, means the isolation of the soul from all that is other than itself."[31] Zaehner observes a deep personal intimacy between a believer and his/her perspective of God. Analogies used by Zaehner reveal the ethos of his vision of "good" mysticism; "The goal is isolation . . . [it] . . . means the isolation of what Christians call man's immortal soul from all its purely psycho-physical adjuncts. . . . The soul in such a state might be compared to that of a new born child; it has reverted to original innocence in which there is neither good nor evil."[32] A more revealing analogy is expressed as follows, "The soul, then, at this stage is comparable to a virgin who falls violently in love and desires nothing so much as to be "ravished," "annihilated," and assimilated into the beloved . . . the raptures of the theistic mystic are closely akin to the transport of sexual union, the soul playing the part of the female and God appearing as the male."[33] A paradigm case of salvation by isolation is found in the Virgin Mary, the sinless holy figure, transcending the standard Jungian image of woman as a depiction of the fourth element (represented by matter). In summary, Zaehner's typology points to two types of mysticism relevant to our analysis: a theistic isolation type of mysticism, in which the mystic accepts the transcendent God with Whom he/she cannot be identified; the other, a nature monistic mysticism, in which the path of self-realization is via integration of the self into nature. Zaehner's contribution to the theoretical analysis of mysticism is commendable; even his critics recognize his sharp distinction between religious and non-religious types of mysticism.

STOEBER'S "THEO-MONISM" AND CRITICISM OF ZAEHNER

In a brilliant move, Michael Stoeber rejects the theist-monist distinction in Zaehner's typology and introduces the new typology of "theo-monism,"

> Phenomenologically . . . [theo-monism is expressed] in terms of mystical self ['s] transformation to divinity. The monistic experience involves a movement towards realization of primary-self, an essence that has its grounding in the very non-dual, static and impersonal essence of a personal Divine. The mystic identifies monistically with the apophatic Source; and this essential association is a purifying movement wherein the mystic becomes a unique medium of elements and energies of the catastrophic Di-

> vine. In experiencing the non-dual, static and impersonal Source, the mystic naturally comes to express distinctively and actively aspects of the personal Divine.[34]

Stoeber moves beyond the theist/nontheist distinction to phenomenal sense of identity; "In theistic mysticism some sense of identity remains in a powerfully affective experience which is expressed in strikingly personal terms . . . [nontheistic] monistic experiences involve a loss of duality or differentiation which rules out personal experiences all together."[35] Stoeber's speaks of "an identification with the Divine," and expresses it by saying that "the Divine expresses both impersonal and personal elements, thus bridging the monotheistic and theistic gap."[36] On a similar theme, C. Hartshorne maintains that although there is a distinction between "the abstract, eternal, necessary essence of deity and the concrete, contingent, partly temporal Divine reality," nevertheless "there are ways of making somewhat more detectable the presence of Deity in all experience;" one way would be to go along with Whitehead "that any direct data of experience are simultaneous with the experience for which they are data, or by which they are prehended."[37] Stace assigns this type of mysticism to a specific type, as he notes that, "According to our view, the essence of introvertive [mystical] experience is the undifferentiated unity, and 'union with God,' [for Western religions, especially Christianity, there] is only one possible interpretation of it."[38] What is the underlying emphasis here? It is on the introvertive mysticism of the relationship between persons and God, as Inge asserts,"

> Religious mysticism may be defined as the attempt to realise the presence of the living God in the soul and in nature, or, more generally, as the attempt to realise, in thought and feeling, the immanence of the temporal in the eternal and of the eternal in the temporal.[39]

The affinity between persons and God is asserted in most sacred texts of monotheism such as the Qur'an, "We are nearer to Him than His own jugular vein."[40] The model of religious theomonism proffered by Stoeber does not account for a symmetric union between persons and God, or an annihilation of persons in God. It is an epistemic pose, or recognition that the inner essence (what the Muslims call *dhāt*) is grounded in the Divine love. I agree with Stoeber that mystics in their devotional ethos, such as prayer, seek to overcome their alienation as an ephemeral entity and relate to the eternal God. But from a non-phenomenological perspective, the dualism remains, because in monotheistic systems, persons and God remain separate. No one can remain a monotheist and claim a symmetrical identity with God. The term 'identification' in its usage as related to 'union,' has many senses. For example, a piece of ice may melt in water and unite with the water. Here the ice melts and the water remains relatively unchanged. In contrast, a patch of blue paint and a yellow paint merge; they unite in a green color and lose their original identity. A male and a female may marry and unite through a child who is common to both of them, while they remain separate entities. A wave in an ocean unites with the rest of the ocean as the ocean transforms through configuration. The last example may be an illustration of Spinoza's "extroverted" mysticism in which monism is preserved; but none of the above senses of identification matches the theistic sense. Why? Supposedly, God is essentially distinct from his creatures; thus no identification or union is possible where God's constituents and a person's constituents merge. It is in this sense that C. Smith notes, "Mysticism as understood by Eckhart is not necessarily a matter of ecstasy or bliss . . . [but] a total surrendering of self and self-will, the creation within oneself of a certain void or nothingness."[41] We have pointed out in another essay that Descartes' ontological argument can be interpreted not as a static logical argument, but a process of phases of increasing authenticity between the apparent and the inner reality.[42] At first Descartes knows that if he asserts that he thinks, then he must exist as a mind; further reflections reveal the finite nature of his self-mind, which can only be actualized on the ground of an infinite being. The epistemic priority of the self as a constituent of a larger Divine-infinite system does not make the Cartesian system ontologically a monistic system. The continuum from self to God does not make the self infinite. R. Carnap classifies this type of mistake as psychologism in logic, which is a variation of Plato's objection to the sophists' position of identifying perception/belief with knowledge; Carnap states that this type of mistake takes place "when the problems themselves are of an objective nature, but the description . . . which the author intends to give . . . [is] framed in subjectivist, psychological terms . . ."[43] Stoeber's insight is correct as long as he is classifying "monism" in a phenomenological language.

An interesting approach to this problem is found in an interpretation of ibn 'Arabī's mystical system that is aware of the distinction between the transcendent and the phenomenon senses of the Divine. Suppose two realms are postulated: Reality [*aletheia*, *ḥaqq*] in itself transcends the phenomenological realm of the believer and the monadic mind-dependent phenomenon world (*dhinī*) of the mystic, in which he/she takes God to be an appearance of Reality, is so far as he/she can prehend. The intimacy (*uns*) that is felt by the mystic is not his/her identification with the Absolute, but with a God revealed by pheomenological icons, such as the ninety divine names.[44]

The self-soul in the theistic mysticism variations of Zaehner and Stoeber, teaches the absolute supremacy and the alienation of God—a God who tests Abraham by requesting the sacrifice of his son. This is very different from the Plotinian soul-self which ascends toward the One; as Plotinus states, "Since the soul is so honorable and divine a thing, be sure already that you can attain God by reason of its being of this kind, and with this as your motive ascend to him" [V.1, 3.1-2].

IV
THEISTIC MYSTICISM AND NEOPLATONISM

Our preliminary step in refinement of "monism," is to present a distinction between it and "theistic mysticism."

MONOTHEISTIC MYSTICISM

Following Carnapian methodology, let us clarify our explicandum of "monotheistic mysticism" using a set of conditions differentiating it from other senses of mysticism in ordinary discourse.[45]

1. *Traditional divine predicates*: The monotheistic God has a mind, a free will and the power to create the world; He is an entity to whom creatures can pray. Note that it would be meaningless to pray to nature or to Aristotle's First Mover.
2. *Absolute transcendence of God.* The doctrine of God's "transcendence" means that it is possible that God exists while the world does not exist. So, creation takes place not by necessity but through God's grace. R. Otto notes on this topic that "All religion, indeed, seeks the transcendent, and salvation in transcendent . . . [that] there remains always the chasm between creator and created."[46]
3. *Impossibility of a unity between God and persons.* God is essentially different from persons. For any person to claim "I am God" is always false.
4. *Mystical proximity in the model of the mathematical "limit."* In this model, persons are construed as processes and not substances. Analogous to the mathematical notion of a "limit," as a person x partakes of mystic states, distinctions between person-like experience and God-like experience decreases toward '0' without ever becoming '0.'

   For any person x, as [$x \rightarrow$ mystical], then [$x \rightarrow$ God-like, or having a God-like perspective]. Embracing mystical states persists not because of x's power alone, but also by God's love, grace, etc.
5. *Normative bifurcation of the world into two casts.* Ethical grace can be achieved while the believer is in an "ontologically lower state." Persons are morally/spiritually inferior to God, prophets, angels, etc. There is always "otherness" between them and the heavenly immortals.
6. *Phenomenological and concrete dimensions of mystical encounter.* In theistic mysticism, the relation between a person and God is closer than the relationship between a person and him/herself, because God is taken to be the inner-essence (*dhāt*) of a person in three senses: the remote efficient cause, because God is the creator, the essence as the cause of persistence of the unity of the entity (which means that a person exists by God's grace), and finally, the final cause, or the

cause of completion (*kamāl, telos*). In a sense, a person does not belong to him/herself, but belongs to the Divine.

SOME DIFFERENCES BETWEEN MONOTHEISM AND MONISM: NEOPLATONIC AND AVICENNAN MONISM

Outside the rubric of western scholarship on Neoplatonism lies a vast domain of Neoplatonic work in the Near East, especially in the Islamic arena.[47] This section focuses on the work of Plotinus as well as Avicenna, who followed Plotinus in emanationism, but differed from his system in many ways. Neither the classic Neoplatonic position nor any one of its major developments, such as Islamic Neoplatonism, is compatible with the theistic notion of God, at least in regard to the following topics:

(a) Plotinus' One is not an entity in the sense of Aristotle's immaterial substance (*ousia*), nor is it a monotheistic God like that of Judaism, who made a covenant with man, and who, like the God of Christianity had a son, and who, like the God of Islam sent an angel (Gabriel) to give moral messages to a man (Prophet Muḥammad) in the cave. These depictions would be meaningful if we substituted "God" for the "One" of Neoplatonism. Plotinus states that "The One is all things and not a single one of them . . . it's the principle (*arche*) of all things and the generator of [entities]" [V.2., 1., 1-3]. The First is beyond (supra) being, and does not think," [*Enneads*, III.8, 1]; the First as the Good is beyond thinking [*Enneads*, III.9, 2-5]. In the world of Plotinus and Avicenna, the ultimate being not an entity but an imminent begetter, a ground of existents, and the beholder [*dāranda*] of the world rather than an existent substance (*ousia, jawhar*).[48]

(b) Unlike the monotheistic God, the One of Plotinus has neither love, grace, nor self-consciousness, nor free will. Thus, according to Plato's *Eythyphro*, one does not pray to Gods, nor does one fear them. The One of Plotinus does not bring floods, does not kill the first-born of the Egyptians to tilt his power in a dispute between believers and non-believers; nor is he instrumental in sending the believers into heaven and the sinners into hell. It is an entity totally different from the monotheistic God shared by the Jews, Christians and Muslims.

(c) The God of Plotinus or Avicenna does not create the world out of nothing by His grace. The world emanates by Necessity; it could not have been otherwise. H. A. Wolfson observed correctly that since Philo believed in the scriptures, Philo parted from Plato, when the doctrines of the Greek philosophers were against religion; whereas Plato's cosmogony takes place by necessity, "Philo, however, following the scriptural conception of God as an all powerful free agent . . . takes the will [of God to mean that] . . . he could have either created the world or created another kind of world . . . [and] can destroy the world."[49] In Avicenna's system, emanation of the world is implied from the "most perfect" (*fauq al-tamām*) feature of the Necessary Existent (*al-Wājib al-Wujūd*). Not only is the latter an existent by itself, it is also the causal generator of other existents. A mere "perfect" (*tamām*) entity, generated by the "most perfect," is persistent due to itself, while an "imperfect" entity (*nāqiṣ*) needs another in order to persist.[50]

(d) Another distinction concerns the nature of the soul and role of the body in human salvation. Inge states, "the essence of Neoplatonic mysticism is the belief that the Soul, which lives here in self contradiction, must break in succession every form in which it tends to crystallize. This is where it differs from Catholicism . . . [which] promises peace as the immediate result of submission and obedience . . . but for the mystics . . . there is no rest from striving . . . to stop short [of union] is to leave the quest unfinished."[51] Stace agrees on the distinctions between theism and mysticism on this point.[52] Like Zaehner, Plotinus too teaches "isolation," for example, in the following context, "Often I have woken up out of the body and have entered into myself, going from all other things" [IV.8.1-2].[53] In a person, the body is a mere icon or an image of his/her soul in its lowest state; while embodiment is the logical end of descent from which ascent takes place. Consequently, embodiment is a positive, natural stage, a necessary phase for later purification, and this theme has been elaborated upon by later Neoplatonists of all traditions. For example, the Ismaili thinker, Nāṣir Khosrow [b1004-1072-78], notes that the particular soul [*nafs-i juz'ī*] needs to be emanated from the universal soul [*nafas-i kulī*] and ultimately to return to it.[54] In Neoplatonic mysticism, the descent is a necessary prerequisite for the mystical union. In contrast, in theistic mysticism, isolation of the self from the body is for the sake of intimacy with God. For example, in the Eucharist in Christianity, the believer partakes of a matter which serves as an icon of the body of Christ. A related topic is the issue of incarnation, as depicted in C. Osborn's recent comparison between Platonic and Christian love; she states, "Unlike the Neoplatonic soul, cast into bodily life as a punishment or imprisonment against its will, Christ's incarnation is chosen for a loving purpose, to redeem the lost sheep."[55] I reject Osborne's interpretation of Plotinus; the embodiment for Plotinus is a free act (but also determined), being a "standard" phase in the drama of salvation; the savior figure in Neoplatonism is a person's intellectual awareness of her/his affinity with the One.

(e) Not only is emanation by necessity, so is ascent free from God's love, affections, etc. By contrast, ascent is due to a person's effort (a person is both free and dependent). Most of the philosophers in the Islamic tradition adopted Neoplatonic emanationism instead of the creation theory. For example, J. J. Houben shows that Avicenna's philosophy is incompatible with Islamic orthodoxy; in Avicenna's system, the mystical union with the Necessary Existent is not a "gift," from God; instead, it is due to the natural knowledge of the Necessary Existent.[56] Through natural knowledge, and not religious calling, we comprehend the cosmos and its Necessary Existent as the beholder of the cosmos. Thus, every entity in this world is a necessity, the first being a categorical necessity, while others are conditional necessities. Incidentally, the difference between nontheistic and theistic models exists not only in an emanation-return type of monism, but also in a more static type, such as Spinoza's ontology. Moreover, the absolute of Neoplatonic tradition resides in its abstract-simple state, whereas, as S. T. Katz states, for the monotheistic tradition of Judaism, it lies in the personal God.[57] W. J. Wainwright presents a similar insight, as he points out that although Plotinus uses the language of love between souls and the One, here love is asymmetrical; the One of Plotinus is loved like the God of the theists, but unlike the God of the theists, the One does not love in return.[58]

(f) The next distinction between Neoplatonism and theism relates to differences concerning the unity of being (*al-waḥdat al-wujūd*). The major role of this doctrine is well brought out by Inge, who asserts, "The Unity of all existence is a fundamental doctrine of all mysticism."[59] It is true that in Neoplatonism there are sharp theoretical distinctions between the One, the intelligence, the soul and matter as a reflection of the soul. But each entity in this descent emanated from its predecessor, contains a dimension of its predecessor, and returns to its predecessor. On this principle of "reversion," Proclus states, "All that proceeds from any principle reverts in respect of its being upon that from which it proceeds" [*Elements*, prop. 31, p. 35], and "Every effect remains in its cause, proceeds from it, and reverts upon it" [*Elements*, pro. 35, p. 39].[60] The monistic vision of the immanence of the ultimate being is at least ontological, as well as phenomenological, as shown by W. Earle, "the experience of the identity of myself and the Absolute."[61] As we clarify, the thesis of "identity among persons and the ultimate being" cannot be construed in a monotheistic system in which persons are particular entities while God is transcendent. In contrast, in Neoplatonism, as Plotinus stated, the moral ethos of a person is judged by the degree of lack of "otherness" between persons and ultimate being [*Enneads*. V. 1., 1]. By the mediacy of abstractions, persons are invited to ascend toward the One. In contemporary language, "otherness" means "alienation," and according to many existentialists, psychoanalysts, and Marxists, alienation is the most significant problem of modern persons.[62] Such a problem cannot be formulated in a truly monistic system, in which a person is not alienated from nature. Plotinus preaches that the soul moves towards a state of "no-otherness" with the One. In societies that officially adopted monotheism, nature mystics who interpreted this union as an identity have often been branded as heretics. In Islam, Manṣūr al-Ḥallāj, the celebrated mystic who expressed the monistic doctrine of "*ana al-Ḥaqq*," was burned to death. Professor Zaehner's reaction to such a monistic idea is less dramatic! I disagree with Zaehner's premises, but I think that Zaehner's system is consistent when he, as a theistic believer, disapproves of extravortive monism.

V
NEOPLATONIC AND THREE OTHER SENSES OF MONISTIC MYSTICISM

Having clarified the first level terminology of "theistic" and "nontheistic" mysticism, this essay advances a refinement of "monism," in four different senses.

STOEBER'S TYPOLOGY OF "THEO-MONISM"

We have already indicated that this type, in its monotheistic context, is ontologically duelist, but phenomenologically monist. This intimacy is nonsymmetric, since persons are not deified, but lose their alienation and relate to God. The theo-mystic experiences concrete bliss and has a rich compassionate encounter with the creation of God and the icons of union and intimacy in prayer with the maker. The sharp differences between any religious mysticism and Eidetic Neoplatonism are evident on many points. For example, Plotinus states that "every soul . . . made all living things itself, breathing life into them, those that the earth feeds and those that are nourished by the sea, and the divine stars in the sky. It made the sun itself, and this great heaven, and adorned it" [V.1. 2. 1-4].

NEOPLATONIC EIDETIC MONISTIC MYSTICISM

Let us begin by clarifying the family of themes which depicts this kind of mysticism:

1. *Abstractness.* Ontologically, the Good and the Real are atemporal and abstract entities. Objects of sense perception or feeling of interpersonal relationship have both ontically and normatively lower status than the abstract entities.
2. *Interconnected Realistic Monism.* The system is monistic in the Leibnizian sense that a total description of any entity includes the One and the other entities in the world. Reality is not depicted in phenomenological terms, but in a system of nonpersonal objective entities which persist outside the consciousness.

3. *Cognitive intelligibility.* Abstract entities are either cognitively intelligible like Platonic forms, or refer to the One which transcends limits of discrete reason and can be encountered only through an allegorical or symbolic theology.
4. *Rationalism.* Faith, sentiment, piety, sense perception, and the like, have a state inferior to reason.
5. *Iconic function of the concrete.* Concrete entities, like a particular flower, or personal temporally indexed experiences such as loving a mate or a relative, are at best, mere icons of abstract entities. They are preliminary steps to ascend toward abstract entity. Philosophy is permitted to refer to the One by making use of icons such as light, mirror and water instead of clear analytical descriptive language.
6. *Ethics of simplification process, and the ethics of self-realization.* The drama of cosmic salvation begins with a descent and culminates with a return. There are two similar models: first, the Neoplatonic emanation-return, and a second, which is embedded in an eschatology of the Divided line, symbolized by the allegory of the cave, as well as love in the symposium. Once again, the encounter with the One is not anti-rational but supra-rational or meta-rational.

Christian theology also has a fall, a sacrifice, and a way of return to the path of God. But in a Neoplatonic system persons do not communicate with the Form of the Good, do not perform prayer, or sacrifice; there is no set of religious rituals; what is demanded is not a blind faith, but a rational state of awareness of the superiority of the eternal over the ephemeral. For example, Plotinus states that the soul is "amphibious," and "in spite of everything, it always possesses something transcendent in some way" [IV.8, 4: 29-31]. As D. O'Brien notes, with respect to natural objects, the soul has a dual function. First, the soul generates matter; then, the soul provides matter with forms which complete matter into a body.[63]

The salient feature of Neoplatonic mysticism, according to John N. Findlay, is depicted in the "the Eidetic Turn." In such a system, the emphasis is no longer on the "individual," but how forms such as "Manhood and Justice are 'this-ified' or 'that-ified,' or 'here-ified' or 'there-ified,' 'now-ified' or 'then-ified' in this or that case."[64]

A key concept is that generic and specific features become the true and primary cases of identity, an identity unaffected by multiple locations in space, or changing location in time."[65] Here, ontic primacy is placed not on particulars, this thing here, but to "*eidos,* idea-form-universal;" moreover, "unity [is treated as] a peculiar instance of itself, having no other attribute but being purely and resolutely single."[66] Thus, individual spatiotemporal objects receive their significance only as far as they instantiate or exemplify a form. In Neoplatonic monism, only the One is the source of its own persistence, as well as being the source of generation of all other entities. Individual souls achieve their appropriate state, not by persisting as they are, but at that stage in their ascent when there is no otherness between them and the One. The essence of a monistic ontology is not sacrificed in Neoplatonism, as the souls are not ultimately distinct from the One; the One is the origin (*arche*, *aṣl*) of all entities. The soul, Plotinus tells us, "possess a power directed to the world here below," [IV.8, 4: 3-4]; but he prescribes that the souls should not "forget their father, God, and be ignorant of him . . . they are parts which come from a higher world and altogether belong to it" [V.1, 1-4]. The process of simplification, the mark of ascent, is in fact, a process of de-individualization, simplification, as clarified by Findlay, which depicts an *unbroken continuity* of the eidetic system.[67] All layers of the emanations from the One-Unity aim to return to the One. Plotinus often hints that this descent is necessary "when it is eternally necessary by the law of nature that it [the soul] should do and experience these things, and, descending from that which is above it, it meets the need of something else in its encounter with it, if any one said that a god sent it down he would not be out of accord with the truth or with himself" [IV.8, 5:13-18]. In a subsequent passage, he notes, "So then the soul, though it is divine and comes from above, enters into the body and, though it is a god of the lowest rank, comes to this world by a spontaneous inclination, its power and the setting order in of what comes after it being the cause of its descent" [IV.8, 5:25-28]. In Neoplatonism there is no contradiction here, as Plotinus states "necessity contains the free will . . ." [IV.8, 5: 4-7]. I agree with the general consensus that alienation is the antithesis of mysticism. How, then, is alienation overcome by the Neoplatonists? The answer lies in a state in which there is "no otherness" between the alienated soul and what is now united with the One. This vision is definitely anti-monotheistic for many reasons. As Findlay states, "the Trinitarian structure . . . is not acceptable from the Platonic point of view . . . there is no place in Platonism for Incarnation theology."[68] This vision is correct if one envisions a static model of Neoplatonism. But the Neoplatonic symmetry could be envisioned from the perspective of "the one" as a process of emanation and from the perspective of matter as a process for potential ascent. In this sense there is a two-fold interpretation of the Universe as a continuum that Plotinus inherited from Plato's allegory of the cave. At each phase an entity is causally linked to a continuum. We have a connected universe. A mystical union depicts our best possible encounter with a total perspective of such a connected vision of the universe. Porphyry reports that Plotinus experienced "being one" four times during his acquaintance with Porphyry.[69] As a matter of fact, as A. C. Lloyd delineates, there are three phases of epistemic-cognitive experiences of the soul: its judgment of sense precepts, its collections and divisions of intelligible objects, and finally its "seeing," and non-discursive encounter in the context of its union with the One.[70] In Muslim epistemology such a state belongs to the epistemic state of 'knowledge by immediate presence,' an incorrigible state. It is very difficult for any one who is not "friend of the forms," to have a comprehension of this vision. Any one who, like Professor Zaehner, prefers a smile of a child to a mathematical equation cannot empathize in the pleasure available to the friends of the forms. A friend of the form appreciates the smile of the child as a mere icon of the form of the Beautiful or the Good. A monotheist is not interested in the abstract One but in the Buberian encounter between the finite created I and the eternal Thou. The Neoplatonic One cannot think; Plotinus states, ". . . if the First thinks, something will belong to it; and will then not be the First, but second, and not one." [V.6, 2, 18-20]. Moreover, The One as the Good "must be simple and without need, it will not need think." [VI.6, 4, 1-2]. Plotinus attacks Aristotle as saying that, "Aristotle makes the first principle separate and intelligible, but when he says that it knows itself, he goes back again and does not make it the first principle" [V.1, 9, 9-12]. Thus, the One of Plotinus, unlike the

God of Monotheism, does not think and does not change. The ultimate aim of the soul-self is to ascend through the various levels and identify itself with the pure entity that is not beyond becoming, but beyond being itself. Eidetic mysticism teaches an agenda which takes a person beyond God's grace. Consequently, there arises the misunderstanding of an acute thinker like the Christian Zaehner, who naively objects to Plato as follows: "Plato seems to have made the enormous, the grotesque mistake of separating Being from becoming, and identifying it with the mathematical abstraction of the Idea. He could never, poor fellow, have seen a bunch of flowers shining with their inner light and all but quivering under the pressure of the significance with which they were charged."[71] A friend of the forms would say that Zaehner resembles a child who plays with teddy bears and wonders why his parent who is a biologist attends to the species of bears and considers teddy bears a copy of a copy of a copy. When Plato, "the poor fellow," inspects a flower, he receives not only the form of the flower but an icon that can relate to him the Form of the good. Zaehner's flower disappears in the snow, whereas Plato's form of the flower is everlasting. Plotinus is not in any sense "against" the bodily dimension of persons; attendance to the needs of the body and to its disciplines is recommended (I.4.4). Being like a musical instrument, a person should give up the body graciously in the same manner that a musician may give the lyre which is no longer to be played (I.4.16.13-29). The body serves as an important element in the drama of salvation of the soul. And evil may be necessary, as it is defined as falling short of the Good (III.2.5.27) and like inferior animals, evil still lies within the natural plan. The world is depicted as a play with some characters that are not heroes; what happens to this play if all inferior characters are eliminated (III.2.11)?

EXTROVERTIVE NATURE MONISTIC MYSTICISM

For a transition from the Eidetic to nature mysticism, let us make a comparison. In agreement with his Eidetic sense of mysticism, Plotinus notes that "the greatest beauty in the world of sense, therefore is a manifestation of the noblest among the intelligibles, of their powers and goodness . . ." [IV.8, 6:24-27]. In contrast to this vision, an extroverted "nature" mystic holds that the beauty of this world is due to itself; and the smile of a child, or a smell of a rose does not need to represent an icon of a hidden meaning for it is beautiful in itself. There are obviously experiences that may be immediately pleasurable, like drugs, alcohol, and unsafe sex, which may lead to insanity, destruction of one's liver and brain, and death from AIDS. But not all pleasures need have such drastic consequences; some stand on their own merit or virtue (*arete, kamāl*).

The most common form of nonreligious mysticism is found in human struggle against alienation; a person feels at home in physical nature, in the mode of ecophilia, without a need to presume the existence of any supranatural, divine entity—his/her will to power, to life, is sufficient. Here we need to distinguish between different senses of living experience as well as different senses of "nature." Philosophers of mysticism often distinguish between introvertive and extrovertive types of experiences. Basically, the former is concerned with the intentional depiction of the world as received by the experience of the subject, while the latter refers to thoughts and sense experience without much reference to the subject. Religiously oriented scholars do not deny "extrovertive experiences," but normally assign to them a lower (moral/normative) status. For example, M. Stoeber notes, "In theo-mysticism, extrovertive mysticism is considered a lower level of aspects of the Divine, not a personal assimilation and integration of this Divine."[72] A paradigm case of an extrovert nature thinker is the Roman poet Lucretius, the author of *De Rurum Natura.*[73] Bailey notes that "Lucretius is an impersonal poet; his subject is all in all, and there is very little which directly reveals his own sentiments or experience."[74] For him all nature consists of matter and void—as proved by the senses.[75] A person is merely part of the temporal complex of ever-becoming that is called nature. He holds that "when I am, death is not; when death is, I am not." In the same way that one should not feel sorry for a movement or a melody in a symphony when it passes away, one should not feel sorrow because of aging or death, as our lives lead to the lives of offspring. For the monist of this type, psychological despair and feelings of alienation and the like are due to ignorance or confusion concerning the nature of the world. The remedy is a philosophy of humanistic naturalism that allows persons to optimize the aesthetic pleasure of their experiences and which includes, according to the Epicureans, relationships such as friendship. Laws are not "above" and "beyond" individuals; they constitute our interpretation of the actual natural processes of entities. Any anthropomorphic interpretation of "laws" of nature is "a category mistake." For example, if the number two were alive, it would not worship the fact that it is an even number, for its being even is a dimension of its inner nature.

Reaffirming Stace's position, Stoeber notes that "Nature mysticism has been called extrovertive mysticism . . . [dealing with an] . . . outward experience involving sensory reality."[76] The latter includes what Spinoza names *Natura Naturata*; as H. H. Joachim states, this is "the eternal systems of God's modes, which is the consequence of the free causality of God [as *Natura Naturans*]."[77] Zaehner correctly identifies Spinoza as a "nature mystic," and Stace takes him to be a pantheist with a mystical consciousness.[78] For Spinoza, substance, nature, and God are one and the same; they designate the single total reality of the world. Spinoza's type of mysticism prohibits any dualism between persons and the world. As M. Wartofsky points out, for Spinoza, ". . . a science of human nature is continuous with the science of nature; that human action and passion are subject to universal laws, and therefore as subject to rational understanding, as in motion of bodies . . . [and concepts] . . . in geometry."[79] Thus Spinoza provides us with an example of nature monistic mysticism, whereas G. Deleuze notes that beatitude lies in the expression of the essence of God-nature, to ". . . be oneself an idea through which the essence of God[-Nature] explicate[s] itself, to have affections that are explained by our own essence and express God's [or Nature's] essence."[80] An analogical account of this system is expressed by a common theme in nature-sufic poetry, in which persons and other modes of the world flow as rivers from the ocean of the One and come back to it; thus we depict a mode of nature as a melody in a symphony or a ray of light from the sun. The One is the ground of our being and the final cause of our return. Mystical virtues include receptive resignation (*riḍā*) and authentic openness to receive (*kasb*) our ultimate true self. We should note that this notion of nature as a totality of all is consistent with the peripatetic view of nature as the source of its own notion and is more extensive than the mere physical aspect of nature.[81]

This type of monism is distinct from the Neoplatonic in the following thematic sense. "Nature," for the nature monist, includes what is received in physical experiences as well as what is received in psychological, aesthetic experiences. It is nobler to think globally, like Leibniz, than to maintain a limited monadic perspective, or, like Spinoza and Lucretius, to universalize one's perspective from the concrete to the universal. All of nature is equally good and moral. In contrast, as J. N. Deck notes, for Plotinus "Nature is the lower part of the world soul,"[82] A paradigm case of "nature mysticism" lies in the so-called "individuation process" of Jungian psychology, where salvation comes from integration into nature.[83] As Inge enumerates, in this context, the major three steps are "purgative," "illuminative," and "unitive" life.[84] Inge remarks that the paradigm of the purgative stage is exemplified in the manuals written for the monks. The unitive, we note, belongs to the extrovertive nature mystics.

EXISTENTIAL NATURALISM AS A TYPE OF MONISTIC MYSTICISM

In this vision of mysticism, ontic priority is given to the temporal experiential field of the subject; the subject here is not the isolated ego-soul, but is analogous to the Heideggerian *Dasein* (being-in-the-world). The ontic status of the God of the theists or the abstract forms/the One of the Eidetic mysticism, is turned upside down on its head. Against Plato's claim that time is the moving image of reality, being-present-in-the-world is the only reality through which all archetypes are actualized. For example, the form of beauty or love is actualized in this very momentary embrace.

The existential naturalism type of mysticism and American pragmatism share many themes in common. For example, in ethics, immediacy of human happiness and choice take priority over the Kantian agenda of primacy of duty and social justice. In this tenor, C. I. Lewis distinguishes between two concerns of ethics: the *summum bonum* and justice. Lewis remarks on Kant's position as follows: "virtue is the supreme good, but the highest and complete good requires also satisfaction of the human capacity for happiness, which is distinct from the moral and even—on his [Kant's] account—opposed to it."[85] The crucial point here is not emphasis on social responsibility and cosmic justice but on the primacy of human happiness in ethics. For both the existential naturalists and modern pragmatists, values are not distinct from and posterior to fact; instead, values are essential constituents of facts. C. I. Lewis explains, "Valuations are a form of empirical knowledge, not fundamentally different in what determines their truth or falsity, and what determines their validity or justification, from other kinds of empirical knowledge."[86] Consider biological urges such as consumption of food, love, or bodily reactions to temperature changes. In these cases, our valuations are dimensions of our actions. It is not true that we think first about the "objective facts," then evaluate the facts, and then act. Satisfactory explanations of actions must include the pragmatic dimension of valuations. Actions are not existents separate from other aspects of reality. Actions are dimensions of existents. This feature of existential mysticism is expressed by L. Wittgenstein as follows.

> *Doing* itself seems not to have any volume of experience. It seems like an extensionless point, the point of a needle. This point seems to be the real agent. And the phenomenologial happenings only to be consequences of this acting. "I *do* . . ." seems to have a definite sense, separate from all experience.[87]

In sum, for existential naturalists, immediate experience, valuing, and doing are not different types of existents but are dimensions of the experience not posterior to the One of Plotinus or Platonic forms.

Family members of this trend have always been present in philosophy, beginning with Heraclitus and the remarks in Plato's *Theaetetus* on Protagoras' theme "Man is the measure of all things." A number of important philosophers attack the Eidetic terms by placing the 'concrete here' above the 'idea' (ειδος). The most celebrated case is Aristotle's insistence that all accidents are actualized via the primary substance. Next candidate could be Kant's view of imagination; for him, concretion of the categories of understanding happens through imagination, which is the temporal indicator of experience. As we shall elaborate later, it is in medieval Islamic poetry that existential mysticism is explicitly stated in the context of the doctrine of the unity of being. The historical roots of this doctrine may be in Eastern Iran, in Zoroastrianism (c. 1200). H. Corbin and others claim that Islamic mysticism in its Iranian context was influenced by Hermetic illuminationism of Zoroastrianism.[88] According to this religion, Ahura Mazda the Wise Monotheistic God personified actuality and battled the myth of evil. Ahriman was the icon of Not-being. To strengthen himself against not-being, Ahura Mazda created human beings and commanded, "Let there be life"—the will to power. By propagating life, learning, and cultivating the land, human beings, who are vicegerents of God, attempt to bring evil—not being—to its knees. Experience is not a passive encounter with facts. In contrast, persons who have a will to power, to life, create realities. F. Nietzsche's intuition that Zoroastrianism supports an aspect of his "will to power" philosophy was correct. But the affinity between the soul-self and God is noticed in many philosophies. Plotinus asserts that "if anyone is going to admit that it knows God, he will be compelled to agree that it also knows itself" [V.3.7]; here he means that if God is known, then God's effects are also known; because self is an effect of God, then God is also known. In existential mysticism, if one knows one's self, then one is aware of the phenomenological outcomes of the self, which includes God. There is a similarity here also with Bergson's concept of *élan vital*, perceived from the existing energy—here the monistic theist's system is turned upside down on its head.

A paradigm case of this theory is found in the medieval poetry of Sheik Mahmud Shabastarī, who rivals Jalāl al-Dīn Rūmī in depth of Ṣūfi mysticism. Shabastarī states in a poem,

> In unity there can never be a multiplicity. Two (distinct) points cannot be the one single center of unity.
>
> I do not know if the One (lit. the beauty mark of the beautiful face *khāl-i ruy-a zībā*) is a mere reflection of

> the heart (self). Or, if this heart is the reflection of the One. . .
>
> This complicated secret is hidden from me. How can our heart be the reflection of the One, as it is in a perpetual state of flux?[89]

This poem is not an accidental passage, as the theme in question is supported by a number of other passages. For example, the Sheikh defends Ḥallāj's famous identification of the *cogito* with the absolute by saying that, "'I am the absolute' is the revealment of [true] secrets, the only speaker of 'I am the absolute' must be absolute itself."[90] In another passage he asserts that, "The universe is found due the light of the Absolute [lit. Him], how can the Absolute be found in the Universe."[91] In another passage, the Sheikh finally answers the primordial question of "Who am I?" as follows, "since one can only refer to the Absolute existence [*hastī muṭlaq*] in an iconic mode, the [wise] refer to it as I."[92] In Islamic mysticism, the depiction of an intimate relationship between the self and the Absolute is a common theme. As al-Ghazālī points out, the "self-soul" and God-world are transcendental conditions of experience.[93] But one finds parallel themes in the Western tradition. For example, Augustine states, "God and the Soul, that is what I desire to know." When asked, "Nothing more?" he answered, "Nothing whatever."[94] Wittgenstein's account of the self in the world corroborates this phenomenological theme as he notes that, "I am my world," and that "The Philosophical self is not the human being, not the human body, or the human soul, with which psychology deals, but rather the metaphysical subject, the limit of the world—not part of it."[95] Even Plotinus emphasizes the soul's unqualified perspective in contrast to the body by asserting that ". . . all soul is present every where, made like the father who begets it in its unity, and its universality" [V.1, 2, 39-41].

In contrast to the Neoplatonic Eidetic view, the primacy of immediate experience has support in everyday life as well as in philosophical traditions. Suppose a plane that carries someone dear to you is late by two hours. For you, the second hour feels much "longer," than the first, while for an impartial bystander, the second hour is the same as the first. When your automobile develops trouble on a trip or it begins to snow heavily, the distance to the destination "seems further." In sum, existential time, a time related to the feeling-space of a subject is an experiential dimension of a reality. In this tenor, Bergson refers to that dimension of "time [which] is at first identical with the continuity of our inner life . . . a melody to which we listen with our eyes closed . . . [which] comes close to coinciding with this time which is the very fluidity of our inner life."[96] Several writers claim that such a phenomenological perspective embeds the language of religion. Thus William Earl notes,

> Phenomenologically speaking, what could be more obvious than that the very *language* of religion and metaphysics, the sense of their terms, the meaning of such terms as eternity, God, Absolute, Reality, Identity, and the rest would be impossible for us, unless there were *in* each self *resources* out of which those terms could draw their sense.[97]

Earle goes further to claim that "Absolute reality has *no value at all*" [Earle's emphasis], it can only be used as an empty center that works as an allegorical principle of the cosmos.[98] Most scholars of Neoplatonism agree on the compatibility of this theme with Neoplatonism. As A. C. Lloyd tells us, "Certainly the (Neoplatonic) genus which contains its species only latently—still more the genus of all genera—cannot possibly be covered by a phenomenological description."[99] In the same manner, R.H. Jones observes, it cannot claim identity with the One.[100]

A salient mark of existential mysticism in its Islamic version is the epistemology of revealment of the hidden (truth). This doctrine has a close affinity with the rise of Islamic phenomenological epistemology after Avicenna, which emphasized knowledge by presence, and by revealment (*kashf*). In perception, the subject is conscious and supposedly receives information about concreta, for example, the distance between the earth and the sun. In conception and deduction, analytical truths and valid structures are contemplated. In mysticism, the gnosis (*ma'rifat)* or sense of knowing is depicted in a process of transformations of the self through different phases of self-realization. The preliminary phase displays alienation from the Divine, the middle phase, love of the mediator figure, and finally, a mystical union in which the alienated soul-self (*nafs*) is annihilated and a person is preserved by incarnation of the divine dimension.

Finally, the salient differences between existential and the other three types of monistic mysticism are its incarnation of the divine (as opposed to the idea in theistic-monism of the absorption of the self into God), its emphasis on the concrete immediacy (as opposed to the abstract dimension of Neoplatonic Eidetic mysticism), and the emphasis on the phenomenology of incarnation of the entirety of nature within the self (as opposed to the idea in nature mysticism of a dissolution of the self in nature).

VI
CONCLUSION

In the monotheistic tradition, Neoplatonism is the most significant source of theistic as well as nontheistic types of mysticism. In spite of this influence, Neoplatonism itself is not a religious type of mysticism, due to its Eidetic monism. Contrary to Zaehner's position, not all monistic systems are anti-religious or irreligious; as Stoeber points out, one could construe an interpretive monistic model which is theistic. Finally, not all nonreligious mysticisms are Neoplatonic; we have described two types of genuine monistic mysticisms which are nonreligious and not Neoplatonic. Hopefully, this essay clarifies some of the key elements in the relationship between Neoplatonism and mysticism.

NOTES

1 For the sake of brevity and precision, our context is limited to monotheistic tradition and to its philosophical counterparts in Ancient Greece, Ancient Near East, Judaism, Christianity and Islam.

2 R. Otto, *Mysticism: East and West*, (New York: Macmillan, 1960), pp. 33-72.

3 Unless specifically stated, all translations of the works of Plato are taken from *The Collected Dialogues of Plato, including the Letters,* trans. E. Hamilton and H. Cairns. (New York: Bollingen, 1966); the references to the Greek

texts are from the Loeb bilingual editions of Plato's dialogues. Cf., D. E. Anderson, *The Mask of Dionysos: A Commentary on Plato's 'Symposium'* (Albany: State University of New York Press, 1993), p. 93.

4 F. M. Cornford, *Plato's Cosmology, the Timaeus*, (London, 1937), pp. 33-34.

5 There is a difference in the Neoplatonic and Avicennian languages. For Avicenna, "being" applies to whatever is significant; thus for him, the Necessary Existent is a "being" but not a substance. For Plotinus, the One is beyond being and is the generator of all existents. Cf., P. Morewedge, "Philosophical Analysis and the Essence-Existence Distinction," *Journal of American Oriental Philosophy* (1972), pp.49-73.

6 R. A. Gilbert, *The Elements of Mysticism*, (Longmead and Rockport: Element Books, 1991).

7 See W. Kingsland, *Rational Mysticism*, (London: George Allen and Unwin, 1924); and W. T. Stace, *Mysticism and Philosophy*, (London: Macmillan, 1960), pp. 31-38. Besides facing Aristotle, as the sharp opponent of Platonism, Plotinus refined Platonic answers to Aristotelian criticisms. Moreover, he differed from Plato concerning several topics, such as the ontic priority of the Good over the beautiful and the cognitive status of aesthetics. For these reasons he cannot be treated as a mere commentator of Plato.

8 J. N. Findlay, Cf., *Neoplatonism and Christian Thought*, ed. D. J. O'Meara, (Albany: State University of New York, 1982), pp. 223-232.

9 Richard H. Jones, *Mysticism Explained: Philosophical Inquiries into Mysticism*, (Albany: State University of New York Press), 1993, pp. 30, 31.

10 W. R. Inge, *The Philosophy of Plotinus*, (New York et al: Longmans and Green), vol. II, p. 142.

11 W. R. Inge, *Christian Mysticism*, (Cleveland and New York: Meridian Books, 1956), p. 78.

12 F. C. Happold, *Mysticism, a Study and Anthology*, (Baltimore: Penguin Books, 1967), p. 18.

13 Steven T. Katz, "Language, Epistemology and Mysticism," in *Mysticism and Philosophical Analysis*, ed. Steven T. Katz, (New York: Oxford University Press, 1978), p. 42. Katz points out that Book VI of *The Enneads* provides the conceptualization of the final ascent toward unity; this description is a paradigm source of this unitive trend in Christian mysticism.

14 R. C. Zaehner, *Zen, Drugs, and Mysticism*, (New York: Pantheon Books, 1972).

15 G. G. Scholem, *Major Trends in Jewish Mysticism*, (New York: Schocken, 1941), p. 203.

16 *Ibid.*, p. 257.

17 M. Idel, *Kaballah: New Perspectives*, (New Haven and London: Yale University Press, 1988), p. 40.

18 Husik, *A History of Jewish Medieval Philosophy*, (New York: Harper and Row, 1966), p. 266.

19 T. M. Rudavsky, "The Jewish Tradition: Maimonides (b. 1135; d. 1204), Gersonides (b. 1288; d. 1334), and Bedersi (b. 1270; d. 1340)," in *Individuation in the Latter Middle Ages and Counter-Reformation, 1150-1650,* ed. J. E. Gracia, (Albany: State University of New York Press, 1994), p. 72.

20 M. A. Fakhry, *A History of Islamic Philosophy*, (New York: Columbia University Press, 1970), pp. 32-44.

21 P. Morewedge, *Essays in Islamic Philosophy and Mysticism*, (Oneonta: Oneonta Philosophy Series, 1995); *Neoplatonism and Islamic Thought* (ed.) (Albany: State University of New York Press, 1992); "Logic of Emanation and Sufism in ibn Sīnā," *Journal of the American Oriental Society*, in two parts. Part I: 91:4 (1971), pp. 467-476; Part II: 91:1 (1972), pp. 425-535. "Critical Observation on Some Philosophies of Mysticism," *International Journal for Philosophy of Religion*, VII: 4 (1976), pp. 409-424.

22 R. T. Wallis, *Neoplatonism*, (New York: Charles Scribner's Sons), p. 173.

23 J. M. Rist, *Plotinus: the Road to Reality*, (London: Cambridge University Press, 1967), p. 214.

24 F. Staal, *Exploring Mysticism*, (Berkeley and Los Angeles: University of California Press, 1975).

25 W. T. Stace, p. 35. Also, see pp. 337-338 for a misinterpretation of Rybroeck's mysticism.

26 Wallis, p. 89.

27 P. Morewedge, *Sufism, Neoplatonism and Zaehner's Theistic Theory of Mysticism*, (Oneonta: Department of Philosophy, SUNY-Oneonta, 1995), pp. 267-296.

28 R. C. Zaehner, *Mysticism, Sacred and Profane*, (London et al: Oxford University Press, 1980), p. 200.

29 *Ibid.*, p. 109.

30 *Ibid.*, p. 66.

31 *Ibid.*, p. 165.

32 *Ibid.*, p. 128.

33 *Ibid.*, p. 151.

34 M. Stoeber, *Theo-Monistic Mysticism, a Hindu-Christian Comparison*, (London: Houndmills et al, Macmillan, 1994), p. 3.

35 *Ibid.*, p. 24.

36 *Ibid.*, p. 87.

37 Charles Hartshorne, "Mysticism and Rationalistic Metaphysics," in *The Monist,* vol. 59:4 (October 1976), pp. 465-469.

38 W. T. Stace, *Mysticism and Philosophy*, (London: Macmillan Press, 1960), p. 341.
39 W. R. Inge, *Christian Mysticism*, (Cleveland and New York: Meridian Books, 1956), p. 4.
40 Qur'ān 50:15.
41 Cyprain Smith, "Meister Eckhart on the Union of Man with God," in *Mystics of the Book: Themes, Topics and Typologies*, ed. R.A. Herrera, (New York, Bern et al: Peter Lang, 1993), p. 237.
42 P. Morewedge, "A Third Version of the Ontological Argument in the Ibn Sīnian Metaphysics," in *Islamic Philosophical Theology*, (Albany: State University of New York Press, 1979), pp. 188-223.
43 R. Carnap, *Logical Foundations of Probability*, (Chicago: University of Chicago Press, 1951), pp. 39, 42.
44 See Toshihiko Izutsu, *Sufism and Taoism*, (Berkeley et al: University of California Press, 1983); William C. Chittick, *The Sufic Path of Knowledge: Ibn al-'Arabi's Metaphysics of Imagination*, (Albany: State University of New York Press, 1989); P. Morewedge, "Theology," in *The Oxford Encyclopedia of Modern Islamic World*, ed. John L. Esposito, (New York and Oxford: Oxford University Press, 1995), vol. IV, pp. 214-222.
45 Carnap, p. 3.
46 Otto, p. 118.
47 Cf., P. Morewedge, *Neoplatonism and Islamic Thought*.
48 P. Morewedge, "Contemporary Scholarship in Near Eastern Philosophy," *The Philosophical Forum*, 11:1 (Fall 1970), pp. 122-140.
49 H. A. Wolfson, *Studies in the History of Philosophy and Religion*, (Cambridge: Harvard University Press, 1973), p. 62.
50 *The Metaphysica of Avicenna (ibn Sīnā)*, trans. P. Morewedge, (New York: Columbia University Press and London: Routledge Keagan Paul, 1973), pp. 255-256.
51 Inge, *The Philosophy of Plotinus*, p. 239.
52 Stace, p. 341.
53 All translations and texts, unless specified, are quoted from *Plotinus, The Enneads, with an English Translation*, trans. A. H. Armstrong, (Massachusetts: Harvard University Press and London: Heinemann, 1966-1988).
54 Nasir Khosrow, *Zad al-Musāfirīn (The Paths of Travellers [Mystic's Path])*, (Tehran and Berlin: University of Tehran Press), pp. 370-377, 388-389.
55 Osborne, *Eros Unveiled, Plato and the God of Love*, (Oxford and New York: Oxford University Press, 1994), p. 177.
56 J. Houben, *Avicenna and Mysticism*, (Calcutta: Iran Society, 1956), p. 219.
57 Katz, p. 50.

58 W. J. Wainright, *Mysticism: A Study of its Nature, Cognitive Value and Moral Implications*, (Milwaukee: University of Wisconsin Press, 1981), p. 36.
59 Inge, *Christian Mysticism*, p. 4.
60 All quotations on Proclus are taken from *Proclus: The Elements of Theology*, trans. E. R. Dodds, (London: Oxford University Press, 1963). Citations are documented by proposition ('prop.' followed by a number) and a page number.
61 William Earle, "Phenomenology and Mysticism," in *The Monist,* vol. 59:4 (October 1976), p. 520.
62 See Herbert Marcuse, *Reason and Revolution*, (New York, 1941); "Symposium on Alienation and the Search for Identity," *American Journal of Psychoanalysis*, 21:2 (1961).
63 Denis O'Brien, "Plotinus on Matter," in *Greek and Medieval Studies in Honor of Leo Sweeney, S. J.* (New York, Bern et al: Peter Lang, 1994), p. 70.
64 J. N. Findlay, "The Logical Peculiarities of Neoplatonism," in *The Structure of Being: a Neoplatonic Approach*, (Albany: State University of New York Press, 1982), p. 1.
65 *Ibid.*, p. 2
66 *Ibid.*, pp. 3-4.
67 *Ibid.*
68 J. N. Findlay, "Why Christians Should be Platonists," in *Neoplatonism and Christian Thought,* ed. Dominic J. O' Meara, (Albany: State University of New York Press, 1982), p. 229.
69 Porphyry, *The Life of Plotinus*, chapter 23.
70 A. C. Lloyd, *The Anatomy of Neoplatonism*, (Oxford: Clarendon Press, 1990), p.165.
71 R. C. Zaehner, *Zen, Drugs and Mysticism*, p. 41.
72 M. Stoeber, p. 5.
73 All quotations are from the standard bilingual edition by C. Bailey (London: Oxford University Press, 1947), 3 vols.
74 *Ibid.*, p. 12.
75 *Ibid.*, p. 197.
76 M. Stoeber, p. 92.
77 H. H. Joachim, *A Study of Ethics of Spinoza*, (London: Oxford University Press, 1901), p. 65.
78 R. C. Zaehner, *Zen, Drugs and Mysticism*, p. 60; W. T. Stace, Mysticism and Philosophy, p. 205.
79 M. Wartofsky, "Action and Passion: Spinoza's Construction of a Scientific Psychology," in *Modern Studies in Spinoza*, ed. M. Greene, (Garden City: Anchor, 1973).

80 G. Deleuze, *Expressionism in Philosophy: Spinoza*, (New York: Zone Books, 1992), p. 320.

81 For clarification of various notions of nature, cf., J. A. Weisheipl, "Aristotle's Concept of Nature: Avicenna and Aquinas," in *Approaches to Nature in the Middle Ages*, ed. L. D. Roberts, (Binghamton: Merts, 1982), pp. 137-160. While Weisheipl is to be commended for his analysis of Aristotle and Aquinas, I take exception to his assignment of Avicenna as an Aristotelian. There are many differences between the two systems. For example, for Avicenna, the Necessary Existent is not a substance from whom the world is emanated, while for Aristotle the First Mover is a substance who is co-eternal with the world.

82 J. N. Deck, *Nature, Contemplation and the One*, (New York: Larson, 1967), p. 4.

83 G. Jung, *Aion: Research into the Phenomenology of the Self*, trans. R. F. C. Hull, (Princeton, 1959), pp. 22-23, 30-32, and 39-40.

84 W. R. Inge, *Christian Mysticism*, pp. 9-10.

85 Lewis, *An Analysis of Knowledge and Valuation*, (La Salle: Open Court, 1962), p. vii.

86 *Ibid.*, p. 365.

87 L. Wittgenstein, *Philosophical Investigation,* trans. G. E. M. Anscombe, (New York: McMillan, 1953), p. 161.

88 H. Corbin, *Spiritual Body and Celestial Earth: From Mazdean Iran to Shi'it Iran*, trans. N. Pearson, (Princeton: Princeton University Press, 1977).

89 L. Wittgenstein, *Philosophical Investigation,* trans. G. E. M. Anscombe, (New York: McMillan, 1953), p. 161.

90 *Ibid.*, p. 85, poem 435.

91 *Ibid.*, p. 71, poem 115.

92 *Ibid.*, p. 78, poems 289-290.

93 R. C. Zaehner, *Hindu and Muslim Mysticism*, (London: Althone Press, 1960), p. 163.

94 See *Soliloquies,* 11, 7, i, in *Writings of Saint Augustine*, ed. W. J. Jones, (New York: Random House, 1948), vol. 1, p. 262.

95 L. Wittgenstein, *Tractatus Logico-Philosophicus*, trans. D. F. Pears and B. F. McGuinnes, (London: Routledge and Kegan Paul, 1921), pp. 117-119.

96 H. Bergson, *Duration and Simultaneity, with reference to Einstein's Theory*, trans. L. Jacobson, (Indianapolis: Bobbs-Merrill, 1965), p. 44.

97 Earle, p. 523.

98 *Ibid.*, p. 531

99 A. C. Lloyd, p. 166.

100 Jones, p. 38.